Turks and Greeks

Neighbours
in Conflict

Turks and Greeks

Neighbours in Conflict

Vamık D. Volkan

and

Norman Itzkowitz

THE EOTHEN PRESS

British Library Cataloguing-in-Publication Data.
A catalogue record for this book is available from the British Library.

First published by The Eothen Press, 1994.

© Vamık D. Volkan and Norman Itzkowitz.

Published by The Eothen Press, 10 Manor Road, Hemingford Grey,
Huntingdon, Cambridgeshire, England, PE18 9BX.

ISBN   0 906719 25 9 hard covers
        0 906719 30 5 paperback
        Paperback reprinted 1995

CONTENTS

Foreword

by former Ambassador W. Nathaniel Howell

The American 'refugees' who landed at Piraeus, the port of Athens, that June morning shared a profound sense of relief. The year was 1967, and the leased cruiseship from which they disembarked delivered them from the stresses and trauma of life in Egypt during and immediately after the six-day war with Israel. Behind us were the official hostility of Egyptian authorities and the rage and anguish of the Egyptian 'street'; Greece represented safe haven, a return to the known, an escape from the 'other'.

As a foreign service officer on my first tour in Cairo, I was not immune to such feelings. Bearing the last diplomatic pouch out of Embassy Cairo, I rode through the streets of Athens in an official car, savouring a feeling of security I had not permitted myself for weeks. The large number of soldiers along my route was not particularly noteworthy to a traveller arriving from Nasser's Egypt. What most struck me was that I was among 'friendly' troops, heirs like myself of a long Western tradition. Intellectually of course, I knew that these were the forces of the 'Greek Colonels' who had seized power by military coup only weeks before. Psychologically, they were assurance of safety for my family and my colleagues; only gradually would the real implications of their high profile crowd out my instinctive relief. The Greece of June 1967 was a military dictatorship, not the 'us' of our emotions. The experience provided me an early object-lesson in the crucial importance of psychological experiences in shaping and conditioning our perceptions of reality.

In this innovative volume, Professors Volkan and Itzkowitz have probed beneath the 'objective' realities of relations between Greece and Turkey. Bringing to bear their considerable knowledge of the historical evolution of the relationship, this interdisciplinary analysis offers significant insights into the underlying psychopolitical factors that bedevil Greek-Turkish interactions and render seemingly straightforward problems and issues resistant to resolution. Their effort should be welcomed by diplomats, scholars, and commentators concerned with these important states and interested in contributing to a normalization of relations between the two neighbours.

In contrast to the authors, my own direct experience with Greece has been more extensive than with Turkey, which has rather been a subject of intellectual and professional interest to me. Ironically, however, tales of the adventures of my uncle in Kemal Atatürk's Istanbul, imbibed in childhood, crystallized my attachment to a diplomatic career and riveted my interest on the Mediterranean/ Middle Eastern arena. In providing a sanctuary for my family not only from the turmoil of Egypt in 1967 but from the chaos of Beirut in 1975-76, Greek people earned a place in my affections balanced by a respect and appreciation for the achievements of modern Turkey in its stunning recovery from the debris of the Ottoman Empire and the Islamic Caliphate. Like many observers, perhaps more than most, I have been saddened and frustrated by the inability of these two 'allies' to regulate their relations, to reconcile my own conflicted feelings.

Volkan and Itzkowitz's application of their expertise and particular optic to the historical interplay between Athens and Ankara highlights key 'chosen traumas' and 'chosen glories' that impede reconciliation. It also exposes a shared thread of expansionism and ill-defined sense of 'national' boundaries. Historically, both the Hellenistic and Ottoman Empires abhorred a vacuum, filling it whenever their military might and cultural influence were sufficient to do so. Today, their heirs and successors still grapple with the 'memories' of their successes and failures in the ebb and flow of their shared history.

If many in the West have forgotten the military and cultural threat posed historically by Ottoman power and energy, it is obvious that the trauma induced by Ottoman conquests remains a living part of the national psyche in Greece and the Balkans centuries after the actual threat has receded. That the Ottoman Empire was integrally expansionist is not in question; the authors concede (p.75) that 'the Ottoman Empire, like those others whose economies depended on agriculture, was originally organized for conquest.' It was, in fact, a threat that was halted and eventually rolled back only by force of arms. Whether the 'Turk' in those centuries of contested power was more brutal or less 'civilized' than his European adversaries, it is not surprising that he was dehumanized in the Christendom of the day. What properly concerns Volkan and Itzkowitz, however, are the psychological processes by which such characterizations and 'displacements' persist in poisoning the atmosphere today.

In February, 1992, I visited Bulgaria under the sponsorship of the United States Information Service (USIA) to lecture on conditions in the Middle East in the aftermath of the expulsion of Iraqi forces from Kuwait. I was struck, during a spirited discussion at the Bulgarian Academy of Sciences, by intense questioning on the subject of Islamic 'fundamentalism'. The exceptional interest in this phenomenon in Sofia perplexed me until I realized what was really being sought - *assurance that the Turks were not coming back!* The idea was incomprehensible to me (as I hastened to point out), but the anxiety was genuine for many of my interlocutors. A few younger Bulgarian academics who suggested that post-communist Bulgaria might have something to learn from the modern Turkish state were a distinct minority. For the majority, the 'chosen trauma' of Ottoman occupation was a vivid reality.

Objectively, the issues between present-day Greece and Turkey, including the vexing question of Cyprus, appear eminently soluble. The mutual benefits seemingly outweigh any advantage of continued enmity and suspicion. But, that judgment reckons without an appreciation of the psychological investment in past feelings of victimization and achievement. As any effective diplomat knows instinctively, the prospects for compromise and negotiation are severely constrained by skewed perceptions or irrational obsessions. Even decades of association as 'allies' within the North Atlantic Treaty Organization (NATO) were not sufficient to exorcise the centuries-old demons in their relationship.

Contemporary Turkey, as Volkan and Itzkowitz demonstrate, has spent decades reinventing itself and developing a secular, democratic tradition. Distancing itself not only from its imperial heritage but from the mainstream of the Islamic world, Ankara abandoned its preoccupation with neighbours in favour of a self-conscious reordering of its internal character and priorities. The Turks' difficulty in dealing with the fact that, for instance, not all Kurds share in the prevailing ethnic identity probably owes much to this single-mindedness. Turkey's impressive achievements, however, are no longer their own reward.

One suspects that the Turks long deeply for release from their 'grand loneliness' (p.190) in the recognition of and acceptance by Europe of the metamorphosis they have wrought. The push for association with the European Union reflects an urge to expunge finally the legacy of the 'Ottoman menace' and the negative caricatures and associations lingering in the Western mind.

Greece, still brooding over the real and mythologized 'losses' of its past, remains wedded to the idea of Turkey as threat and victimizer. Unable to mourn fully its losses, Greek identity remains integrally tied to an obsession more with Turkey's historical antecedents than its present reality. Like their Turkish counterparts, the Greeks find it difficult to abandon the myth of ethnic homogeneity within their frontiers. Circumlocutions, such as 'Muslim minority' or 'Slavophone Greeks', reflect an effort to square reality with emotion. The opposition of Athens to the full integration of Turkey into the modern European system of nations seems to reflect a fear that Turks may, in fact, turn out to be 'like us', an anxiety implicit in the Greek editorials adduced by the authors (p.167). For if Turkey is accepted into European civilization, not only is the unique character and mission of Greece called into question, but a recognition of both the good and bad aspects of their own and Turkey's impulses and character must be accommodated within the Greek sense of identity.

Though Athens and Ankara have avoided open conflict for decades and neither represents a credible threat to the other's integrity or security, a relationship of trust and tolerance has eluded them. Condemned by geography, historical experience, and psychological conditioning to coexist in close proximity, they have proven incapable of benefiting from positive co-operation, despite the efforts and urgings of friends and allies. Volkan and Itzkowitz, by peeling away layers of their complex and conflicted interrelationship, reveal important elements of the psychopolitical barriers that, paradoxically, link them in dysfunctional ways.

The distance between tentative diagnosis and effective cure remains immense. Severing the unhealthy linkage and replacing it with a more constructive relationship of trust and empathy would clearly necessitate painful introspection and growth. It is far from evident that the will to reopen and treat ancient wounds, to complete the process of mourning historic 'losses', to give up the crutches that prop up the concept of popular identity, exists. Without inspired leadership or compelling reasons, it is, alas, human nature to cling to familiar, self-defeating habits however great the cost in future possibilities.

The end of the Cold War, which forced Turkey and Greece into reluctant alliance against the Soviet threat, has opened new horizons for each. With the collapse of hostile and impenetrable frontiers, both Ankara and Athens face new foreign policy opportunities and outlets that could dilute their bilateral relationship, possibly in more healthy ways. For Turkey, the lure and needs of new states in Central Asia and Transcaucasia have been substantial enough to overturn a decades-old policy of non-involvement in the affairs of Turkic peoples outside its own borders (p.161). Ankara has moved quickly, within the limits of its resources, to capitalize on these new opportunities.

Greece likewise possesses enlarged vistas in the Balkans and Eastern Europe, but can it overcome the crippling sense of victimization that is already poisoning its new relationships? The petty bickering over the use of the term 'Macedonia', for example, raises questions about the capability of Athens to benefit from its newfound opportunities. Rather than utilizing the new circumstances to diversify relationships and compensate for decades of obsession with Turkey, some in Greece seem intent on multiplying hostile relationships and turning their anger and sense of humiliation inward on citizens who question government policy (*The Economist*, 14.8.1993, p.46). Persistence in this path can only deprive the Greeks of opportunities for positive, confidence-building experiences to work through, or offset, well-entrenched 'chosen traumas'.

For readers who share a respect and concern for both Greece and Turkey, this analysis offers a new way of thinking about the basis of the tensions that have marked their modern relationship. Understanding the historical development of that relationship and the unresolved traumas that have shaped the interaction of the two peoples illuminates the persistent influence of humiliations and enmities long after the events that provoked them. Above all, the authors challenge us all to re-examine our own perceptions and assumptions and to find ways to help the Turkish and Greek peoples come to grips with the psychopolitical barriers that lock them into so predictable and sterile an embrace.

Preface and Acknowledgements

Confucius was asked to name the principle concerning the best way people could live with others. His answer was, 'Is not reciprocity that word?' This book is about reciprocity–about how one neighbour treats the other and, in turn, how that second neighbour treats the first one. Specifically, we are going to study the Turks and Greeks as neighbours.

Turkish-Greek problems fall into the category of regional conflicts. They are already of an historical, long-standing nature and have been awaiting a solution for many years. As a result, clear-cut adversary images have already been created in both countries. Often the technical, legal, and political aspects of these problems have been long forgotten, giving way to a mythical and mystical confrontation laden with fear, animosity, and psychological preoccupation. As the decade of the 1990s began, the world was experiencing sweeping changes at an unprecedented pace, but the obsessions between Turks and Greeks have remained basically unchanged.

When communism as a state ideology and political force began to collapse, the bipolar post-World War II international balance was replaced by the unipolar hierarchical one with the United States as the only superpower. The sudden decline in international tensions raised hopes for finding peaceful solutions to regional conflicts on the basis of the 'rule of law'. Indeed, after Iraq invaded Kuwait a coalition was formed to enforce the 'rule of law'. The coalition forces repelled the invasion of Kuwait and restored the 'rule of law' to the region. However, heavy damage was inflicted upon the aggressor and the area's Kurdish population suffered. It is highly likely that the

West will no longer feel bound to condone the 'guilty party' in regional conflicts as it used to do out of regard for the perceived acute security interests in the highly competitive former bipolar world. The West's involvement in Bosnia has not been as drastic as its involvement in Kuwait.

Nevertheless, the question remains whether peaceful and democratic solutions can be worked out for domestic and international conflicts without resort to military action. While we are witnessing the emergence of the institutional foundations of an integrated western Europe, we are also experiencing a disintegration process in the former Soviet Union and the horrible events in the former Yugoslavia which threaten the territorial integrity of several new republics. The beginning of the 1990s saw an estimated one hundred and twelve armed conflicts worldwide, thirty-two of which were major wars, with 'major' defined as having caused one thousand or more deaths. Most of these were heavily influenced by ethnic conflicts.[1]

To have a post-communist and peaceful 'new world order' major obstacles must first be faced. Since the normative aspect of the 'new world order' is still in an elementary stage in terms of under-developed international law and institutions, solutions promoted by the West for regional conflicts can hardly escape the religious or moral preferences of the West. The Turks, for example, claim that this seems to be true of Nagorno-Karabakh and Bosnia-Herzegovina.

The regional Turkish-Greek conflict in this book is approached within the general framework of the above-mentioned characteristics of the emerging 'new world order'. We believe that this story of Turkish-Greek relationships sheds the necessary light on the Eastern-Western, or Moslem-Christian, dilemma that has been resurrected especially after the events in Bosnia-Herzegovina. We shall dwell on the psychological structures embedded in the policies pursued by the two countries. We focus on the psychological aspects because, as Harold Saunders, a former career diplomat who served under five United States presidents as a member of the National Security Council, has noted, some of the traditional concepts we associate with relationships among nations, and how they are conducted, do not fully explain the issues that dominate today's world. Some of the traditional tools of statecraft with which we are familiar can no longer be relied on to produce the results we expect from them. There are clear signs that we need to reorganize our thinking about how nations and ethnic groups relate. Saunders states: 'When old lenses no longer bring the world into focus and a traditional vocabulary does not accurately describe it, it is both realistic and prudent to grind new lenses and introduce fresh language.'[2]

Following Harold Saunders' lead, the purpose of this book is to grind a psychological lens, one that can help us integrate our observations with other paradigms in order to understand international dynamics more fully and to help formulate suggestions for action. Policymakers and diplomats often utilize some degree of *surface* psychology to influence the enemy or to obtain the upper hand for propaganda purposes. When we refer to psychology here, however, our allusion is to an in-depth understanding of generally unconsciously-motivated forces which are commonly present in large group interactions and in large group experiences with their leaders.

Our aim is to analyse Turkish-Greek relations in order to illuminate their psychological foundations and to explain irrational attitudes while differentiating fantasy and unconscious phenomena from reality. We want to use this conflict to offer an example *par excellence* of inter-ethnic neighbour psychology and to show how this psychology may become a pathological, unseen focus dominating political, economic, legal, and military factors. No such analysis is possible without knowing the parties' histories and the unconscious ingredients of their political cultures. In this book we shall first provide a general overview of the psychology of large group neighbours and then discuss the encounters and hostilities, as well as the partnerships, between the Turks and the Greeks beginning in 1071 when the Turkish Seljukid leader Sultan Alp Arslan defeated the Byzantine Emperor Romanus Diogenes IV at Manzikert. We are *not* interested in parading all the exact details of the complex interaction between the Turks and the Greeks, but we will attempt to observe the flow of history through a psychological lens.

This book is written by a psychoanalyst with a long-standing interest in international relations and an historian with a psychoanalytic background. The senior author, Dr. Volkan, is of Turkish origins, while Dr. Itzkowitz lived in Turkey for three years during his early studies of Turkish history. We are aware that no totally neutral or absolute truth regarding ethnic or national positions is possible. On the positive side, however, the authors' backgrounds make them 'participant observers', to use a psychoanalytic term, in Turkish-Greek studies. They are aware of the impact of emotions and psychological processes in international relationships. The authors have collaborated in writing two previous books, one being a psychobiography of the Turkish leader Mustafa Kemal Atatürk which provided a better integration of psychoanalysis and history in considering various historical and political events.[3]

Large ethnic or related groups, such as large religious or national groups, interact with each other by utilizing extensively shared, often primitive and unconscious, mental mechanisms, such as sharing projections onto another group of unwanted aspects of themselves. This book is unusual because the authors 'belong' to the group which receives the projections of the Greeks. While this work at times deals more with Greeks than with Turks, we try to provide a balance. Perhaps those who are 'targets' of projections are able to feel and to examine the nature of them more sensitively than those in whom the projections originate. A quick examination of the literature written in English on Turkish-Greek relationships provides an abundance of books written by individuals who are of Greek origin or have a strong connection with the Greeks, while it is seldom possible to find books dealing with the same topic written by individuals examining opposing viewpoints. This book may help immensely to overcome the stereotyping of one area of historical inquiry.

Our basic premise is that the psychological analysis of enemy image structures, once fully understood, could gradually facilitate the development of an attitude more amenable to a peaceful solution to the differences that separate the Turks and the Greeks. Our purpose is to help the Turks and the Greeks, as well as any third party involved, to understand the deep and complex psychological needs, motives, and anxieties beneath so-called national sovereignty interests, rights and obligations of states, prestige and dignity of nations, tactics-policy-strategy calculations, and 'realpolitik', which are usually considered to be determinants of foreign policy and international relations. We also hope that this book will be an example of how an in-depth psycho-historical and psycho-political analysis can be carried out.

PREFACE AND ACKNOWLEDGEMENTS

Kurt Volkan was involved in this project from its beginning and he assisted us in our research and preparation of this book. We are indebted to him. We thank Professor Jouni Suistola, of Oulu, Finland, and Nail Atalay, of Nicosia, Northern Cyprus, who read the first draft of this book and gave valuable suggestions. We would also like to express our appreciation to Virginia Kennan, Dr. Volkan's editorial assistant for over twenty years; Lee Ann Fargo, Administrative Assistant to Dr. Volkan; and Lisa Beard, Co-ordinator for the Center of the Study of Mind and Human Interaction at the University of Virginia, for their efforts in making this publication possible.

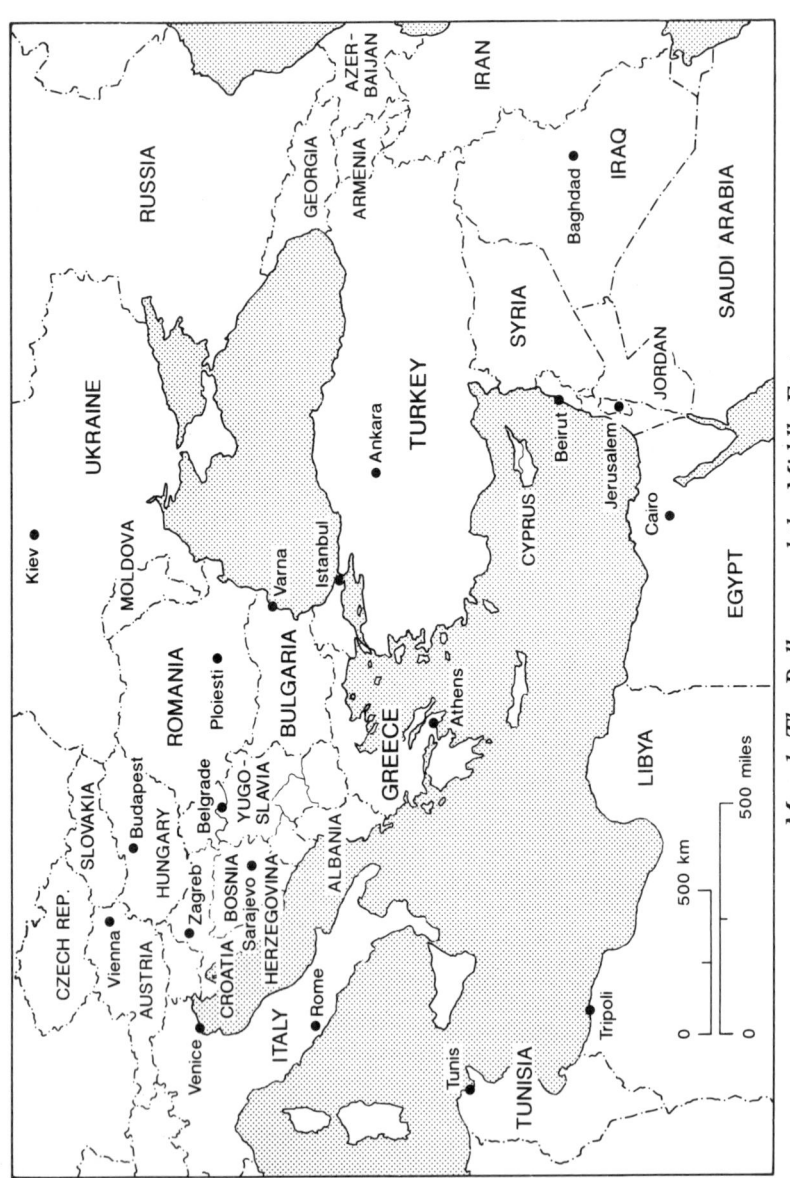

Map 1: The Balkans and the Middle East

| 1 |

History through a Psychological Lens

Today's realities in Turkish-Greek relationships cannot simply be understood only with a focus on real world issues in the legal, political, economic, and military arenas. We need to understand how the history of a group results in conscious, and perhaps more importantly unconscious, psychological phenomena which become an 'unseen power' in the interaction of neighbouring countries. Images, perceptions, thoughts, fantasies, and feelings (the combination of them are called *mental representations*) of past traumas and glories, sometimes hundreds and hundreds of years old, and mental defences associated with them are transmitted from generation to generation.[4]

The Psychology of Large Group Neighbours
The basis for the psychology of ethnic relationships comes from the psychology of large group neighbours. For centuries, tribes living in close proximity had only one another with whom to interact due both to their natural boundaries, sparsity of population, and the limitations imposed by the state of their technology. Neighbouring groups had to compete for food and physical goods for their survival. Eventually, we assume that this primitive level of competition took on greater psychological importance. Physical essentials, besides retaining their status as genuine necessities, took on mental meanings as well (i.e., of prestige) and evolved from being tokens of survival to becoming symbols for large groups of self-esteem and glory. Anthropologists have taught us, for example, how items such as arrows, spears, and drums, essential to the hunt for food, take on a special meaning and

often become the symbols of power and authority.

Psychoanalyst Erik H. Erikson coined the term 'pseudospecies' in reference to mankind's tendency to portray itself as 'the human beings' and other groups as less than human.[5] Erikson theorized that primitive man sought a measure of 'protection' for his unbearable nakedness by adopting the armour of the lower animals and wearing their skins, feathers, or claws. On the basis of these outer 'garments', each tribe, clan, or group developed a sense of identity as well as a conviction that it alone harboured the *one* human identity.

Erikson's postulations clearly fall within the realm of speculation. However, many independent observations corroborate his thinking.[6] Anthropologist Howard Stein says this type of pattern 'cannot be literally generalized to all cultures, but it shows in the extreme a universal proclivity in feelings toward, perception of, and action taken against those who were not "the people"'.[7] We can state that men's preoccupation with a shared 'other' is real, not simply a theory.[8] Furthermore, from childhood on, the values and memories associated with one's group are passed on from generation to generation. Issues of 'us and them' and 'enemies and allies' are inherent to both human evolution and the development of the human mind. Such divisions are so much a part of our humanness that we cannot simply wish them away.

We have learned from psychoanalytic child researchers that no matter how much potential and ability an infant possesses, early in life no one has a separate sense of self; the human mind during infancy can be conceptualized as being in a creative state of confusion. One's sense of genuine and cohesive 'I' (self) evolves slowly within the first three years of life.

Furthermore, a very young child is not capable of integrating discrete experiences. He knows a pleasurable ('good') experience when he has one and a not so pleasurable ('bad') experience, but he cannot recognize that sometimes the source of both experiences can be one and the same person; in psychoanalytic language this person is called an *object*. The mother who satisfies her child by feeding him and the mother who frustrates her child by not feeding him are not experienced as the same source in the infant's mind. Again, the development of the ego's ability to integrate opposing experiences and opposing self and object-images with their accompanying emotions is a time-consuming process. Eventually, as the child's integrative functions evolve, the child is able to unite opposing images and make 'grey' (*integration*) from black and white experiences.

One of the ways the child prepares himself for this process is by learning to attribute to other individuals or things certain parts which belong to him (*projection*). Projections serve to make the sense of 'I' cohesive. Two types of projection are utilized:

(1) The child projects his unintegrated, unpleasant, 'bad' aspects onto others in order to maintain the cohesiveness of parts that he keeps inside himself.

(2) Interestingly enough, the child also projects unintegrated, pleasurable, 'good' aspects of himself onto others, as if to keep them safe for use on a rainy day. If the child becomes anxious about losing these 'good' aspects, he projects them onto idealized objects at the time of integration to ensure their preservation and as a step in the grey-making process.

During the developmental stages it is possible for a child to re-own 'good' and 'bad' projections from the past that have not been integrated and incorporate them into his ever-evolving self-representation. The significance of this process in relation to the psychology of neighbours is that certain projections are never completely re-owned. Some become sanctioned by the adults in the group to which the child belongs—due to the influences of the group's historical, cultural, and social expectations—and then stabilized as group projections.

By belonging to a large group (i.e., an ethnic group) children accumulate what is known as *shared reservoirs*, which are supported and sponsored by the adults in the group. The function of these reservoirs is to serve as a receptacle for the projections ('good' and 'bad') of all the children in the group, especially at the peak of their grey-making period. Vamık Volkan has theorized that 'bad' shared reservoirs represent the beginnings of a shared 'other' (enemies) and 'good' shared reservoirs stand for the beginnings of 'we-ness' (allies). This 'we-ness' is the core of ethnicity whether the reference is to a clan or to any large group label or marker, and the 'other' usually is a neighbouring group.[9]

In the modern world, even if we are not neighbours physically, all ethnic groups are linked at least figuratively by telecommunications and other advanced technological means. Thus, with the world shrinking as much as it has been, it is possible to identify derivatives of behaviour that are based upon the psychology of neighbours in groups who are not even close geographically. The prototype of ethnic conflicts, however, is seen in areas where two groups are physical neighbours, e.g., Armenians and Azerbaijanis, Croatians and Serbians, and Israelis and Palestinians. These are all ethnic groups sharing the same ground or claiming ownership of the same piece of land. The Turkish-Greek confrontation is another paradigm. The Turkish-Greek relationship shares certain common elements with the other ethnic conflicts though it also has its own unique characteristics. The study of any ethnic conflict will be beneficial in understanding large-group phenomena, but we also need to consider that each case merits specific consideration. For example, although we find Koch bacilli in every case of tuberculosis, the nature of the illness will appear to be different in each ill individual—the individual's specific inner and outer conditions, therefore, must also be considered. Likewise, in examining the identities of large groups the mental representations from history pertaining to each group must be understood.

Ethnicity

Although ethnicity is not something that can be measured, its presence is palpable, and one would think that it would be rather easy to describe. Turks and Greeks so clearly insist on how they are different and separate from one another in certain aspects and how they are similar in others, that it should not be too difficult to isolate a description of ethnicity and the reasons for ethnic differences. Yet, the fact is that it is impossible to find one single description of ethnicity that would be acceptable to most scholars. Ethnicity, like nationalism, is a term that changes in scope and substance according to the discipline by which it is being studied. In the late nineteenth century both these terms took on new meanings and have continued to do so ever since. Furthermore, the nature, values, and even the symbols of a group's ethnicity or nationalism undergo changes throughout the group's history.

Many social scientists have wrestled with the problem of a definition for ethnicity. Max Weber in referring to ethnicity speaks of a 'subjective belief' in a 'common descent ... whether or not an objective blood relationship exists'.[10] Horowitz, a lawyer and political scientist, adds to Weber's conception 'a minimal scale requirement, so that ethnic membership transcends the range of face-to-face interactions, as recognized kinship need not.' He goes on to add, 'So conceived, ethnicity easily embraces groups differentiated by color, language, and religion; it covers "tribes", "races", "nationalities", and "castes".'[11] As Stein, a psychoanalytic anthropologist, states: 'As a marker of personal and social identity, ethnicity is a model of thought, not a category in nature.'[12] We agree with Horowitz and Stein; in this book we are more interested in large political processes than we are in identifying the exact label that should be attached to large political groups.

Some authors pair the concepts of ethnicity and nationalism and others use the term ethnonationalism to attest to the inseparability of the two concepts. A phenomenological approach to ethnicity and nationalism, however, falls short of explaining the dynamic forces associated with these concepts as well as the emotions invested in them, which, at times, may become rather intense. Historian Boyd C. Shafer focuses on the human factor. Citing Jean Piaget's finding that children between the ages of six and ten learn patriotism from their parents, Shafer states that love for one's country and hatred of foreigners are learned sentiments and maintains that the form of government, the economic organization, education, family training, and propaganda all influence these sentiments.[13]

What makes ethnicity or nationalism 'hot'? What makes the Greeks preoccupied with the Turks and the Turks preoccupied with the Greeks? Why does one's sense of self rise and fall according to the standing of one's ethnic or national group? Why is it so difficult—if not impossible—to change one's established ethnic sentiments once they are established, especially following the adolescent passage? Why are we, under certain circumstances, willing to die rather than change our ethnic identities? Why does a large group cling to its identity all the more when political and/or military pressure is intensified? Why do we seem to need shared 'others' (enemies) in order to define ourselves?

For the purpose of carrying these thoughts one step further, we must progress from a static/phenomenological understanding of ethnicity or nationalism to a psychodynamic formulation of it. Real-world issues (i.e., political, economic, legal, or military) are there to be observed and even measured. After all, enemies who are attacking us are real. Psychoanalysis, however, has taught us that real-world issues are intertwined with issues of psychic reality and that one constantly influences the other. The inner demands, feelings, perceptions, fantasies, expectations, and the defences against these psychological phenomena interact with the environment and influence the development and modification of one's psychic structure.[14] Through psychoanalytic research on the child's developing sense of self and others and ego functions, we are learning more and more that the early experiences of the child-mother (or her representative) environment (which is a restricted one) are crucial to shaping the child's psychic structure.[15] The child's genetic potentials, physiological capacities, the influence of the family, education, and culture, as well as his nurturing ('good') and traumatic ('bad') experiences go through the 'channel' of child-mother interactions in providing the child's psychic building blocks. In ethnic groups certain ingredients that come from the real world initially go through the child-mother channels and are, therefore, shared by all children in the group. There are also other shared experiences when children in the same group expand their worlds and relate to other important individuals, such as fathers and teachers, who respond to them according to the traditions and the customs of the group. Thus, we understand Stein's remark that the enemies of an ethnic group 'are neither "merely" projections, nor are they "merely" real'.[16] They are both. The enemy who kills us is real, but he is also a reservoir of our shared projections supported by the people in our own group.

Ethnicity and related large group labels do not become a 'force' in any human drama without one large group's interaction with another large group in peace or, more importantly, in conflict. We do not mean to belittle the influence of these real world issues (all have a profound impact on one another), but it is becoming increasingly evident that psychological issues may dominate in episodes of ethnic conflict, especially if they become chronic, as in the case of the Middle East in general and in Turkish-Greek relations in particular.

Did not the late Egyptian President Anwar al-Sadat surprise the world in 1977 when he told the Israeli Knesset that he believed seventy per cent of the long-standing problems between the Arabs and the Israelis were psychological? Before Sadat, Bülent Ecevit, who was the Turkish Prime Minister in 1974 when the Turkish military intervened in Cyprus, indirectly addressed the importance of psychological factors between Turks and Greeks in a poem he wrote while in London more than a quarter-century before the Turkish military became embroiled in Cypriot affairs. He describes his own ambivalence toward both parties, an attitude shared by many Turks and Greeks:

> Only when homesick do you realize
> you have become brother to the Greek.
> When he hears a Greek melody abroad,
> how transformed is the child of Istanbul.

> With pungent Turkish we have abused you
> to our heart's content.

> We have become mortal enemies.
> Still, there is affection within us,
> Hidden away during more harmonious days.[17]

Chosen Traumas and Chosen Glories

We use the term 'chosen trauma' to refer to an event that invokes in the members of one group intense feelings of having been humiliated and victimized by members of another group. A group does not, of course, 'choose' to be victimized and, subsequently, to lose self-esteem, but it does 'choose' to psychologize and mythologize—to dwell on the event.

The group draws the emotional meanings (mental representations) of the traumatic event and mental defences against emotional hurts into its very identity, assiduously passing these mental representations of hurt and shame and defences against them from generation to generation. The mental representations of chosen traumas and defences against them become vital markers of ethnic identity. Once a trauma becomes a chosen trauma, the historical truth about it does not really matter.[18] The central role that the mental representation of the event and defences associated with it play in the group's ethnic identity becomes most significant. Usually a major chosen trauma becomes condensed with similar traumas from the past and the future.

Mourning is an obligatory human response that is initiated by loss or change.[19] If a loved one dies, it is obligatory that we go through a mourning process. If we are successful in mourning, we accept the changes and losses, adopt new internal and external realities, and continue with our lives. Members of a group who experience a shared loss or change, like individuals, must mourn. We do not mean to say that a group is like a flesh and blood organism, but its members will share reactions to drastic events. For example, after such disasters as Challenger 7 or the Mexican earthquake, dozens of distasteful jokes started to appear. The 'creation' of jokes was the beginning of group mourning. The jokes reversed the sad affects of the event and dealt with the survivors' shared guilt. When drastic losses occur, the survivors experience unconscious guilt for outliving the relatives, friends, or important other persons who have perished. Depending upon the impact of the event, society will provide means (i.e., reviving the memory of the event in ceremonies, in legal processes, in art, and in songs) to perform a shared work of mourning. Drastic events that are politically and militarily humiliating, unlike those caused by nature, are more difficult to mourn.[20]

An incident that occurred in 1864 demonstrates how a chosen trauma may evolve. Approximately eight thousand Navajo Indians in New Mexico were left homeless when US soldiers, under the direction of Kit Carson, burned and destroyed their property. The Indians were forced on a three-hundred mile march to Fort Sumner, New Mexico, where they were cruelly imprisoned for four years; during the march and after, two thousand five hundred of them died. The march became known as the 'Long Walk'. David A. Maurer, a Charlottesville newspaper reporter, interviewed two local pastors, Neal Knight and Harold L. Bare, Sr., who were involved in a project with Navajo Indians. The pastors relayed to Maurer their perception that for many Navajo, time had stopped in 1864 when Kit Carson and his men destroyed their way of life. Pastor Bare remarked: 'The Indians were telling me about the "Long Walk", and at first I thought they were talking about something that had happened the day before. I was really taken aback when I realized they were talking about something that had happened more than 125 years ago ... to the Indians, the "Long Walk" is as real as the morning sunlight.'[21]

The work of mourning often needs to be completed before such political compromises as yielding territory to an enemy group can be accepted, even if such a compromise would result in a mutually beneficial peace. But, under certain circumstances, mourning may be very difficult. The victimized group may be too humiliated or too angry to mourn. An event evolves into a chosen trauma as a participating group, for various reasons, finds itself unable to complete its work of mourning. The inability to mourn the chosen trauma influences the social and political ideologies of the particular group. Thus, the ethnic identity evolves through history.

As a chosen trauma passes from one generation to another, it may change its function or, by being linked to a more recent trauma, acquire a renewed emotional power. In his study of teenage pregnancies, violence and psychosomatic conditions (such as anorexia nervosa) among African American youth, Maurice Apprey suggests that the chosen trauma of slavery has changed its function. The victimization of blacks by whites in the United States, he believes, has become internalized as *self*-destructive behaviour by means of which black teenagers, as part of their ethnic identity, unconsciously recount the chosen trauma of their ancestors.[22]

When shared mental defences associated with a group's chosen trauma are omnipotent, paradoxically the reactivation of the chosen trauma may raise the group's self-esteem. Members of each new generation may share a conscious and unconscious wish to repair what has been done to their ancestors and to release themselves from the burden of humiliation that has become part of the group's identity. Various ritualistic outlets are available (such as ceremonies or demonstrations when the political atmosphere is suitable, artistic creations, and so on). There are also other outlets that operate at the unconscious level that especially fuel prejudices, thereby affecting politics and international relationships.[23] For example, the inability to mourn a chosen trauma and the evolution of shared mental defences against it will influence the social and political ideologies of large groups. In effect, an attitude is created that says: '*We* have been hurt enough. Now *we* should be given what others owe us.' This may result in a new generation embracing an ideology of entitlement.[24]

The inability to mourn the mental representations of past traumas most often results in various purification rituals. Even when a traumatic event has ended, if a group has not been able to resolve issues associated with the event, linkage with the enemy will remain. Especially when a large group frees itself from the influences of an oppressor, it may feel too resentful to its change in status. When the group views the enemy as being so contaminated and so dirty, it will feel the need to cleanse itself. This practice may range from harmless to harmful. When a group cannot grieve and move on to its new status, it tries to shed all 'foreign' elements in order to achieve a 'new' cohesive identity that will replace the former 'injured' identity.[25]

Sometimes, if the group remains powerless, the people may seem to surrender to its fate of being victims.[26]

When referring to a chosen trauma, the group holds on to the principle of what John E. Mack called 'egoism of victimization'. This refers to a phenomenon of little or no empathy for one's enemy's losses, 'even if the victimization on the other side is palpably evident and comparable to or greater than one's own. ... The lack of empathy, the inability to identify with the anguish experienced by the members of a national group toward whom one bears hostile feelings, removes one of the central deterrents to the waging war.'[27] When a new conflict—a war or war-like condition—develops, the current enemy's mental image becomes contaminated with the image of the enemy in the chosen trauma. The new enemy may be in fact descended from the original enemy, or they may not be in any way related.

'Chosen glory' refers to an event that induces in the members of a group intense feelings of having been successful or of having triumphed deservedly over the members of another group. Chosen glories serve to bolster a group's present self-esteem and, like chosen traumas, are heavily mythologized.[28] These events, too, become part of the group's self-identity and are not easily relinquished. The chosen glory is reactivated again and again to summon support for a group's self-esteem. In certain situations, it supports the group's shared sadism and masochism to 'recreate' or live up to the chosen glory. Both chosen glories and chosen traumas are introjected by the child, as it were, along with his mother's milk and, as he grows, through the media of parental stories, communal festivals, and history lessons. They shape indelibly his sense of ethnic identity. The inter-generational transmission of chosen trauma and chosen glory is more than the child's hearing stories, reading books, etc. about the event. Such a transmission occurs mostly in a silent fashion within the child's relationship with important others and through what psychoanalysts call 'identifications'.[29]

The Shaking of the Ethnic Tent

Individual self-esteem and ethnic identity inevitably intertwine.[30] The success of an ethnic group uplifts the individuals in that group, and an attack on their ethnic identity hurts them. A comment by a Greek hero from Greece's War of Independence in the early nineteenth century clearly conforms to this view, as General Makriyannis wrote in his memoirs: 'As I love my country I love nothing else. If one comes and tells me that the country will go forward, I consent that he put out my two eyes. For if I am crippled and the country is well, it nourishes me; if the country is sick, ten eyes let me have, a cripple will I be.'[31]

Ethnic identity can be expressed adaptively in energetic but ordinarily peaceful rituals of competition, such as sporting events, or by a greater affection for the diet, costumes, symbols, and cultural artifacts of one's own group over those of another. Under certain circumstances, however, it can take the form of maladaptive belligerence and violence. In order to understand this, consider that, from childhood on, an individual wears two layers of clothing.[32] The first 'garment', which belongs only to the individual who wears it, fits snugly. This is his or her self-identity. The second set of 'clothes' is a loose covering that shelters many individuals. It is, if you like, a large canvas tent. This is the individual's group or ethnic identity. Chosen traumas and chosen glories are woven into the fabric of the tent, and the column that supports the tent is held by the group's leaders. Their dominant role is to sustain the group's identity and their own authority by keeping alive the memories and emotional meanings of chosen traumas and chosen glories and by presiding over the group's relationships with its neighbours.

The second set of clothes, the ethnic layer, protects us like a mother, or other caregiver. It is the shared 'good' reservoir mentioned earlier. As far as ethnicity is concerned, all the individuals under this tent, whether they are men or women, are equal. If the individuals happen to be Greek, their Greekness is not affected by such factors as social status or level of wealth. All members of the group share equally in the Greekness of the group. As long as the tent remains strong and stable, the members of the group need pay it little heed. They will go about their daily lives without constantly rehearsing and proving their ethnic identity. If the tent is shaken or disturbed, however, this attracts more notice, and all the individuals under the tent collectively become preoccupied with trying to shore it up again. Under these circumstances, the group identity supersedes individual identities. Certain 'cultural amplifiers',[33] such as legends, myths, flags, foods, songs, dances, and other traditions, are utilized in ritualistic ways to preserve both layers of clothes, that is, the individual and group identities.

However, a leader may be driven to act out his own personal drama in the historical arena and, in the process, may shake the tent. The tent may also be disturbed by a neighbouring group's attitudes and behaviour; by what a neighbour projects on the first group's tent; by the insensitivity of a national government dominated by members of a rival ethnic group; by economic changes; natural disasters; man-made disasters, such as Chernobyl; or any number of other real-world issues. Here, psychological and real-world issues become intertwined, for the more stress a group experiences, the more it wants to retain, at all costs, its own identity. The fear of identity loss—of the tent, as it were, collapsing or being torn to shreds—is a fear of psychological death. It occasions such anxiety that physical death may be preferred. Beginning with the next chapter, we examine the ethnic tents of the Turks and the Greeks; we focus on the textures of the fabric and the support columns.

| 2 |

Anatolia Before the Turks

Momentous events that alter the flow of history often take place far from the centres of political power. The 1914 assassination of Archduke Francis Ferdinand in Sarajevo, far from Vienna, London, Paris, Berlin, or St. Petersburg; Columbus' arrival in the New World in 1492; and Vasco Da Gama's rounding of Africa in 1498 far from Madrid and Lisbon are cases in point. A similar event took place in August 1071, in eastern Anatolia. The Byzantine army, under the leadership of Emperor Romanus IV Diogenes, met Alp Arslan's Seljuk army near Manzikert,[34] hundreds of miles from Constantinople and Baghdad, the respective seats of the Christian and Muslim leaders. Romanus Diogenes IV had left Constantinople with his troops in an attempt to keep Anatolia (Asia Minor) safe from Turcomans. Having rescued the Abbasid caliphate from the domination of the Shi'ite Buyids (Buwayhids), under the leadership of Tuğrul Bey (Toghril Beg), in 1055, the orthodox Seljuk Turks became the caliph's faithful client. Intent upon establishing themselves in the heart of the Islamic world, the Seljuks needed to find employment for their Turcoman military retainers who felt that booty was a legitimate end of military action. The Turcomans were directed into Anatolia.

Responding to anguished demands from his subjects in eastern Anatolia for relief from the incursions of the Turcomans, who in 1059 had raided as far west as Sivas, the Byzantine emperor resolved to march into Anatolia at the head of a large army. His plan was to attack the Seljuk Turks in Armenia. At this juncture, the Seljuks under Alp Arslan, who had succeeded his uncle Tuğrul in 1063, were preoccupied with trying to defeat the rivals of the Abbasids, the Shi'ite Fatimids of Egypt. Learning of the projected Byzantine attack, Alp

Arslan turned his troops northward towards Anatolia.

While the exact date and place of the battle are still unresolved issues,[35] the result was definitive. The Seljuk Turks thoroughly defeated the Byzantine emperor himself. Alp Arslan, however, did not exploit his victory. He freed the emperor in return for a ransom, restitution of all frontier strong points captured by the Byzantines in the past half century, and a projected future alliance. With his western flank pacified, Alp Arslan veered towards Central Asia to do battle with the Karakhanids. Having engraved his name in the annals of Turkish history at Manzikert, Alp Arslan died far from home at the hands of a prisoner of war. As for Anatolia after Manzikert, the plateau was open not just to raids by the Turcomans, but to their eventual permanent settlement as well. Thousands came into the new territory, together with their families, horses, and flocks, seeking fresh pasturage. Compared with the heat and aridity of Iraq and Iran, Anatolia presented a more hospitable environment to the newly arriving Turcomans.

Greek Migrations

When the Seljuk Turks arrived, the predominant language of Anatolia was Greek. The Taurus Mountains had formed an effective barrier to Arab incursions in earlier centuries. The dual processes of Arabization in language and Islamization in religion that had washed over the Fertile Crescent under the Umayyads and the Abbasids stopped at the mountains separating Syria from Byzantium. As a consequence, the Anatolian plateau had remained Greek-speaking and Christian.

Greek itself was an importation into the coastal area of western Anatolia, arriving at the end of the Bronze Age with the onset of Greek migrations, spurred on by the collapse of the Mycenean Empire. The Greeks who came to this area after 1200 BC by ship across the Aegean found the region devoid of any central authority. The people whom we call Greeks, so named by the Romans, would call themselves Hellenes. They were bound together by a common culture, the most important elements of which were a common language and a common religion. The process of settlement, which saw them build their own political environments after having been driven out of the northern Peloponnesus took many generations. Ionia would be the name given to the region they settled, and they would be called Ionians. Herodotus in the fifth century BC recorded twelve cities in Ionia, but there could easily have been more. Ephesus and Miletus were the leading cities of the area. Though seaports originally, centuries of natural geological processes have caused them to be far removed from the sea that first nurtured them.

There were two other groups of Greeks who settled along this coast as neighbours to the Ionians; one was the Aeolians in the north and the other was the Dorians in the south. The Aeolians, contemporaries of the Ionians, are said to have come from the eastern flanks of the Greek mainland.[36] The Dorians arrived after 900 BC, moving on to the mainland from bridgeheads on Rhodes and Cos. Halicarnassus was one of their major cities. Ionian expansion took place in north and north-eastern directions. They wrested Smyrna from the Aeolians, and soon planted colonies along the Dardanelles. The city of Miletus was their crowning achievement. This city, in turn, began to send out its own colonizers who set up establishments around the Sea of Marmara. In their northern expansion the Ionians soon ran into colonies established by the Dorians sent out from Megara in Greece itself. Along with the Ionians, it was the Megarians in the seventh century BC who pushed Greek culture into the Black Sea regions after establishing a colony at Byzantium located where the Sea of Marmara and the Bosphorus meet. The Ionians gave the Black Sea its name, Pontus, meaning 'open sea' from its vastness.[37] By 500 BC the entire Black Sea coast was dotted with Greek trading posts and agricultural settlements. The Ionians were prevented from penetrating into the Anatolian plateau by the Phrygians, who were the other great power in Asia Minor with Gordium as their capital.

Enriched through the presence of timber and good pasturage for flocks on the plateau, the Phrygians prospered until attacked from the east by the Cimmerians, who had been pushed out of the steppes by the Scythians. The Scythians established their short-lived hegemony between the Halys and the Euphrates Rivers in the eighth century BC, but they also ranged westward over the next half century, sacking Gordium in the process. While Gordium subsequently recovered, Phrygian power was seriously undermined as they ceased to be a factor in Asia Minor politics.

This active process of colonization experienced along the western coast of Asia Minor was not replicated along its southern coast. Here access to the interior was inhibited by the presence of precipitous mountains. Settlement was possible at only two places, one around

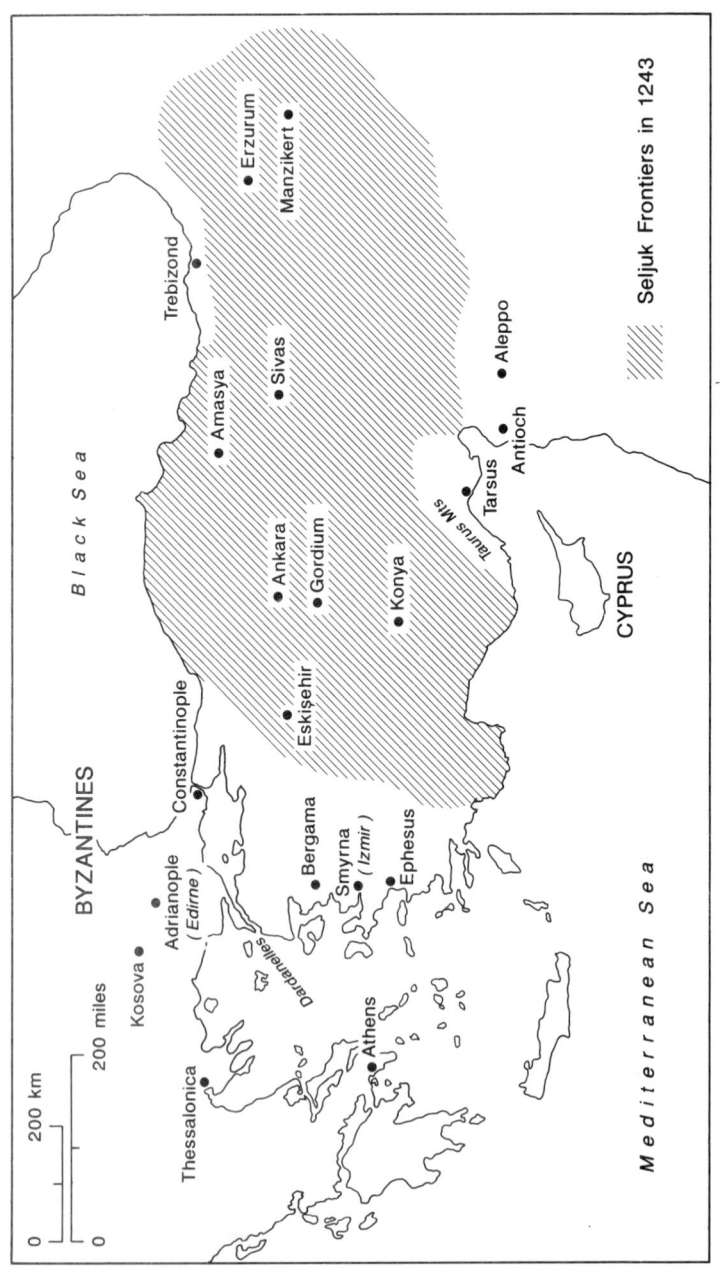

Map 2: Seljuk Turks in Anatolia (1243)

Antalya, and the other at the eastern end of this land mass.

Sixth-century BC Asia Minor is the scene of the emergence of new powers, especially the non-Greek Lydians led by Croesus, who came to the Lydian throne in 561 BC, and the Persians. Croesus attacked the Persians under Cyrus, who followed him into Asia Minor and defeated him before his capital of Sardis. Earlier, Cyrus, an Archaemenid, had in 549 BC taken over the Median empire before he added Lydia to his realm. Lydia was demilitarized, and Sardis became the centre of the western sector of the Persian Empire. The Persians then set about to conquer as many of the Greek colonies in Asia Minor as they could. With the principal exception of the city of Miletus, the Greeks of Asia Minor soon fell under Persian control. The loss of their freedom signalled the end of the Ionian achievement in Asia Minor.[38]

Compared with his predecessors, the Assyrians, Cyrus' rule did not weigh too heavily upon the various elements of his empire as long as they sent their tribute, usually in gold, to his imperial treasury. In anticipation of the satrap system, Cyrus decentralized his empire and respected the culture and institutions of his newly acquired subjects. The Medes and the Babylonians, however, tried to regain their independence after his death, but they were defeated by Darius (522-486 BC). Enveloping himself in the title of 'King of Kings', Darius pushed his empire to the Indus River in the east and Macedonia in the west. Darius introduced the satrap system, dividing the empire into twenty provinces, each administered by a satrap who was a prince or a noble.

Perhaps emboldened by the failure of the Persians to establish themselves permanently in Macedonia in the face of Scythian opposition, the Ionic cities of western Asia Minor rose up in rebellion against their overlords and managed to burn Sardis. Despite the fact that Athens, which had developed into a formidable political and commercial entity bolstered strongly by the discovery of great deposits of silver at Laurium, assisted the Asia Minor Greeks, the Persians triumphed. Athens was now faced by a Persian Empire bent on retribution.

The Persian Wars
Greek culture, based on its language and its religion, in which the Gods interacted with humans and exhibited all the virtues and follies

of human beings (but in epic proportion), and supported by slavery which was mainly of the household variety (it has been estimated that twenty-five per cent of the population were slaves at the height of Athenian prosperity), now clashed with the Persian Empire. Greek antagonism towards the Persians smacked of the flavour of ethnic hostility.

Darius' empire was Ayrian (Aryan) in language and Zoroastrian in religion. Zoroastrianism was characterized by its dualistic emphasis on the struggle between the god of good (light) and the god of evil (darkness). For those who upheld the god of light there would be life everlasting after death. This tenet would be put to the test as the Persians sent their fleet against Athens. Initially, things went well for the Greeks. In 492 BC the Persian fleet was wrecked near Mount Athos, and two years later, another fleet was destroyed at the Battle of Marathon. In their next attempt a decade later, the Persians landed a large army, perhaps eighty thousand strong, under their king, Xerxes I, in Thrace. The brunt of the land war was borne by Sparta, but the pendulum swung for the Persians, who defeated the Greeks at Thermopylae. Retreating to Corinth, the Greeks then focused their fleet in the bay of Salamis where they gained a huge victory over Xerxes' ships. Deprived of their naval support, Xerxes' troops on the Greek mainland were defeated the following year, and his navy suffered another crushing blow at Mycale.

Basically, the Persian Wars were at an end. These victories were followed up with similar gains in Asia Minor as the Persians retreated back to their homeland. Asia Minor began its dual existence as either the furthest reaches of Europe or the beginnings of Asia. The great classical age of Greece was ushered in on the wings of enthusiasm engendered by these victories. Immortal names of places and people are associated with this era—Athens and Sparta, Socrates, Plato, Aristotle, Herodotus, and Thucydides, to mention only a few. This age of glory lasted until another world conqueror burst upon the historical scene in the second half of the fourth century BC.

Alexander and Hellenism

Alexander! His very name represents a watershed in human history. He was the son of Philip II of Macedon, who, in 359 BC, began to unify and expand the kingdom over which he had become regent and then ruler in his own right. Relying upon an army that employed heavily armoured cavalry, phalanxes of pikemen armed with extra long pikes, and heavy siege weapons, Philip, in 355 BC, entered into a nine-years long war against Athens and emerged in control of central Greece. In 336 BC as Philip prepared to move eastward in the hope of driving the declining Persian empire out of Asia Minor, he was assassinated. His son Alexander succeeded him.

Personally brave to the point of recklessness, learned through his years of tutoring by Aristotle, politically creative, and desirous of the approbation of others (especially of his mother through whom he identified himself as being descended from Achilles), Alexander threw himself into the creation of his empire. In 334 BC he headed his army into Asia Minor. After cutting the Gordion Knot at Gordium, which stamped him as the Conqueror of Asia according to the oracle's prediction, Alexander unleashed a decade of conquest that carried him all the way to the valley of the Indus River in India. Tired of constant campaigning, his soldiers forced him to head back home. On the return trip he contracted what was most likely malaria and died in Babylon in 323 BC.

Alexander's conquests and achievements were monumental in extent and scope. He established Greek dominion outside the Greek mainland from Ionia to India. Great as those lifetime accomplishments were, the spread of Greek culture into the areas ruled by Alexander and then by the successor states, usually headed by his generals and their descendants, was an even greater achievement. Historians have called this infusion of Greek culture Hellenism and the resulting culture Hellenistic. The dynasties which were especially influential in this process of Hellenization were the Seleucids who, ruling from Antioch, claimed dominion over Alexander's former empire from Bactria across Afghanistan and Iran into Asia Minor, and the Ptolemys, in Egypt, whose rule lasted until the death of Cleopatra in 30 BC.

Throughout the Near East during the Hellenistic age Greek became not only the official governmental language but the language of most of the people as well. Colonization, that is, the importation of people of Greek origin and the creation of scores of cities by Greeks, was the policy of the era, with the intention of fostering the Hellenization of the people on the scene. These new cities, notably those in Asia Minor, were not in the classical Greek mode with a highly developed sense of self-consciousness and independence. The Seleucids were autocratic and continued the Persians' satrap government system. In places such as Pergamum near the Ionian coast of Asia Minor, intellectual life was fostered by the Attalids, and elsewhere in the Near East Greek learning was kept alive, added to, and transmitted, but with less of the innovative and creative spirit of earlier days. Greek culture mixed with the ever-present Oriental heritage of the Near East, producing the Hellenistic civilization which was pre-shadowed in the mass marriage of Alexander's troops to local women, the symbolic marriage of East and West.

The Romans and Christianity

Hellenistic civilization reigned supreme in the Near East until the advent of the Romans. Roman rule was extended over the Near East, including Asia Minor, commencing in the middle of the second century BC and continuing until 58 BC when Cyprus was annexed, giving Rome effective control of the Near East from Egypt to the Black Sea. The process of Hellenization continued under Roman rule, facilitated by the era of peace ushered in under the Roman empire. While the internal history of Rome, characterized by the growth of huge landed estates, struggles for power often involving manipulations for control of the military, revolutions, and murders (including that of Julius Caesar himself), is beyond the scope of this chapter, it is sufficient to say that with respect to the Near East, Roman rule continued to be extended from the coastline of Asia Minor and the Near East into the interior.

One highly significant element in the expansion of Roman rule was its confrontation with the Jews of the Fertile Crescent, who had managed to re-establish their independence in 142 BC only to lose it, in 63 BC, to Pompey, who then established Roman authority in the area. Out of these mundane events came the origins of Christianity. In AD 26 Pontius Pilate was named governor of Judea, and, as they say, the rest is history, for it was he who condoned the sentence of execution passed against Jesus of Nazareth by the Jewish religious court on a charge of blasphemy which led in AD 33 to Jesus' crucifixion. Christ's teachings were kept alive by a small group of his disciples and then propagated by Paul of Tarsus who undertook several trips to preach the new religion in the eastern Mediterranean area. The new religion broke with Judaism, out of which it originated, on the doctrine of the divinity of Jesus, and it began to set down roots in Rome itself.

Constantinople and the Byzantine Empire

Over the course of the next three centuries, Christianity was to undergo several severe persecutions, the last begun in AD 303 under Diocletian. The fortunes of Christianity turned for the better after Constantine (who reunited the Roman Empire under his sole rule in 324) converted to Christianity. Through his own person he linked the new church and the Roman Empire. To free his new creation from the association with paganism so prevalent in Rome, he moved the centre of the empire. Building upon the ruins of the old Greek colony of Byzantium where the waters of the Black Sea, emerging from the Bosphorus, mix with the Sea of Marmara before entering the Dardenelles to spill into the Aegean and then into the Mediterranean, he erected a new capital which would bear his name, Constantinople.

Out of the cultural and religious crisis that Rome passed through in the fourth century arose a new synthesis of Christian, Greek, and Eastern cultures which would come to be known as Byzantine. The new Rome became the centre of this new politico-religious dispensation upon its dedication in May 330. Sitting astride both east-west and north-south trade routes, Constantinople would prosper, and its founding would be one of Constantine's greatest achievements.

Byzantine government quickly became characterized by a centralized, bureaucratic government headed by an increasingly autocratic emperor-god based on Oriental, largely Persian, models. By the time of the second church Council which was held in Constantinople in 381, the bishop, or patriarch, of the city was ranked second to the bishop of Rome, an indication of the status the city had achieved in half a century. A major point of contention was still the issue of whether the state was supreme over the church or if the church remained outside the temporal authority of the state. At the same time, paganism lost its final battles with Catholicism in the decrees of Theodosius in 392. More troubling than religious issues to the Byzantines in the fifth century were their relations with the fierce Germanic bands, the Visigoths led by Alaric, on their western flank and the Huns in the middle Danube region.

Culturally, Constantinople came to replace pagan Athens, which had gone into decline as the intellectual centre of the Roman Empire once Christianity became established. While Latin still remained the official language of the empire, recognition of the fact that Greek was the dominant language of the people in the eastern part of the empire was demonstrated in the organization of the new higher school in Constantinople under Theodosius II in 425. Thirteen teachers were assigned to teach in Latin, but fifteen would teach in Greek.[39]

Theodosius II was also responsible for the production of the codex of laws which bears his name and the construction of the walls of Constantinople, which were built to protect the city that had outgrown the original wall built by Constantine. The codex was written in Latin and became one of the principal means by which Roman law was mediated to western Europe.

Religious problems, once thought resolved by the second ecumenical council, continued vexatiously. In 451 the fourth council convened in Chalcedon to deal with the issue of Monophysitism, the question of whether Christ had one or two natures. The council reversed the decision of the second ecumenical council and affirmed the two natures of Christ. The schism became hardened, and the eastern provinces of Syria and Egypt were firmly alienated, creating fertile ground for the success of the Arab Muslim invasions of the seventh century. The fifth century also witnessed the increased presence of Slavs in the Balkans coupled with the first Hunnic (peoples of Turkic origins) invasions.

Byzantine culture grew out of an amalgamation of three influences that occurred slowly from the fourth to the sixth centuries. These were Christianity, Hellenism, and the Orient.[40] This work of cultural synthesis was spurred on by Emperor Justinian against a background of his almost incessant warfare carried out in the west against the Germanic tribes and in the east against the Persians. Justinian also engaged in legislative work for which he has gained lasting distinction. Under his orders, the great compendia of Roman law, the Code, The Digest, and law handbook, The Institutes, which were designed as guides for students of the law, were created from 529 to 533. These works were all in Latin, and spawned a number of commentaries and 'ponies' in Greek which greatly facilitated their usefulness in everyday life. Justinian led the way for the reconciliation between Roman law and the practices of the East which were so heavily influenced by Christianity and the Orient.

Justinian's wars inflicted severe economic hardship on the empire. The treasury was exhausted. Prolonged confrontation with the Persians weakened Byzantium both financially and militarily. In their turn, the Persians were similarly hard pressed. Neither the Byzantines nor the Persians would be successful in resisting the advance of Islam into the Fertile Crescent and on to the Iranian plateau.

History remembers Justinian more for his politics than his wars. He is the archetypical exponent of Caesaropapism, the notion that held the Byzantine emperor to be both Caesar and Pope, supreme in all matters temporal as well as spiritual.[41] Justinian, under the influence of his wife, Theodora, sought reconciliation with the Monophysites, but he failed to unite the church behind a common policy. Seeking to bolster Christianity, he stamped out the last stronghold of paganism by closing the philosophical school of Athens in 529, an action that would have disastrous repercussions for Greek learning, especially in Asia Minor.

Internally, Justinian was faced with economic hardships induced by the rise of great landed estates in the hands of local magnates and the church as well. In this, as in many other areas, he failed to achieve lasting victory despite confiscating many large estates. Taxation and official corruption were two other areas in which Justinian sought to achieve reform. War made efficient collection of taxes imperative and demanded honest, incorruptible government agents. Needless to say, he failed on both accounts—corruption spread and tax income dropped. The peasantry was impoverished. Despite all these difficulties, Justinian created a lasting monument to his fame, the construction of the Church of St. Sophia which was dedicated on Christmas Day, 537.

Justinian died in 565 and his immediate successors were no more successful in matters religious, military, or economic. Under attack in Italy by the Lombards, in North Africa by the Berbers, and in Greece itself by the Avar-led Slavs, who basically would put an end to the Hellenes of old, a significant military reform led to the creation of the position of exarch, a military ruler who assumed responsibility for civil administration (both financial and judicial) as well. An exarchate was established in Ravenna and another in Carthage. Out of this structure would come the organization of the *themes*, the provincial structure, that would breathe new life into the Byzantine empire.

As the periphery of the Byzantine empire was peeled away by the Arabs in North Africa, Egypt, Palestine, Syria, and Iraq, the Slavs in Greece, and the Bulgars in the Balkans (among others), only the kernel, Asia Minor, remained.[42] As war became chronic, the civilian-oriented government of the empire could not cope with the problems.

First the exarchate and then its linear descendant, the *theme*, were organized, which turned civilian government into martial law under the military governor or *strategos*. This system is attributed to Heraclius, based on the earlier work of Emperor Maurice.

Under Heraclius (610-641) the Byzantine Empire achieved its classical form, in which two elements predominated. These were the Greek language and the Orthodox church. Greek became the official language of the state, giving its peoples, who came from a variety of cultural and ethnic stocks, a common heritage. This was achieved *without* any affinity for ancient Hellas—the Byzantines remained Romans who now used Greek as their written and spoken language. In matters of religion the state supported the view of the Chalcedon Council that Christ 'was complete in humanity as well as divinity, and the same Christ in two natures, without confusion or change, division or separation, each nature concurring into one Person and one Substance' over against the monophysite view that Christ had possessed one single divine nature.[43] These two views proved to be irreconcilable and have continued to be so.

After the Sassanians, the Arabs presented the next threat to the existence of the Byzantine Empire. Much territory was lost to the Arabs, but the dual processes of Arabization and Islamization were halted at the Taurus Mountains despite deep penetrations into Anatolia and two sieges of Constantinople. Anatolia remained Greek speaking and Christian. Anatolia was kept safe through the elaboration of the *theme* structure, the Armeniac, Anatolic, and Byzantine *themes*. Each *theme* was populated by free peasants organized in communes who grew the food that supported the peasantry and the military of the *theme* and provided tax income for the state. The head of the family or its eldest son served as a soldier, responsible to receive the proper training and provide his own horse and weapons when called upon to serve, which was often. It took a great deal of campaigning by Leo II and his son at the beginning of the ninth century, combined with internal weaknesses in the caliphate, to push the Arabs out of Anatolia.

From the time of Constantine the Great to the beginning of the ninth century, the Roman world considered itself as one entity, ruled by the emperor of the Romans with Constantinople as the centre of that world. The emperor was the embodiment of Christ on earth and had the dual duty of preserving political unity and Christian orthodoxy.[44] This unitarian view was almost destroyed by Charlemagne, who became emperor of the West in 800 and sought to reunify the Roman world by marrying Irene, the empress in Constantinople. This was not to be, and in 802 Irene was driven from her throne by the usurper Nicephorus. The concept of the unitary Roman world was destroyed as Charles, as King of the Franks, created his own western empire on the Byzantine model and claimed equality with the emperor in Constantinople and independence from the papacy. Alongside these two emperors there arose a third, the Pope of Rome, who sought to use this period of internal weakness to strengthen the papacy's claim to superiority over any emperor. Instead of a struggle for superiority, what happened was a gradual separation between the church of the west, which became Latin in spirit, and the church of the east, which became Greek. Just as the empire had been split so, too, the church would be bifurcated.

In Constantinople, the court, weakened by a succession of incompetent emperors, nevertheless kept up the spectacle of imperial greatness. Financially this created a great strain on the provinces, especially in Asia Minor. Increasingly, the peasantry in Asia Minor found itself at odds with the capital, where the military and the upper echelons of the bureaucracy were engaged in a struggle for power. The high ranking military figures extended their control over provincial estates and the former free proprietors who had inhabited them. These military landed magnates intermarried and came to form an aristocracy which was antithetical to the old thematic system. The *themes* had provided government on the local level and a proficient fighting force, but now they were in severe decline. It was against this background that the Turks began to infiltrate into Anatolia and eventually defeated the Byzantine emperor at the Battle of Manzikert in 1071.

Following Manzikert and in the absence of great organized military resistance from Constantinople—due largely to the fact that the bureaucratic party had systematically destroyed the military establishment since the death of Basil II in 1025—the Turks began their conquests of Asia Minor under the impetus of the dual processes of Turkification and Islamization. To the Arabs before them and now to the Turks, Asia Minor was *Rum*, meaning the land of the Romans and its Byzantine Greek inhabitants. The language used by the overwhelming majority of the area's population gradually would become Turkish and the religion, Islam. After the ninth century the language of the elite-bureaucratic, religious, and militarily-centred elements in Constantinople was Greek, replacing Latin. In addition, there was a renaissance in learning in the early eleventh century centred in the newly reopened University of Constantinople in 1045, but we are less well-informed about the status of Greek and Greek learning in the countryside. Anatolia had been Hellenized along its coastlines first, and only later did Hellenism spread throughout the peninsula. With respect even to the capital, Anna Comnena remarked: 'From the time of the Emperor Basil the Porphyrogenitus down to the Emperor Monomachus the study of letters, although neglected by the majority, had nevertheless not entirely died out.'[45]

In the countryside the process undertaken by the emperors of repopulating Anatolia as a defensive measure must have had some impact on the exclusiveness of Greek as the local language. They used peoples of non-Greek origins, especially Slavs and Armenians, who were moved into Anatolia in large numbers at the end of the seventh century. The sources as well as the scholarship are neither clear nor unanimous on the issues of the size of the Anatolian population and the linguistic situation there on the eve of the Turkish invasion.[46]

| 3 |

From Manzikert to Constantinople

The First Encounters

The people who would establish, first the Seljuk state in the twelfth century, and then the Ottoman enterprise in the thirteenth century in Anatolia, were Turks. The meaning of the word Turk is unknown,[47] but the first mention of Turks in written records was in Chinese and Byzantine sources of the sixth century AD. The Turkish language belongs to the family of languages known as Ural-Altaic, which makes them linguistically related to the Finno-Ugrian speakers, which include the Finns, Hungarians, and Mongols.[48] As such, the Turks are related to the Huns, best remembered for their empire in Europe under Attila in the fifth century. Turks had established an empire in Central Asia from the Jaxartes to the Siberia, from the Altai to the Volga Rivers. They were pastoral nomads relying on sheep and camels for their wealth and material needs and their ability to shoot their bows and arrows while on horseback for their military superiority. Gradually at first, and then more quickly by the tenth century, Turks began to migrate westward. Some groups followed routes that took them north of the Caspian Sea, and others to the south of that body of water. In this way Turks came into Europe, where they were known by various names, including Pecheneg and Cuman. Others came into Khorasan and Iran, the Fertile Crescent, and Asia Minor. These were mainly the Oğuz (Oghuz) of whom tradition says there were twenty-four tribes. The Kınık were the most important of the twenty-four tribes, and the Seljuks were of the Kınık tribe of the Oğuz. The Ottomans would later also claim to be Oğuz.

Along their journey the Oğuz were Islamized and adopted the Arabic script for their language. The vanguard of Turks making their way into the central Islamic world were a group known as 'Iraqi Turks', who were a part of the Seljuks. The main body of Seljuks under their leader, Tuğrul, reached Khorasan by the third decade of the eleventh century and took the area from the Ghaznevid Turks after the battle of Dandanaqan in 1040. From then on Tuğrul concentrated his efforts on the conquest of the central Islamic world, and in 1055 he took the caliphal seat of Baghdad. He converted himself from the head of a large group of nomads into a sultan—someone who exercised power and authority due to the military might at his command rather than through religious sanction.

Assuming the role as the sword of Islam under the banner of the caliph, the Seljuks, with their regular troops, expanded southwards towards Egypt. The irregulars, or Turcomans, were directed against Anatolia.[49] There a combination of their military skill and the breakdown of Byzantine control over the area (due to a variety of causes that included the decline of the military under the bureaucratic regime in Constantinople and the redirection of what forces were available in Anatolia to the west in order to meet the Pecheneg threat on the Danube) opened Anatolia to the incursion of the Turks which resulted, as described earlier, in the battle of Manzikert in 1071.

Following Manzikert, the Turcomans flooded into Anatolia. The obvious Turkish threat had little impact on the warring military and bureaucratic factions in Constantinople, each of which sought to hire Turcoman warriors in support of its cause. By this time there were a number of Turkish groups setting up their own little states, or emirates, throughout Anatolia. These included the Danishmends under their leader Malik Danishmend, and Süleyman ibn Kutulmus, who was the representative of the Seljuks in Baghdad. He set up his centre in Nicaea (İznik), but with the intention of forming a large Turcoman army to go back and defeat his Seljuk family members in Baghdad. He died on one such campaign in 1086. It would take several decades before his heirs would come to see Anatolia as a worthy prize in its own right. They then settled down in Konya and organized the sultanate of the Seljuks of *Rum* which was an Islamic state based on the traditions of High Islam in its culture and civilization. They built mosques, *medreses* (colleges for instruction in the Islamic sciences), caravanserais, *imarets* (soup kitchens), irrigation systems, roads, and bridges. They distributed *iqtas* (incomes derived from a share in agricultural taxation in return for military service) and educated slaves for governmental service (*ghulams*).[50] High Islamic culture tolerated other scriptural religions, and life in Seljuk Asia Minor was characterized by a semi-symbiotic relationship among the Turks and non-Turks and Muslims and non-Muslims. Konya attracted the great mystic Mevlana Celâleddin-i Rumi, spiritual leader of the Whirling Dervishes. He represents, among other things, the inclusivity and tolerance of Islamic culture rather than exclusivity. He urged:

> Whether you are Arab or Greek or Turk—
> Learn the tongue without tongues![51]

At his death he was mourned by Turks, Greeks, and Jews alike according to the comments of his son:

> The people of the city, young and old
> were all lamenting, crying, sighing loud,
> The villagers as well as Turks and Greeks,
> They tore their shirts from grief for this great man.
> 'He was our Jesus!'—thus the Christians spoke.
> 'He was our Moses!' said the Jews of him.[52]

The Crusades

In typical Islamic fashion, the Seljuks settled groups, some of recent nomadic heritage, in their march lands to protect the frontiers. This was especially necessary when the Byzantine emperor was driven out of Constantinople in 1204 by the Latins of the Fourth Crusade who diverted the venture from the Holy Land to the conquest of the Byzantine capital. The first crusade had been preached by Urban II in Clermont on 22 November 1095. Ostensibly, the crusade was intended to deliver the eastern Christians, who were depicted as being slaughtered by the Turks. The Pope painted coming to the aid of the Greeks as an act of charity. The crusade also had the aim of delivering Jerusalem from the hands of the infidels. European stereotyping of the Turks as violent, marauding nomads and as the enemies of Christianity stems from the occupation of Jerusalem by the Seljuks. By the time the crusaders reached Jerusalem in early June 1099, however, it had been taken from the Turks by the Fatimids of Egypt.

The crusades would also serve to divide the Mediterranean world into the Christian West and the Muslim East.

As preached by Urban II, the crusade would also have the added benefit of getting rid of unemployed military men who were engaging in brigandage and disturbing the Truce of God in France and other areas of Europe. The idea of a crusade caught on quickly, assisted by the experience gained since 1085 in waging holy war in Spain against the Muslims. Hope of booty was another incentive to participate in this holy venture, as was the grant of an indulgence—the remission of the penance which the church imposed for sin.[53] The crusaders sewed on crosses to indicate that they had taken a vow to pray at the Holy Sepulchre. And pray they did after the conquest of the city on 15 July 1099, after massacring the Muslims and the Jews in the holy city - which aroused enormous resentment against Christianity in the Near East.

Initially, the crusaders saw the lands of the Levant which they conquered as the patrimony of the Latin Church. Quickly, however, they organized the Kingdom of Jerusalem with its three fiefs, the County of Edessa, the Principality of Antioch, and the County of Tripoli. Through their mistreatment of both the Muslims and the eastern Christians, the crusaders wore out their welcome. The second crusade in 1101 was designed to ensure control of the Holy Land, but it ended in failure. The crusaders were mauled near Merzifon on the Anatolian plateau, precipitating a general panic and hasty retreat all the way back to Constantinople and beyond to western Europe.

In 1187 Saladin retook Jerusalem, much to the satisfaction of the Greek Christians who had suffered under the Latin Christians, thereby provoking the Third Crusade (1189-1192). It is interesting to note that once Saladin had destroyed the Latin Kingdom of Jerusalem, the Latin churches were converted, or reconverted into mosques, but the Greek establishments were left unmolested. The Third Crusade featured such renowned European personalities as the Holy Roman Emperor Frederick Barbarossa and Richard Lion Heart. Frederick died early in the Crusade in an Anatolian river, and Richard left the Holy Land on 9 October 1192, ill and more concerned about political events in England than praying in the church of the Holy Sepulchre. He departed after arranging a truce with Saladin. As the twelfth century drew to a close, Pope Innocent III promoted the notion of a Fourth Crusade to liberate the Holy Land again. While this crusade was still in the talking stage,

Boniface of Monteferrat emerged as the designated leader. In return, he asked for the return of the fief of Thessalonica (Salonica) which was in Byzantine hands. From the outset, the Fourth Crusade was more Byzantium than Jerusalem-oriented. The crusade was diverted from its goal of the Holy Land to Constantinople because of the interests of its principal backers, Boniface, the Holy Roman Emperor Philip of Swabia, and the Venetians. Philip was related by marriage to the Angelus family, who were pretenders to the Byzantine throne. In the end, in 1203 the crusaders attacked Constantinople and drove the emperor into exile, electing two members of the Angelus family as co-emperors. They were slow to act on the proposed reunion of the Latin and Orthodox churches, and they soon fell out with the crusaders. In April 1204, the Latins took the city after an uprising had resulted in the deaths of the co-emperors and the usurpation of the throne by another pretender. The crusaders then submitted the populace of Constantinople to three days of organized terror for which the Greeks still harbour great resentment. This sense of violation was summed up by the Greek historian Nicetas Chonistes: 'The accursed Latins ... lust after our possessions and would like to destroy our race ... between *them and us* [italics added] there is a wide gulf of hatred.'[54]

On 16 May 1204 Baldwin was crowned emperor in Hagia Sophia (St. Sophia), beginning the Latin Empire of Constantinople that would last until 1261. The Byzantine territory was divided up among the emperor, the Venetians, and the non-Venetian crusaders. The Byzantine leadership fled to Asia Minor. One group under Alexius and David Comnenus captured the city of Trebizond (Trabzon) on the eastern shore of the Black Sea and initiated a Byzantine state in exile. Theodore Lascaris took refuge in the interior of Anatolia in Bursa. He had himself crowned emperor in 1208 and organized a Greek state in exile around Nicaea. There the emperor-in-exile sought to shore up his Anatolian defences. A stalemate of sorts was created in Anatolia between the Greeks and the Turks that was shaken first by the defeat of the Seljuks in 1243 at the hands of the Mongols and then in 1261 when the Byzantines regained their capital.

The Beginning of the Ottomans
Following the defeat of the Seljuks, the groups of Turks who had taken up residence on the frontier to engage in raiding of non-Muslims in order to gain booty, and a place in heaven if they should fall in

battle, and whose numbers had been increased by those fleeing the Mongols, were called *ghazis* (*gazis* - those who carried out raiding, *ghazza*). One such group started out in Söğüt, near Eskişehir, under their eponymous founder Osman, and would be known to history as the Ottomans.

Benefiting from their strategic position closest to the Byzantine trade routes, which offered opportunities for booty, and developing into the paramount *ghazis* on the frontier, the Ottomans quickly attracted other *ghazis* to their banner. From march warden for the Seljuks the Ottoman leader was now an emir, the head of his own small state or emirate. He extended his territory at the expense of the local Byzantine population who found themselves alienated from their own rulers (now back in Constantinople and seeking to extend their dominion into the Balkans rather than in Anatolia). The Ottoman ranks were swelled by alliances with Greek war lords, by conversion of local Greeks and others to Islam, the peaceful absorption of other *ghazi* groups, and at times by the annexation of lands belonging to other emirates.

Soon, the Ottoman emir became a factor in Byzantine royal politics as the aid of the Ottomans was sought by one or another faction in the struggle for the position of emperor. After Osman's son, Orhan (1326-62), followed up his father's work by taking Bursa in 1326, İznik in 1331, and İzmit in 1337, he entered into the service of Emperor John VI Cantacuzenus to assist him in the near-perpetual struggles for the throne. The Byzantine-Ottoman alliance was strengthened through the marriage of John's daughter Theodora to Orhan. By 1352 the Ottomans had established a bridgehead at Tzympe (Cinbi) on the Gallipoli peninsula which they had used as the point through which they shuttled their forces back and forth between Asia Minor and Europe.

Once established in Europe, the Ottomans began to act in their own interests rather than as mercenaries in Byzantine political struggles. In 1354 they took Gallipoli (Gelibolu) after the local people left in the aftermath of an earthquake, and by 1361 they had advanced as far as Adrianople (Edirne). By means of a three-pronged attack that took them to Serres (1383) and Salonika (1387) on the left, Sofia (1385) and Nish (1386) in the centre, and the Black Sea on the right, the Ottomans began their centuries-long occupation of the Balkans. Behind the expanding frontier, Turks from Anatolia, some attracted by the possibilities and others forcibly relocated by the emir, populated the conquered regions.

In the first stage of their conquests the Ottomans converted conquered Bulgarian and Serbian Christian overlords into vassals whom they allowed to continue to rule in return for contributions of troops to be used in their Anatolian campaigns. Murat I pressed on with the conquest of the Balkans, but the Bulgars and the Serbs revolted against their conditions of vassalage, and Murat had to bring the full force of his army to bear on them. On the plain of Kosova in 1389 Murat's army defeated the Serbs under Lazar, but it was a costly victory. Murat was slain by a Serb at the battle's end. His son Bayazit (Bayezid) succeeded him immediately, and Lazar was slain along with his son. This entire series of events was amalgamated into the legend of Kosova that is still alive today in the current tragedy in the former Yugoslavia.

Bayazit increased the intensity of the Ottoman drive into the Balkans, and successfully petitioned the caliph in Cairo for the right to use the title sultan. He also extended the Ottoman domains in Anatolia, which brought him into conflict with the central Asian conqueror Tamerlane. In 1402 the armies of the two parties met outside Ankara. The Ottomans were defeated and Bayazit was taken prisoner. He died while in captivity, and Tamerlane reinstated all the Anatolian emirs dispossessed by the Ottomans. It took the Ottomans just over a decade to restore their sultanate during a period that has come to be termed the Interregnum. Upon the reconstitution of their holdings, the Ottomans began to renew their conquests.

Great strides were made under Murat II, but Constantinople still remained outside the Ottoman orbit. Murat died in 1451 and was succeeded by his son Mehmet II. Constantinople became the centre of discussion in Ottoman councils. The 'war party' was urged on by Zaganos Pasha, Mehmet's slave-tutor, and Çandarlı Halil Pasha represented the 'peace party' which sought an accommodation with Byzantium. In the end, the Ottomans decided to press on with the attack on Constantinople. After a long siege, which Halil Pasha urged abandoning, the Ottoman army breached the walls of the city, and on 29 May 1453 the Ottomans took the Byzantine capital, thereby uniting the Anatolian and European parts of their domains. Mehmet allowed his troops three days of pillaging in accordance with the dictates of Islamic law, then restored order as a prerequisite to turning the city into the greatest capital of the Islamic world. Later Constantinople would be renamed Istanbul.

| 4 |

Greek Inability to Mourn over Constantinople

Continuity is coveted by the human mind. When a link breaks and a loss is sustained, we feel anxious. Without a successful period of mourning over the loss of people, things, land, and pride, no realistic internal or external adaptations can occur. In a clinical situation, we usually study the process of mourning in an individual after the death of a loved one, and we see that after an initial shock comes disbelief, denial, bargaining, and anger followed by a painful struggle over either the surrender or retention of the lost person (or thing). The mourner settles into a slow sandpapering process, called the work of mourning.[55] If everything goes without complications, the mourner accepts the discontinuity and change, making the loss a futureless memory.[56]

Some mourners cannot let the image of the dead rest in peace; they are locked into a seemingly endless struggle between the hope of regaining the loss and the ability to let it go. We call such individuals perennial mourners. Most of us have met perennial mourners at one time or another. Years after the loss they speak of the dead person (or thing) in the present tense; they seem to have an active relationship with him or her; they are interested in reincarnation. In short, their minds are actively populated with the images of the dead person. The individual's inability to mourn has various causes. For example, the loss may be too great to be assimilated; the mourner may be too dependent to give up his/her need for the now dead love object, or he/she may be too angry about what happened to accept reality.

Intellectually, the perennial mourner knows that the link is broken, but consciously and, even more importantly, unconsciously, dreams about the return of the unbroken link while wishing that he could accept the reality fully and unburden himself from hopeless efforts once and for all. He seems doomed in a continual struggle between keeping what is lost and fully accepting a new reality. In his mind, the event in which the loss occurred remains fresh as he expends most of his energies to find echoes of this past in the present. He becomes obsessed with this major topic, the loss, and how to deal with it. Passing a graveyard, reading obituaries, or seeing a morgue on television can reopen the old wounds, causing him to bleed anew. The lost person or thing, over many years, does not become a futureless image. The mourner keeps the image to respond to his internal mind's eye's wishes, thereby keeping the illusion that the wound can be repaired.

Groups also mourn.[57] When the members who compose the groups share a loss, a drastic change, or a narcissistic blow, they too may, like individuals, become to one degree or another, perennial mourners and may pass this attitude on from generation to generation.[58] The Turkish victory on 29 May 1453 ended one era in history and began a new one as the Byzantine Empire was replaced by the Ottoman Empire. Constantinople was captured by the Turks on a Tuesday, and every Tuesday thereafter has been treated by the Greeks and some other Christians as an unpropitious day of the week. Reality, fantasy, rituals, and myths have been linked throughout history due to a loading of our perceptions of events with shared emotions. When chronicles were a primary form of historical writing in Europe during medieval and early modern times, chroniclers were not much concerned with reality in their pantheon of causal factors in history. For them the prime mover of human history was the hand of God. Constantinople's fall to the heathen Turks was attributed to God's judgement brought down upon those Christians 'because of the sins of Christians everywhere'.[59]

On that memorable day in May 1453 a link had been broken. The loss belonged to the entire Christian world. When news of the capture of Constantinople reached Rome and other European centres, shock and disbelief prevailed, despite Byzantium's earlier calls for Latin help against the Turk and the anger that arose when no such help was forthcoming. The Turkish victory was experienced as a knife plunged into the heart of Christianity. On 12 July 1453 Aeneas Sylvius

Piccolomini, a future Pope, wrote to Pope Nicholas V that the Turks had killed Homer and Plato for the second time.[60] The fact was that the loss of Constantinople could not be mourned. After the initial shock, disbelief, and anger, the shared work of mourning could not take a 'normal' course—it was contaminated. It should be remembered that we use the term 'work of mourning' here in the psychoanalytic sense—the sum total of obligatory human reactions initiated to deal with the changes, losses, and threats around them until a new internal adaptation sets in and a relationship with the new environment crystallizes. Furthermore, the loss of Constantinople reopened the wounds caused by the loss of Jerusalem. The two losses were condensed. While Jerusalem had been 'regained' and then 'relost', the reaction to the defeat at Constantinople was only helplessness. The fall of Constantinople to the Turks, which came three hundred years after Manzikert, became the major chosen trauma for the Christian world. Some Christians referred to the conqueror of Constantinople, Mehmet II, as 'the Beast of the Apocalpyse' or the 'Satan'.

The Seed of the 'Megali' Idea
Following the capture of the city, the wish to deny the loss of Constantinople among Christians, especially among the Greeks, in order to escape from the blow of this trauma, could not be maintained fully as the reality of the presence of the Turks in the city set in. The desire to undo the loss expressed itself in the form of rumblings about the organization of another crusade. Nothing came of such talk, but the idea still lingered on. A few years after the fall of Constantinople, songs were shared among the Christians of the Ottoman domains in an attempt to deny the change and recapture the loss. They sang: 'Again with years, with time, again they will be ours.' As Young observed, 'Thus was born again the "Great Idea" that haunts many Greeks to this day.'[61] The fact is that the 'Great Idea' (*Megali Idea*) became an ideology only in the mid-nineteenth century, but the Greeks reached back to the fall of Constantinople as the origin of this ideology. The 'Great Idea' is 'the doctrine of Greek irredentism whereby all the lands of Classical and Byzantine Hellenism should be reclaimed for the reborn nation'.[62] It refers to a pan-Hellenistic ideology in which the aim is to activate a dream of someday recapturing Constantinople and restoring the Byzantine Empire. Markides states, 'One could argue that the 'Great Idea' had an internal logic, pressing for realization in every

part of the Greek world which continues to be under foreign rule.'[63]

Linking and Unlinking

If a continuity or link between the Turks and the Byzantines could be established, there would be less of a need for the Byzantines and other Christians to feel hurt or wounded. Schoebel examines, through historical documents, how the legend of Troy was invoked to identify the Turks. A preoccupation existed among Westerners to search for the antique origins of the Turks. A humanist, Giovanni Maria Filelfo, declared that Mehmet II had a Trojan ancestry; therefore, he had a right to possess Asia Minor but added ambivalently, that if Mehmet II was truly Trojan, he had no right to seize Greece proper. A German, Felix Fabri, also traced the origins of the Turks as descended from Teucer, son of the Greek Telamon and the Trojan princess Hesione. It should be recalled that Telamon was a friend of Hercules. Felix Fabri did not accept Teucer as the origin of the Turks, but he believed that the Turks came from Turcus, a son of Troyas, whose grandfather was Laomedan.[64]

Those involved in the literary preoccupation described above tried to find a 'link' between the Greeks and the Turks, their 'old' neighbours.[65] While efforts by Christians to find a continuity or link between the two sides continued in an effort to make the loss or change more tolerable, the process of mourning also required an opposite attempt—to unlink the two sides so that Byzantines could maintain their identities; this, in turn, led to further stereotyping of the Turks.

Berkes states that 'the Fates' played a trick; the Turks were the recipients. Because they conquered Constantinople (condensed with the mental representation of their conquering Jerusalem), the Turks became the unconsciously selected targets of a stubborn, systematic, negative stereotyping by Europeans and, therefore, by Western historians. These scholars, according to Berkes, never stereotyped other peoples who are 'strangers' to Europeans (i.e., Chinese, Arabs, Japanese) as much as they stereotyped the Turks.[66]

Mehmet the Conqueror and Oedipal Themes

A closer look at Mehmet II, also known as the Conqueror or the Grand Turk, who at the age of twenty-one brought an end to the Byzantine Empire, may illuminate the initial tone of the relationship between the conqueror and the conquered, between the Turks and the Greeks (most of whom would soon fall under Turkish domination for centuries to come). Also we shall try to show that, besides dealing a narcissistic blow to the Christian world, the Christians' chosen trauma pertaining to the fall of Constantinople includes a less apparent symbolism that connected it with oedipal and sexual issues.

Mehmet, the fourth son of Sultan Murat II, was born on 30 March 1432 in the Ottoman palace of Edirne built by his grandfather, Murat I. His mother was Huma Hatun (the name Huma, meaning bird of paradise, was also borne by the mother of Xerxes). Some writers have claimed that she was Italian or French, but she appears to have been a Serbian or a Macedonian slave. One recent Turkish writer claims she was Greek.[67] In any case, the young prince was soon given over to the care of a nanny named Daye Hatun, and it was she who raised him.[68] Following the contemporary Ottoman practice of sending young princes out to govern provinces under the tutelage of their mentors (*lalas*), Mehmet was sent as governor to Amasya, in Anatolia, in the Spring of 1443 together with his two mentors. Later that year, upon the death of his older brother, Mehmet was left as the sole surviving Ottoman prince. Thereupon, his father, who was contemplating stepping down from the sultanate, recalled him to Edirne. Murat II then arranged a peace treaty with the Serbs and Hungarians in June 1444. With peace assured and with an eye towards preventing a struggle for the throne threatened by a pretender named Orhon, who was appointed by the Byzantines in Constantinople, he brought his twelve-year-old son to the throne and went into retirement in Anatolia in July 1444.

Young Sultan Mehmet inherited his father's grand vizier, Çandarlı Halil Pasha, who immediately entered into a serious rivalry with Zaganos and İbrahim, the sultan's two *lalas*. Halil represented the entrenched Turkish ruling class. He was from the religious element, the *ulema* who were the guardians of the High Islamic tradition. He represented the party that favoured a policy of peace and compromise towards Byzantium. Opposed to him were Zaganos and İbrahim from the military class. They represented the rising power of the *devşirme* people, those young boys who were levied from the Christian Orthodox population, enslaved (the best of whom were trained and educated for Ottoman service with the rest eventually becoming Janissaries), converted to Islam, and given access to the most important military/administrative positions in the empire. Their policy called for stepped-up conquest, especially the conquest of Constantinople.

While this struggle for control of the sultan and the direction of Ottoman policy was being waged within the palace, the conduct of state affairs was not as carefully supervised as it should have been. On 8 September 1444 there was a serious uprising in Edirne itself led by a heretic of the Hurufi dervish order, a group known to espouse Shi'ism. This event, in which the Hurufi propagandist lost his life, led to further deterioration of relations between Halil, who felt that young Mehmet had supported the heretic, and Sultan Mehmet. The rift between the two was further enlarged by the news that a crusader army had crossed the Danube and was planning to lay siege to Varna. Not trusting the young Sultan Mehmet and his supporters to defend the Ottoman domains successfully, he sent for Murat to return from his retirement in Anatolia to repel the invaders.

Murat brought his army to *Rumeli* (Rumelia) to deal with the various Balkan rulers who were throwing off their status as vassals of the Ottomans in the hopes that this crusading force would restore their independence. At the Battle of Varna, 10 November 1444, the Ottomans crushed the invaders and re-established Ottoman control all along the frontier. Murat did not reassume the sultanate until 2 August 1446 following Çandarlı Halil Pasha's secret inciting of the Janissaries to revolt in support of their demands for higher wages and better conditions.

It is important to remember that Halil Pasha engineered this dethronement when Mehmet was fourteen years old, going through an adolescent passage, and while his mother was still alive. She did not die until 1450. The possible oedipal implications of this series of events for the young Mehmet were many and deep. An adolescent goes through a 'second individuation'.[69] He (or she) loosens up his emotional ties to the parents of his childhood and revisits oedipal issues which cause internal turmoil, but the adolescent's regression is in the service of development. After the internal turmoil, if there are no complications, the youngster crystallizes his character organization.

It should be noted that young Mehmet replaced his father while still under the psychological influence of the adolescent passsage and renewed oedipal issues. We assume that his oedipal struggles were rekindled when he struggled against Halil Pasha (the extension of the fantasized 'bad' oedipal father) and especially when he was dethroned at the age of fourteen after being 'number one' for two years. Mehmet's father, however, in reality was 'good' to the teenager. Mehmet, therefore, might have had a difficult time in expressing his anger directly at his father while expecting to regain the throne once more. It is likely that Mehmet displaced and externalized his oedipal struggles onto the historical arena. Some of the significant events which immediately followed the conquest of Constantinople will be played back against the screen of these experiences and memories.

Murat's second reign was initiated as a response to the Janissary revolt concocted by Halil Pasha. The sultan sent Mehmet, together with his *lalas*, to the governorship of Manisa. Murat still wished to see his son succeed to the throne. He took Mehmet on campaign with him against the Hungarians in 1448 and the Albanians in 1450. Murat II died shortly after Mehmet was married off in a diplomatic marriage to the daughter of the Dhu'l Kadr leader, who was an Ottoman ally against the Karamanids of eastern Anatolia. On 18 February 1451, at the age of nineteen, Mehmet came to the Ottoman throne for the second time.

Mehmet's mother, with whom he had had relatively little contact since he was handed over to the care of his wet nurse, had died between his first and second enthronements. A recent work on Mehmet the Conqueror claims that over these years of separation the sultan had forgotten his mother. Those of us who have worked psychoanalytically with adults who were separated from their biological mothers when they were children know that these individuals never forget their mothers. Indeed, the separation calls for more fantasies pertaining to the mother-child relationship while these fantasies develop with certain 'psychic realities'. Though we do not know and have no way of knowing Mehmet's psychological make-up, it is more likely, however, that the peculiarities of his childhood, his becoming sultan at puberty, and his dethronement and subsequent return to power played a role in keeping his oedipal struggles alive.

It is entirely possible that when Mehmet was brought to the throne for the first time, and then dethroned, he experienced these events as an oedipal 'triumph' followed by 'humiliation'. Leaving a psychological mark on him, these events could easily have left him resolute in the determination never to be humiliated again. He concentrated the major share of his energies in planning for and executing the conquest of Constantinople. This he achieved through the support of Zaganos Pasha over and against the cautious policy urged on him by Çandarlı Halil Pasha. Although Constantinople had been isolated by the earlier Ottoman absorption of the surrounding territory on both the Asia Minor and European sides of the city, the walls of the city remained a formidable obstacle which required the Ottomans to cast a huge cannon on the scene with which to breach the walls. Mehmet constantly visited his troops and urged them to press the battle.

As the final Ottoman assault surged through an opening in the walls, Emperor Constantine was killed in the attack. Shortly after order was restored in the city, Halil Pasha was arrested and put to death. In this act Mehmet II consciously demonstrated that the period of Ottoman history in which a decisive role was played by the leading Turkish families who had supported the Islamic religion (*din*), as well as the Ottoman's state (*devlet*), was coming to an end. Henceforth, the slaves of the sultan (the *kapıkulu* or products of the Palace School who were recruited through the *devşirme*) would exercise predominant power. At the same time, he reasserted his control over the Janissaries by demonstrating his martial skills and devotion to the cause of expanding the Abode of Islam (*Dar al-Islam*) at the expense of the Abode of War (*Dar al-Harp*), that is, winning territory for the Ottoman state from the Christians and others who were seen as suitable opponents.

On the unconscious level it is possible to talk of the condensation of two events with respect to Mehmet's oedipal struggle without reducing the capture of Constantinople to the oedipal struggles of its twenty-one year old conqueror. One of those events was the death of Emperor Constantine, who might also have stood for the 'bad' oedipal father who had attracted his 'son's' death wishes. After the emperor's death, the young sultan declared that he was the new chief protector of the Christian Church (the mother). A 'son' was replacing his 'father' as this theme appears in the oedipal (unconscious) fantasy. The other event was the demise of Halil Pasha who had been responsible for Mehmet's dethronement. Here, Sultan Mehmet II reaped his revenge upon Halil Pasha which can be seen as the achievement of an oedipal triumph, and gave the message that he would not allow himself to be humiliated again.

Allegations still circulate that Sultan Mehmet slept with the daughter of the dead emperor Constantine and that he tried to persuade her to convert to Islam.[70] We can imagine that this material, true or not, also echoes an oedipal theme. The father (Constantine) was killed, and the son (young Mehmet) sleeps with his woman. The mental representation of the fall of Constantinople after its wall was bombarded by the biggest cannon which existed at that time was sexualized *as a rape*, while the victim's refusal to give in voluntarily and to become a Muslim was idealized. The Turkish cannon might be perceived as powerful phallic symbols, and they were an object of interest to many Christians for years to come.

Perhaps the sultan's young age (twenty-one) also influenced many to look upon the conquest of Constantinople in sexual terms. What was difficult to assimilate was the fact that the 'rape' was performed not by the father, but by the son, who had achieved an oedipal triumph. Europeans writing their versions of history, assigned to the young sultan endless 'lust'. For example, the noted nineteenth-century historian of the Ottoman Empire, von Hammer-Purgstall, writing in 1835, stated that Mehmet lusted after the youngest son of Grand-Duke Lucas Notaras, who had led the Byzantine fleet in its defence of the city.[71] In *Mehmed the Conqueror*, Franz Babinger repeated the story of Notaras' refusal to heed the sultan's demand that he allow his son to appear in his presence. Thereupon, Mehmet had Notaras and both his sons executed.[72] Over time, Constantinople (Istanbul) took on the symbol of a fallen or bleeding woman for Greeks and Turks alike.[73]

The Greeks and other Christians obviously suffered other chosen traumas at the hands of the Ottomans before the fall of Constantinople. For example, in 1389, sixty-four years before taking Constantinople, the Turks had defeated the Serbians at Kosova. On the 600th anniversary of this event, an ambitious Serbian Communist leader, Slobodan Milosevic, reactivated the Serbs' chosen trauma, declaring at Kosova 'Never again!' and the coffin of the defeated Serbian commander began a year-long pilgrimage, visiting every village in the country.[74]

The Serb's chosen trauma did not generalize but remained only a part of the Serbian identity. The fall of Constantinople did generalize and influenced many Christian nations. Its mental representation, condensed with that of the Turks' seizure of Jerusalem and the consequent launching of the Crusades, was for Christians a 'chosen trauma' of such magnitude that it functioned like a black hole in space.

Western eyes, accordingly, saw Turks as possessing qualities in which were condensed mental representations of the 'aggressive and lustful' Mehmet the Conqueror and Turkish acts before as well as after 1453.

Preoccupation with the Turks as conquerors of Jerusalem and Constantinople became globalized as Europeans began discovering new parts of the world and colonizing them. For example, in 1539, Mexican Indians took part in a dramatic pageant representing the liberation of Jerusalem from the Turks by the armies of the Catholic world joined by those of the New World.[75] Even today, a variation of this pageant is still re-enacted in Mexico, halfway around the world from Turkey.[76]

Mutual Curiosity

Sultan Mehmet's interest in Byzantium and in the Greeks was not solely bellicose in nature. In this he was firmly within the long tradition of Muslims and Christians who had demonstrated their interest in each other since the incursion of the Muslims into the Fertile Crescent in the seventh century. This mutual interest was heightened during the period of the Crusades, and in the Near East, when Christian clergy and Muslim *ulema* often engaged in theological debates in defence of the supremacy of their religions. One such classical debate took place early in the Ottoman-Byzantine confrontation when the Ottomans captured Gregory Palamas, the bishop of Salonika, in 1355. He was taken to the court of Orhan, where a theological debate was arranged between Gregory and some Ottoman clergymen.[77]

Beyond this historical context of mutual curiosity between Muslims and Christians in the mid-fifteenth century, there are some questions raised by recent Turkish scholars. One has indicated his opinion that Mehmet's interest in things Greek stemmed in part from the fact that his stepmother, Despoena Maria, was Greek and probably taught him some Greek.[78] Another maintains, as stated earlier, that Mehmet's biological mother was Greek.[79] It is also maintained that a Greek prince, who was probably a hostage kept in the Ottoman palace, was Mehmet's childhood companion.[80]

While the idealization of the Conqueror made him someone who knew, besides the Turkish language, Arabic, Persian, Greek, Latin, and Slavic languages, the truth is no doubt considerably less. Most likely Mehmet knew some Greek individuals and was familiar with Greek mythology. Apparently he was familiar with the Iliad. Kritovoulos writes of Mehmet's expedition into Phrygia during which he visited Ilium where he inquired about the tombs of Achilles and Ajax:

> And he praised and congratulated them, their memory and their deeds, and on having a person like the poet Homer to extol them.

Kritovoulos further reports that Mehmet spoke of his campaign in the Peloponnesus:

> God has reserved for me, through so long a period of years, the right to avenge this city and its inhabitants. For I have subdued their enemies and have plundered their cities and made them the spoils of the Mysians. It was the Greeks and Macedonians and Thessalians and Pelopponesians who have ravaged this place in the past, and whose descendants have now through my efforts paid the just penalty, after a long period of years, for their injustice to us Asiatics at that time and so often in subsequent times.[81]

Mehmet the Conqueror's interests in religious and metaphysical topics are also known from Turkish sources. The sultan loved to have discussions on these topics and, therefore, had an active interest in Christianity.[82]

After the conquest of the city, Mehmet set about the task of repopulating it and restoring economic, social, and religious stability. One aspect of his policy was to extend extraordinary privileges to the Orthodox church which included the banishment of all Latin Catholic organizations from his empire. Mehmet's 'generosity', in addition to being related to real world political, cultural, and religious issues, might also have sprung from his internal demands. Most likely the real world issues and the psychological ones were condensed.

Cross-Identification

We shall now mention one more mental mechanism clinically associated with the mourning process—identification. It affects the mourner's identity. When someone dies, we keep 'contact' with him or her by identifying with some aspects or functions of the dead person. If these identifications are adaptive and healthy, at the end of a painful work of mourning we enrich ourselves. We usually hear stories about a 'no good' son changing after his father's death and taking over in a serious manner the father's business. In complicated or perennial mourning, when there is too much anger, too much dependency or other conflicts, or a suddenness of loss which does not allow the mourner to be prepared for the change, the identification may be with undesirable and/or conflicted aspects of the lost person. Instead of the mourner enriching himself, he may embrace the struggle, now felt within himself. An example of an unhealthy identification is provided by a widow who, after the death of her husband due to a heart attack, develops chest pains. In short, losses and changes in our lives influence our sense of self due to the unconscious mechanism of identification.

When Constantinople fell, both the Turks and the Greeks faced losses and changes. The Turks had become a 'world power'. They had to change their identity. The Greeks had lost their Byzantium. They had to re-evaluate themselves. In the process of each party re-examining themselves, consciously and unconsciously, a great deal of cross-identification occurred.

In summary, the Turkish-Greek relationships in that period of history were complicated. Linking and unlinking, being different while being the same, being enemies while still collaborating, are all a part of attempting to know who they were. After the long war and after the fall of Constantinople, there were active psychological processes which left their marks on the conquerors and the conquered.

George Scholarius Gennadios, whom Mehmet II had appointed Patriarch of the Orthodox Church, had wondered earlier who he and his people were. He wrote: 'Though I am a Hellene by speech, yet I would never say that I was Hellene, for I do not believe as the Hellenes believed. I should like to take my name from my faith and if anyone asked me what I am, answer, "A Christian". Though my father dwelt in Thessaly, I do not call myself a Thessalian, but a Byzantine, for I am of Byzantium.'[83] Who was he after the fall of Constantinople? Ottoman rule over the Greeks lasted until 1829 (the Treaty of Adrianople). Their identities changed further as their relationships changed. After examining the Turks' mourning, the next chapter focuses on the Turks' and the Greeks' 'togetherness'.

| 5 |

The Mourning Process of the Turks

In the psychoanalytic sense mourning is viewed as an inevitable response to loss and change; accordingly, the Turks, although victorious, had to mourn the change in their image occasioned by their long-awaited conquest of Constantinople and their success in putting an end to the Byzantine Empire.[84] They had to adapt to a new identity and restore their inner psychic balance. Pollock noted that 'to be able to mourn is to be able to change. To be unable to mourn, to deny changes, carries great risk to the individual and to the organization.'[85] The loss of Constantinople was too great to be mourned by the Byzantines, and we have noted their attempts at denial. Throughout this volume, we indicate the effects of their inability to mourn, its condensation with the effects of other losses, and their behaving like perennial mourners.

A change for the better is easier to accept than a change for the worse, provided that the gain does not induce great guilt. After 1453, it took decades for the Turks to mourn and adjust to their new identity as a major power. As we shall see, their mourning is evident in the work of Sinan, the great Ottoman architect (1490-1588), which reflects the mood and unconscious processes of the Ottomans.

St. Sophia
The church of St. Sophia in Constantinople was, at the time of the city's conquest, the sacred architectural masterpiece of the Christian world, unlike anything previously seen by the Seljuk or Ottoman Turks. It was said by Greeks to have been made by divine powers

according to a heavenly design, and it struck awe in the hearts of the Turkish conquerors. Begun by Constantine in 325 and rebuilt by Theodosius and Justinian in the wake of fires and earthquakes, the basilica had been the setting for magnificent celebrations, such as coronations and royal weddings. According to popular belief, an angel would protect it against the Turks, but no such angel appeared as Mehmet II took the city on 29 May 1453. The sultan had heard of the beauty of Constantinople and told his troops on the eve of their final assault:

> You will enjoy the beauty of the churches and public buildings and splendid houses and gardens, and many such things, suited to look at and enjoy and take pleasure in and profit by. ... you will capture a city whose renown has gone out to all parts of the world. It is evident that to whatever extent the leadership and glory of this city has spread, to a like extent, the renown of your valour and bravery will spread for having captured by assault a city such as this.[86]

Prepared accordingly to anticipate much, the reality of St. Sophia dazzled the Turks. Other examples of Byzantine architecture, so unlike their customary architecture, impressed them greatly, caused a 'loss' in their self-esteem and required considerable adaptation in their new position as the owners of the city. Thus, the Turks, also, had to mourn. Christianity's sacred building, with its soft curves and its lighting that suggested infinity, was turned into a mosque and much later would become a museum.

Following older Islamic custom in urban development, Mehmet the Conqueror urged his highest ranking officials to begin the process of converting Christian Constantinople into Muslim Istanbul by taking the crowns of the city's major hills and other important urban sites and constructing there Islamic complexes consisting of mosques, religious schools (*medreses*), soup kitchens (*imarets*), hospitals, and baths. These were financed through the institution of pious endowments (*vakıf*). Sultan Mehmet II showed the way by co-opting a prime site on which, ten years after first beholding St. Sophia, he had the mosque that would bear his name constructed. He also had the fabled Covered Bazaar (*Kapalı Çarşı*), which still stands, constructed so that the rents from the shops would support the pious works of his Fatih Mehmet Mosque complex. Work on the mosque began in 1463 and was completed in 1471. Compared to St. Sophia, the mosque of Fatih Mehmet is less grand, attesting to the fact that the conquering

Ottomans had not yet conquered Byzantine architecture.

The Age of Koca Mimar Sinan

Impressive as Mehmet's mosque is (the original mosque was destroyed in an earthquake on 11 May 1677, and rebuilt a century later from 1767 to 1771 in the reign of Mustafa III), it is still only a lesser edition of St. Sophia. It was not until the age of the illustrious Ottoman architect, Sinan (1490-1588), known in Turkish as Koca Mimar Sinan (the Great Architect Sinan) that an Ottoman architect was able to 'separate and individuate', as a psychoanalyst would say, from the Byzantine influence to achieve greater things than those characteristic of St. Sophia. During the work of mourning, the individual identifies (unconsciously) with aspects of the mental representation of the lost or dead person or thing. To some extent he becomes like the lost person or thing. Identification serves two purposes: (1) to keep aspects of what is lost; and (2) to gain freedom from the influence of what is lost. By analogy, it would appear that the process Koca Sinan went through in his creativity paralleled the Turkish mourning process—the internalization and assimilation of aspects of Byzantine influences, the working towards freedom from other influences, and the ultimate discovery of a new identity.

According to Vogt-Göknil, the Turks, when they came into contact with Christians, already had their own artistic laws and forms. Political victories compelled them to measure up to 'Christian architecture',[87] but at first they were paralysed as though in mourning. In spite of the relative success of the Conqueror's Mosque, other mosques they built were less accomplished than those they had built in Edirne and Bursa, their previous capital cities, before the fall of Constantinople. Their paralysis continued for half a century until the activities of Sinan helped them work through their mourning to reach a new identity and to separate themselves from the trauma brought about by the change occasioned by their victory.

Koca Mimar Sinan, a contemporary of Andrea Palladio (1508-1579), was born a Christian. He was levied in the *devşirme* in 1512 and taken into Ottoman service. According to his testimony, he was levied in the first *devşirme* carried out near the Anatolian city of Kayseri. Originally the *devşirme* was limited to the Balkans. The fact that this was the first levy in his area might also account for the fact that he was taken at an advanced age—most boys were taken between the ages of eight and twelve. According to most accounts, he was trained and became a Janissary in 1521 on the eve of Mehmet II's great grandson's, Sultan Süleyman the Magnificent's, Belgrade campaign. He served with the Janissaries on campaigns in the Arab world and Iran, and in the Balkans, including Hungary and southern Austria. He distinguished himself as a military engineer, creating pontoon bridges and other bridge structures to assist the army in crossing marshes and rivers. At the age of fifty, he became chief architect and by the time of his death, almost five decades later, he had created some three hundred and sixty-four structures across the panorama of Islamic construction, including mosques, *medreses*, mausoleums, caravanserais, bridges, aquaducts, and bathhouses. It is known that in building his first imperial mosque, the Şehzade Mosque in Istanbul, Sinan felt challenged to surpass St. Sophia, a feeling he shared with his fellow members of the Ottoman elite.[88] In addition, he may have felt himself pitted against the ghosts of Anthemius of Tralles and Isidor of Miletus, the designers of St. Sophia, and determined to separate his creativity from theirs. Some indication of the intensity and depth of Sinan's feelings in this regard can be gleaned from some lines of poetry in his book of professional memoirs, *Tezkiret-ul-Bunyan* (*A Book about Buildings*) which he related to Sai Mustafa Çelebi, who wrote them down in prose and verse:

> As a capable architect, I wished to leave
> behind me
>
> Works that would remain in this world.
>
> I prayed that God would see me worthy
> To build a soaring mosque.
>
> What I had prayed for was granted, for God
> In his Divine Wisdom allowed me to become
> the Sultan's favourite.[89]

In building the Şehzade Mosque (1544-48), Sinan experimented with four semi-domes buttressing the main dome. St. Sophia has two semi-domes. The use of four domes changed the axial symmetry of St. Sophia into a perfect central symmetry. This design was familiar to the Byzantines who used barrel vaults instead of semi-domes to cover the four side aisles. Sinan has taken the symbol of the cross (four barrel vaults) and modified it according to Islamic principles. The link between the 'lost' Byzantine Empire and the conquering Ottoman

Empire persisted. Twelve years after building the Şehzade Mosque, Sinan tried an even more daring scheme in designing the Mihrinah Mosque with a dome resting directly on walls without the support of semi-domes. It seemed that he was experimenting with designs which differed from the design of St. Sophia. His next major imperial commission was the design and construction of Sultan Süleyman's own mosque (Süleymaniye Mosque) and its attendant buildings. In the *Tezkiret-ul-Bunyan*, Sinan, with his characteristic combination of pride and humility, remarks:

> One morning the idea of building a mosque entered the blessed heart of our Sultan, who is the sun of the age of refinement ... Sultan Süleyman Khan, son of His late Blessed Majesty Sultan Selim Khan—may God grant him peace and forgiveness. Summoning his pitiful and humble servant Sinan ... to his presence, a consultation about the mosque took place...
>
> The order of our glorious Sultan was given
> I was bidden to build him a fine mosque.
>
> I removed the remains of the Old Palace (Greek)
> and carefully built a mosque upon the site.
>
> Men of perception will appreciate how much
> Art and skill went into its building.[90]

It is clear that both the sultan and his architect wished to surpass the Greeks and free themselves from the influence of Emperor Justinian and the Eastern Orthodox Church. Clearing away the old Greek Palace was both a symbolic act and an architectural necessity. The Süleymaniye Mosque was begun in 1550 and completed in 1557. It is generally acclaimed as a superb edifice. Evliya Çelebi, the famed Ottoman traveller of the seventeenth century who is equally famous for his unsubstantiated embellishments, presents an encounter he says he had with ten visiting European Christians inside the Süleymaniye. They were so struck by the magnificence of the structure that they commented, he says, by exclaiming, 'Mother of God!'[91] Clearly, it was important for the Muslim Ottomans to surpass the Christian Byzantines.

Although the Süleymaniye repeats to some extent the structural scheme of St. Sophia in respect to having a main dome supported by two semi-domes, and its exterior resembles that of St. Sophia, the interior departs from the Byzantine model. Decoratively, Christian mosaics are replaced by a calligraphic presentation at the top of the dome of a verse from the Koran (*Surah* XXXV, verse 41, the Creator [*al-Fatir*]):

> Lo! Allah graspeth the heavens and the earth
> that they deviate not, and if they were to deviate
> there is not one that could grasp them after him.
> Lo! He is ever Clement, Forgiving.[92]

Dedicated to using only the best materials and master artisans, Sinan enlisted the services of the calligrapher, Hasan Karahisarı, 'Lord of all calligraphers'.[93]

Illumination inside the mosque was originally provided by thousands of candles. Sinan oversaw every aspect of the mosque's interior, including the floor coverings, with the same dedicated energy he devoted to the exterior. The dome of the Sülemaniye is slightly smaller than that of St. Sophia. Despite its magnificence, Sinan considered this mosque to be representative of his work as a journeyman.

Sinan felt that only with the construction of the Selimiye Mosque in Edirne (1569-1575) built for Süleyman the Magnificent's son, Sultan Selim II, did he achieve the rank of master builder. With this edifice, built a little over a century after the Turk's conquest of Constantinople, Sinan sought to bring to its fullest realization the small Turkish single-domed mosque. He created a single dome, supported by eight pillars, slightly larger than the dome of St. Sophia. Sinan was aware of the competition between Eastern and Western architecture. He thought that the West did not see any value in oriental architecture because the East could not match the dome of St. Sophia. Now the master builder had succeeded in doing so. He even regarded the minarets, architecturally speaking, more significant than the dome. The Selimiye mosque is embellished by four minarets so perfectly aligned that when approaching the city by automobile it appears for a rather long time that the mosque has only two minarets. Equally remarkable is the fact that neither the interior nor the exterior of the mosque shows any observable signs of Byzantine influence.

| 6 |

The Ottoman Empire

After succeeding the Seljuks of *Rum* and then defeating the Karamanids, also centred in Konya, to become the predominant Muslim power in Anatolia by the early decades of the fifteenth century, the Ottomans extended their sovereignty over Constantinople in 1453 and then over the other parts of Anatolia, such as Trabizond (Trabzon), that had eluded Seljuk control. They also pushed further into the Balkans, a process that had commenced as early as the beginning of the fourteenth century and would last well into the seventeenth, and brought Ottoman rule into the Arab world through their conquest of the Fertile Crescent and Egypt in 1517. In addition, they spread their dominion over North Africa to the eastern border of Morocco and over Arabia as well. The Black Sea, as far as the Crimea and the Sea of Azov, became an Ottoman lake, and the eastern Mediterranean and its principal islands of Rhodes (1522) and Cyprus (1571), likewise fell under Ottoman hegemony. Indeed, the Ottoman sultan was, as one of his favourite titles claimed, the lord of the *Berreyn* and the *Bahreyn*, the two lands—*Rumeli* (the Balkans) and Anatolia, and the two seas, the Black and the White (that is, the Mediterranean) Seas. During the reign of Süleyman the Magnificent (1520-1566), the Ottoman Empire encompassed the area from the gates of Vienna in the west, to Azerbaijan in the east, and in the north from the Crimea to Egypt and across North Africa to Morocco in the south. With the empire at its height during this period, the Ottomans ruled over a multinational, multireligious, multilinguistic, and multiethnic empire.

Western historians, as well as Orientalists, have long been interested in the similarities between some significant Byzantine and

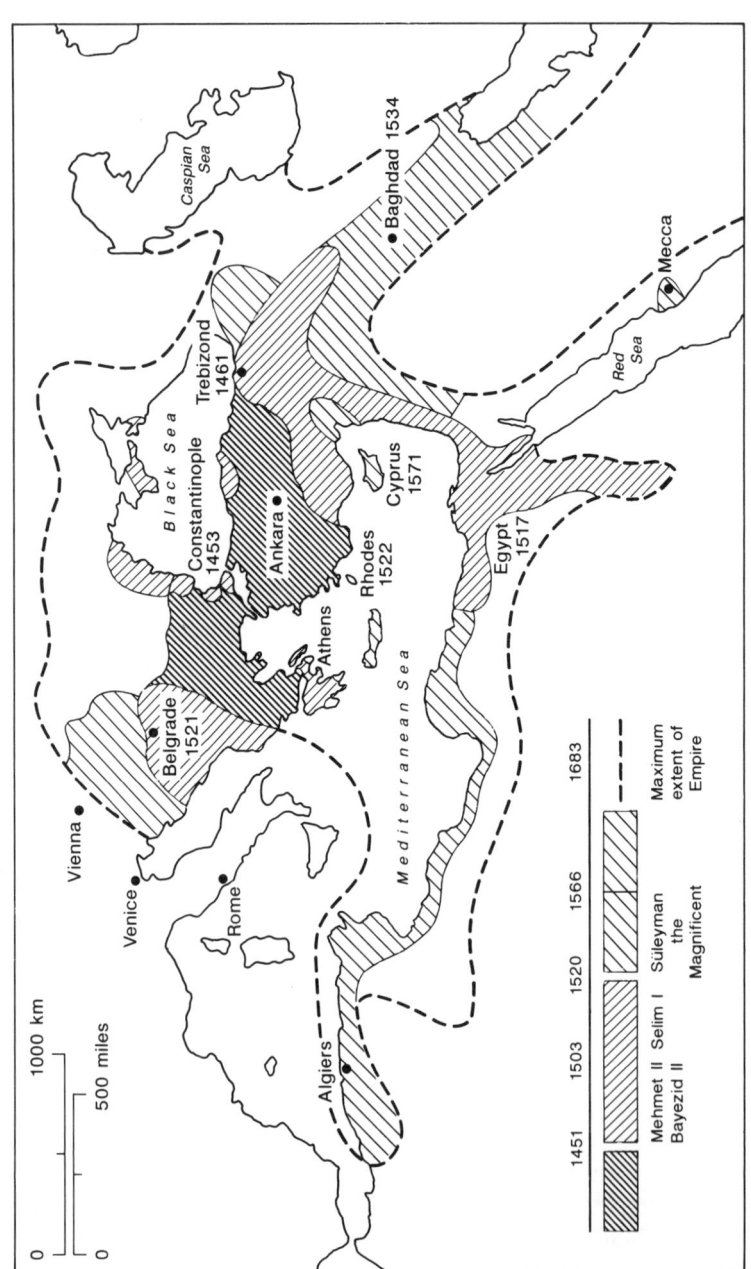

Map 3: The Ottoman Empire

Ottoman institutions and customs that persisted for centuries after the fall of Constantinople. The distinguished Turcologist, M. Fuat Köprülü, devoted a long article to this topic in 1931 which was translated into Italian in 1935 as, *Alcuni osservazioni intorno all'influenza delle instituzioni byzantine sulle instituzione ottomane*.[94] While there are many similarities between Byzantine and Ottoman institutions, the Islamic historical experience provided the Ottomans with ample models. In many cases, behind the Islamic experience there stand the Persian institutions of statecraft that helped to shape early Islamic practices. Writers, especially westerners, continue to seek comparisons and relationships, for if the Ottomans borrowed institutions from the Byzantines, that somehow makes Byzantium superior. Similar opinions frequently appear in the popular press and books for tourists. Kelly, for example, erroneously equates the Ottoman sultan with the Byzantine emperor, establishing a parity between the sultan in his status as caliph with the divinity of the emperor.[95] Muhammad always made it clear that he was but a man, and the caliphs never pretended to possess divinity. The Ottoman sultans' claims to the caliphate, since they were not of the tribe of the Prophet, the Kuraysh, rested simply on power. The Sa'dian dynasty of Morocco in the sixteenth century challenged the Ottoman claim to the caliphate because they could, and the Ottomans could not, trace their descent back to Muhammad. In any case, caliph was not a title the Ottomans traded on much until the late nineteenth century as they retreated from the Balkans, leaving behind Muslims and Muslim property. Claiming authority based on the fact that he was the most powerful Muslim sovereign, the sultan sought to intervene in European affairs to protect those Muslims and that Muslim property. Empires, perforce, have been interested in stability and continuity. It is not surprising, therefore, that they have come up with similar institutions to deal with similar problems, but it is equally obvious that they have often produced dissimilar solutions to similar problems.

Institutional Arrangements
It would be a mistake to consider, as some have, the Ottoman Empire simply as a modified continuation of the Byzantine. While similarities exist between certain institutions, it is difficult, if not impossible, to say that many Byzantine institutions directly influenced Ottoman institutions.[96] The *timar* system was a central institution for the

Ottomans. It superficially resembles the Byzantine *pronoia*, but the Islamic institution of *iqta* appears more likely to have been its actual inspiration. A *timar* was a grant constituting a stated share in the agricultural tax revenue of a stipulated area. The *timar*-holder also received a grant of land on which he could build his house and create a farm for the support of himself and his family. In return, the *timar*-holder became part of the provincial cavalry and would then participate in the imperial campaigns of the empire under the provincial military/administrative leadership. Terms of service were related to the amount of income assigned to the *timar*-holder. The basic grant required the *timar*-holder to present himself, together with his horses and weapons, for service. Greater income could require the *timar*-holder to equip and bring additional horsemen, arms, tents, or soup kitchens to the campaign. This system provided the Ottomans with a vast cavalry force without putting pressure on a treasury short of precious metals.

Ottoman genius for government expressed itself in the changes wrought in the basic four-fold structure of earlier Islamic society described by Nasireddin Tūsi (d. 1275) in his book on ethics:

> First came the Men of the Pen such as the masters of the sciences and the branches of knowledge, the canon-lawyers, the judges, secretaries, accountants, geometers, astronomers, physicians, and poets, on whose existence depends the order of this world and the next; among the natural elements these correspond to Water. Secondly, the Men of the Sword; fighters, warriors, volunteers, skirmishers, frontier-guardians, sentries, valiant men, supporters of the realm and guardians of the state by whose intermediacy the world's organization is effected; among the natural elements these correspond to Fire. Thirdly, the Men of Negotiation, merchants who carry goods from one region to another, tradesmen, masters of crafts, and tax-collectors, without whose co-operation the daily life of the species would be impossible; among the natural elements, they are like Air. Fourthly, the Men of Husbandry, such as sowers, farmers, ploughmen, and agriculturalists, who organize the feeding of all the communities, and without whose help the survival of the individuals would be out of the question; among the natural elements they have the same rank as Earth.[97]

Tūsi's depiction indicates a highly structured society. The early Ottoman frontier society had a simpler structure differentiating the rulers from the ruled: The former were the *askeris*, the military, and all others were *reaya*, the subjects. As the productive element in the society, tending their crops and their flocks and paying taxes, the *reaya* produced the wealth that supported the members of the *askeri* group, whose privileged status was buttressed by their tax exemption. In this early period of Ottoman history which can be said to have lasted until Christian *timar*-holders revolted in the first half of the fifteenth century, the term *reaya* covered Muslims and Christians alike, and the *askeris*, as well, contained Muslims and Christians in their ranks. Following those revolts, Christians generally were no longer granted *timars*, and the term *reaya* came to designate the non-Muslim subjects of the sultan. As Ottoman history unfolded, members of the *reaya* would seek to cross the line and become part of the *askeris*. One of the sultan's main functions was to maintain the distinction between the *askeris* and the *reaya*. One can characterize Ottoman society as a system in which there was a place for everyone, and the sultan's role was to keep everybody in his place.

As the Ottomans began to expand both in the Balkans and in Anatolia, they experienced a need for more men to administer the newly conquered territories and for more warriors to press the attack forward. As new areas were added to the imperial domains, they were surveyed as to their sources of wealth (mostly agricultural) and the extent of the population. These surveys provided the sultan with information about the taxable wealth of an area and the number of fighting men it could support. *Timars* were then allocated on the basis of these cadastral surveys.

Timar-holders were required to participate in imperial campaigns through a hierarchy that led from their local officials to the provincial governor and ultimately to the *beylerbeyi* (bey of the beys), the overall regional commander. They were also responsible for the collection of taxes and the maintenance of law and order in their area. For a rather long time, the *timar*-holders provided the glue that kept local society together and produced the stability and continuity that were hallmarks of the Ottoman Empire.

Another hallmark of Ottoman society was its character as a *ghulam* state. *Ghulams* were slaves educated and trained for state service and as an institution date back to the time of the Abbasid caliph al-Mutasim (833-842). Al-Mutasim was the first Muslim ruler to purchase pagan Turkish youths (from Samarkand), import them into the central Islamic world, and train them for military service. This institution prospered in the Islamic world, and the Ottomans were familiar with it from the practices of the Seljuks of *Rum*. The Ottomans then took this institution and gave it a new twist by recruiting these future state servants from their own Christian Orthodox population through the *devşirme*. Levied at a young age, the best of the youths passed through the various *odas* (training rooms and dormitories) of the Palace School, converted to Islam and were educated in the traditions and languages of High Islam. Those who successfully completed the course were moved out at about the age of twenty-five to take up high positions in the provincial structure, the Janissary Corps, or in the Palace itself. The rest of the youths were hired out to Turkish farm families where they were converted to Islam, were educated in the traditions of folk Islam, and learned to speak the common Turkish language. At about the age of eighteen, they were brought back to Istanbul and placed in the companies of the Janssaries to see service as soldiers.

In this fashion, the Ottoman state provided itself with both its military/administrative elite and its awesome Janissary corps. Both groups were made up of slaves of non-Muslim origins. Collectively, they were known as the *kapıkulları*, the servants of the Porte. While this system lasted for many, many decades, it quickly broke down under pressure applied by its own members who wanted to assure a place in it for their children. Sultan Selim I (1512-1520) was the first sultan who allowed the *kapıkulları* to get married, and his successor, Süleyman (1520-1566) made room in the system for children of the *kapıkulları* who had been allowed to marry.

Careers

This development went hand-in-hand with another one of equal significance—social differentiation within the *askeri* group. This differentiation took place primarily along occupational lines. There came to be essentially three main groups, or careers, within the original *askeri* classification. There were men of the sword (*seyf*), the men of the pen (*kalem*/bureaucracy), and the men of the religious establishment (*ilim*/religious knowledge). Each career had its own recruitment and education methods, but essentially, each member was trained in three 'Islamic' languages of the region—Arabic, Persian, and Ottoman Turkish. The latter was the court language composed of grammatical and vocabulary elements from Arabic and Persian together with the basic structure and vocabulary of Turkish. The men of the sword were drawn essentially from the *devşirme* and educated in the palace school. Bureaucrats were trained in the bureaus of the bureaucracy from about the age of twelve on, and they also attended lectures at the main mosques of Istanbul in the subjects that interested them. They were largely the children of bureaucrats. The men of religion were educated in the religious school system, the *medreses*, and they, too, were largely the sons of fathers who were already established in that career.

While exact membership statistics in each career are difficult, if not impossible, to obtain, their numbers are small. Although the Ottoman bureaucracy produced enormous amounts of paperwork, by the end of the eighteenth century, the central bureaucracy composed of the bureaus of the *Divan-i Hümayun* (The Imperial Council) and the financial administration numbered no more than one thousand scribes. Far larger in numbers was what Albert H. Lybyer called the Religious Institution.[98] This career also had two main components, the religious schools, and the *kadıs* or Islamic juristconsults. The *medrese* was the educational institution that trained these future religious careerists, and the recruits came mostly from Muslim families who already had a connection in that career. Graduates of this educational system went on to teach in *medreses* throughout the empire, with positions in the leading *medreses* of Istanbul being the most coveted, or else served as *kadıs* in the various provinces. Since the *kadıs* administered both the religious law (the *şeriat*) and the administrative law of the empire, there was some bias against becoming a *kadı* because in some significant areas the administrative law ran counter to the dictates of the religious law. There was always the possibility, then, that a pious Muslim could run the risk of placing his soul in jeopardy through inflicting the punishments embodied in the administrative law that did not exist in the religious law.

Osmanlı (Ottoman)

In the process of differentiation mentioned earlier, another feature of Ottoman society came into prominence—the meaning and use of the term Ottoman. Originally, Ottoman (*Osmanlı*) was the term that designated the followers of the eponymous founder of the dynasty, Osman. Later, the term Ottoman was used to designate the family of Osman and the dynasty that was created by and rooted in that family.

By the time of Süleyman the Magnificent, the term Ottoman became a cultural term, designating those members of the *askeri* group who served both the religion and the state and knew the Ottoman Way. One served the religion by being a Muslim and served the state by holding a position in the careers discussed above. Knowing the Ottoman Way entailed being fully conversant with the High Islamic cultural tradition and with the Ottoman Turkish language, which was the vehicle for that tradition.

Under this definition of an Ottoman, the group is severely restricted in number. For example, most of the youths who were levied in the *devşirme* wound up in the Janissaries. While they still had the status of being among the *askeris* and had the privileges of such, including tax exemption, they cannot be considered Ottomans because they lacked the education necessary for the knowledge of the Ottoman Way. The *timar*-holders, equally part of the *askeri* group, for the most part are similarly disqualified for the same reasons despite the fact that they served the religion and the state. In terms of numbers, if one had to hazard a guess, the Ottoman group (families included) probably numbered no more than two hundred and fifty thousand to three hundred thousand out of a total empire population in the late sixteenth century of about twenty-five million.

The 'Millet' System

Only with the conquest of the Arab world in 1517 by Selim I did the Ottoman Empire become, for the first time, a society in which Muslims were the majority. One of the major instruments through which the Ottomans ruled this society was the *millet* system. Identity in the Ottoman Empire was corporate rather than individual, and one's main identity derived from one's religion. Ottoman relations with non-Muslims were based on traditions stemming from the Islamic experience when the Arab Muslims first conquered great areas inhabited by large numbers of non-Muslims, mostly Christians and Jews. Protection and tolerance were extended to those groups due to their possessing revealed, written scripture. These peoples were called *ahl al-Kitab*, people of the book, as well as *ahl al-dhimma*, people of the pact, that document which regulated their relationship with the Muslim state. They were also referred to as *dhimmis*. These religious communities were extended a certain degree of autonomy, especially with regard to issues of personal status—marriage, divorce, and inheritance—to adjudicate these matters according to their own religious law. In return for this autonomy, the *dhimmis* were subjected to special capitation taxes, which in time became known as the *cizye*, and to a series of sumptuary laws that regulated what they could and could not wear, what animals they could ride, and deprived them of the right to bear arms.

When Mehmet the Conqueror succeeded in conquering Constantinople and then in extending his dominion over additional areas of the Balkans and Anatolia, he became the heir to Byzantium and ruler over vast numbers of Christian adherents of the Orthodox faith. He was faced with the task of giving a structure to his new status. One of the ways he did that was to install, some time after the conquest, George Scholarios as patriarch in Constantinople. (The exact date is in dispute, but one thing is certain—it was not immediately, most likely in 1454.) The new patriarch then took the name Gennadios II. This was the origin of what has come to be known as the *millet* system. The word *millet* in the nineteenth century came to mean nation, but earlier it referred to an organized religious community whose head was responsible to the Ottoman government for the good behaviour of its members, payment of the *cizye* tax and other aspects of the relationships between the *millet* and the government.

The Orthodox ('Greek') Millet: As head of the *Millet-i Rum* (the 'Greek' *millet*), the religious community of the Orthodox Christians, the patriarch was granted ecclesiastical, and in some matters civil, control over his co-religionists. The Orthodox were not an ethnically homogeneous group, made up as they were of Greeks, Bulgarians, Serbs, Vlachs, and others, but the Greeks, and especially the Phanariote Greeks, dominated the Patriarchate, the Holy Synod, and the more important positions in the Orthodox ecclesiastical hierarchy.[99]

Over time, two processes were at work within the Greek communities of Anatolia and elsewhere in the Ottoman Empire. Through the first process, so much of the Turkish language entered the Greek language that the resulting dialect could only be understood by those who had a knowledge of both languages. By the second process, many Greeks became Turcophone, speaking Turkish, but writing their language in Greek letters. They became known as *karamanlı* Christians. Both ecclesiastical and civil matters, such as issues of inheritance, marriage, divorce, and tax collection devolved upon the patriarchate whose authority encompassed the entire empire. In many ways, the patriarch was more powerful under the Ottomans than the Byzantines.

The Jewish 'Millet': With respect to the Jewish community, it would be more accurate to speak of communities, for the Jews never recognized a single head under either Byzantium or the Ottomans. Although it is often repeated by historians that Mehmet the Conqueror established Moses Capasali, a Jew of Istanbul, as *haham başı,* or chief rabbi, over the empire's Jewish community, in reality his authority did not extend much beyond Istanbul. Jewish communities throughout the empire continued to exercise control over their own communal or *millet* matters.

Under the same umbrella of the *millet* system, the Ottoman Empire sheltered the Jews who were expelled from Spain in 1492. The expulsion of the Jews and the hostility Europeans were beginning to demonstrate towards other unwanted elements within their societies, such as heretics, homosexuals, and lepers, was part of the process of nation-building which would see multiethnic and multireligious empires replaced by nation-states based on exclusivity of race and religion.[100] This rise in anti-semitism, and the fear of heretics, homosexuals and lepers, point to the apparent requirement that the cohesion of developing nation-states needed shared 'suitable targets of externalization' for groups to 'purify' themselves and solidify their identities.[101] Jews, accused of the killing of Jesus, were a threat to the Christians' identification with the Son of God. Some Jews were forced to convert to Christianity, but the possibility that one could become a Christian through conversion made Christians anxious since they needed people unlike themselves upon whom to externalize and project their unwanted aspects.[102]

Iberian Jews found a warm welcome in the Ottoman Empire. A Christian traveller, Nicolay, in the Ottoman domains in 1577 commented that the arrival of the Jews had damaged the position of Christians there.[103] Jews and their Turkish protectors were lumped together as the enemy. While the Ottomans, unlike the Jews, were not considered deicidal, they did pose a threat to the Son of God as the conquerors of Jerusalem and Constantinople. The Turks weighed heavily upon the consciousness of the Europeans. Luther considered them a fitting visitation from God upon Christians for their sins. Well into the seventeenth century, Catholics viewed not just Islam but 'Turcism' as the antichrist.[104] Jews, being without military power, were persecuted. The Turks, who instilled fear in their adversaries as the terror of the world, escaped persecution, but they were ritualistically regarded as evil. Both anti-Semitic and anti-Turkish sentiment lay, at least unconsciously, at the central core of the developing European nation-states in the nineteenth century.[105]

The Armenian Millet: Armenians constituted another *millet*. Although, in this case as well, legend holds that Mehmet the Conqueror established the bishop of Bursa, Yovakim, in Constantinople as patriarch (in 1461) over the Armenians, it appears more than likely that the Ottoman state dealt with the Armenians in much the same manner as they had with the Jews. Initially, a number of Armenian communities under their own bishops or chief prelates were recognized as independent entities, but the Armenians as a whole constituted the Armenian *millet*. Complicating the situation was the fact that the majority of Armenians lived outside the jurisdiction of the Ottoman state until the Ottoman conquests of the central Islamic lands in 1517. The emergence of a stable, ecumenical patriarchate in the person of the patriarch of Constantinople was a long process which was accelerated in the seventeenth century and completed in the eighteenth century. This process owed much to the Armenian cultural renaissance initiated by the Mekhitarist Congregation of Venice in 1701 whose monks set up a network of schools throughout the Ottoman Empire to spread knowledge of Armenian literature, history and language. This revival fostered a sense of Armenian unity, and the Armenian patriarch in Constantinople came to embody that sense of unity.[106]

Ummah: Given the concepts of *dhimma* and *millet*, the Muslims constituted the *ummah*, the community of God or of Muhammad. Until the emergence of the Turks as the dominant political force in the central Islamic world, the Arabs had been the rulers both politically and culturally. With the decline of the Arabs and the rise first of the Mamluks and then the Ottomans and with the resurgence of the Persians under the Safavids as well, the Arabs lost ground politically and even culturally, but not so much in terms of religion. With these new factors in play, there developed some tensions within the Islamic community which we could label in the light of present day problems as ethnic conflicts. There was no love lost among the Arabs, the Turks, and the Persians mostly for ethnic reasons. Each group focused on elements that fed its sense of identity and pride. The Arabs were first in Islam, long-time intellectual leaders of the Islamic world, and expanders of the original frontiers of Islam. The Turks were in the process of creating one of the greatest and most powerful Islamic empires, coupling their military prowess with outstanding poetry and prose traditions. The Persians had experienced a renaissance in their language, expunging the Arabic elements that had filtered into the language over the centuries and, basing their emerging empire on a revitalized Sh'ism, they hoped to be able to lord it over both the Turks and the Arabs.

This system, through which Muslims and non-Muslims lived side by side in relative peace and tranquility within the Ottoman Empire and which has come to be called the *millet* system, was efficient well into the nineteenth century. Under the system, Jews did not suffer the pogroms inflicted upon their co-religionists in Russia and Poland, and the Orthodox did not engage in the mutual violence with Catholics that is an everyday occurrence in contemporary Yugoslavia or what is left of it. In the Ottoman Empire everyone was equal, but the Muslims were more equal. There was a place for everyone in the empire, but the sultan's role was to keep everybody in his place.

The Nineteenth Century

Most Ottoman institutions depended upon ongoing conquest to sustain their vitality. Imperial conquest gradually ceased with the ending of the sixteenth century; in the nineteenth century, it had almost totally disappeared. This decline was brought on by a combination of internal Ottoman decline and structural, societal, political, intellectual, and technological changes in Europe. The Ottomans were faced with a deteriorating situation on the diplomatic front and institutionally as well. The corrosive ideas of nationalism and ethnicity made their appearance in the Balkans, challenging the efficacy of the *millet* system. Stability, so necessary to the life of the Ottoman Empire, was seriously challenged on two fronts simultaneously—within the *millets* themselves and between the *millets* and the Ottoman state.

Within the Orthodox *millet* (the 'Greek' *millet*), for example, ethnicity and nationalism urged the Bulgarians and the Serbs to seek first a measure of autonomy within the *millet* by the establishment or re-establishment of their own patriarchate, which resulted in communal strife, and then ultimately the establishment of their own national states which led to terrorist activities and full-scale wars. The disintegration of the millet system was exacerbated by the intrusion of the European powers into the system as they championed one or another of the *millets*, the prime example being Russia, who became the protector of the Orthodox. The Ottoman response to this challenge was 'too little too late', as the nineteenth-century Ottoman reformers developed the concept of 'Ottomanism' and sought to offer the non-Muslims of the empire status as Ottoman citizens. This still carried with it too much of a second-class citizen aura, as the Muslims still found it difficult to divest themselves of the notion of being more equal. Militarily, service for non-Muslims was a serious sticking point for both Muslims and non-Muslims alike in much the same manner that the issue of American gays serving in the military has become an emotional flash point for America in the 1990s. In addition, by the late nineteenth century Bulgarians preferred having a Bulgarian state to being Ottoman citizens, and in the same mould, Serbs wanted a Serbian state. Nationalism and ethnicity, including Turkish identity, had become the rocks on which the Ottoman state would founder.

The End of the Ottoman Empire
Steering its course among those rocks had preoccupied the Ottoman Empire in a major way since the partition of Poland which started in 1792 with the first partition and ended with the third in 1795. The extra territory made available by the dismemberment of Poland served to create a new European equilibrium to replace the status quo established since 1648—a status quo based on the view that all states then existing should continue to do so. With Europe now having run out of territory that could be sacrificed on the altar of compensation in the interests of European equilibrium, the Eastern Question—what would be the division of the spoils should the Ottoman Empire disappear—came to loom larger and larger in European affairs.

Shocked by the dislocation engendered by the Napoleonic era, the European powers sought to reconstitute some notion of stability, peace, and order in international affairs. This new order was codified by the Congress of Vienna. The new map of Europe would be maintained through the mechanism of the Concert of Europe. While the Ottomans were excluded from the general guarantee of the peace, they emerged from the settlement with new found diplomatic support from Great Britain. Peace was preserved by the Concert of Europe through two periods of major revolutionary upheaval, 1830 and 1848, until Europe 'blundered' into the Crimean War.

Humiliated by her defeat in that debacle, Russia embarked upon a policy to rid herself of the encumbering conditions set down by the Peace of Paris, which she did unilaterally in 1870 while Europe was distracted by the rise of Bismarck and the Franco-Prussian War. Russia had also set in motion significant military, economic, and social reforms, including a policy of expansion first in Central Asia and then in the Black Sea area and the Balkans. As Russia pressed in on the Ottoman Empire, absorbing the northern Black Sea littoral and extending her frontier westward river system by river system, the Ottomans were busy on both diplomatic and internal fronts. British support, in the person of Disraeli at the Congress of Berlin following the Ottoman-Russian war of 1877-1878, limited Russia's gains. Gladstone, seeking to unseat Disraeli as Prime Minister, took up the cause of the Bulgarians without any serious knowledge on his part of the situation in Bulgaria, and called for the Ottomans to be driven out of Bulgaria 'bag and baggage'.

Gladstone was referring, of course, to the communal strife taking place in the Balkans in the name of nationalism and ethnicity. Eventually, the Ottoman Empire was unable to resist the demands for independence on the part of its Balkan peoples. Following the earlier examples of Montenegro (1799), Serbia (1804), and Greece (1821), independent states proliferated with the birth of Romania (1856), Bulgaria (1878), and Albania (1913).

Following the Russian-French alliance in 1905, Europe began to organize itself into two camps, Germany and Austro-Hungary against Britain, France, and Russia. Unresolved ethnic and nationalist demands in the Balkans ultimately resulted in the First and Second Balkan Wars which still left many of the nationalist and ethnic issues unresolved. Austria and Germany drew closer together. The Anglo-Russian Convention of 1907 had served to patch up relations between those two former rivals in the east. In 1914, when relations between Serbia and Austria degenerated and a member of the Serbian Black

Hand secret society murdered the Austrian Archduke Ferdinand in Sarajevo on 28 June 1914, the end result was the engulfment of the world in what was termed the war to end all wars. We would be remiss if we did not note that 28 June is also the anniversary of the Battle of Kosova in 1389. Enver Pasha, a leader of the Young Turks, who had sought to pressure Sultan Adbülhamit II to institute a policy of reform intended to revitalize the nearly moribund Ottoman Empire but who ended up forcing the sultan into exile and taking over the government, led the empire into the war on the side of the Central Powers.

Caught in the necessity of having to fight a two-front war—in the east against the Russians and to the west against the British, Commonwealth, and French forces—the empire's internal situation took a disastrous turn. With the Russians advancing against the Ottoman army, Armenians in eastern Anatolia saw supporting the Russians as a means toward the realization of their national ambitions. For a long time, the Armenian *millet* had been considered the most loyal *millet*. The Ottoman response to what they perceived as a strategic military threat was to relocate Armenians from eastern Anatolia in Syria and Lebanon. Tragically, the central government lost control of the situation on the ground, where in war-time it took very little to ignite the passions of communal strife. Hundreds of thousands of Armenians lost their lives. Those events have embittered relationships between those two peoples ever since.[107]

Having chosen the wrong side in the war, the Ottoman Empire emerged from the conflict thoroughly defeated and destitute. The Allies occupied Constantinople, and in the peace arrangements they sought to satisfy their imperialist ambitions according to the secret treaties made during the war but which were rendered null and void by the Russian revolution. Within Turkey a resistance movement arose against the actions of the sultan and his government, which were seen as a complete sell-out of the country. When Greece grew tired of waiting for her share of the Ottoman pie from the peace conference, she, with the connivance of Great Britain, landed troops in western Anatolia. This action united the several Defence of Rights Associations in Anatolia which found their leader in the person of Mustafa Kemal (Atatürk). He succeeded in driving out the Greeks, and then outmanoeuvred the French and the Italians who sought to take possession of the Turkish territory they deemed part of their war spoils. Under Mustafa Kemal, an alternative government to the sultan's was established in Ankara which became the modern Republic of Turkey in 1923. The sultanate and the caliphate were abolished, and a modern, secular state took the place of the Ottoman Empire.[108]

The View of the 'Turk'

As part of the internal deterioration of the Ottoman Empire, and especially due to the ethnic and nationalist struggles that persisted throughout the nineteenth century on into the early twentieth century, the view of the 'Turk' in the West underwent a severe denigration. Western diplomats, politicians, writers, and travellers alike, most particularly those of British and Greek origins, tended to view the Greek *millet* as living in constant suffering at the hands of the Turks, who were seen as nomads or uncivilized, sadistic people. Gladstone portrayed the Turks as stamping out civilization wherever they went,[109] and Achilles Rose, a Greek-American writing in 1898 for the members of the Hellenic Association of America, described the Ottoman Turks as filthy, lazy, fanatical, and given to sensual excesses.[110] Sir Charles Eliot, British ambassador to Constantinople, called the Greeks 'a superior class of Christians' who 'constituted a counterpoint to the Turks'.[111] Vacalopoulas saw the Turks as an undisciplined and predatory horde that 'trampled upon countless men, women, and children'.[112] This stereotyping was even incorporated into Webster's dictionary under the definition of 'Turk': One exhibiting any quality attributed to Turks, such as duplicity, sensuality, or brutality.[113]

Few, if any, nationalities other than the Turks have 'qualities' included in their definitions—this scurrilous definition is a product of stereotypical thinking which continues until this day. In discussion about other empire-builders, such as the Romans, British, and Russians, references to Turks imply in their aggression a special 'bad' quality that distinguished them from other conquerors in history whose 'aggression' came to be viewed with the passage of time as an expectable human response and somehow more 'civilized'. No doubt, the Greek *millet* did suffer like others, including the Turks themselves, when the empire started to decline, disintegrate, and dissolve. But it is the reputation of the Ottomans, added to the suffering of the Greeks, that underlies, even today, the psychology of Turkish-Greek relations.

What these comments may be reflecting is the absorption on the part of these westerners of the Greek sense of having been humiliated by living under the domination of the Turks for a long time. This sort of humiliation actually is shared—as are the psychological defences against it. It is internalized and conveyed from one generation of those humiliated to the next. Clearly, the Greeks had felt humiliation under Ottoman rule and took pride in having been able to maintain their own traditions, sentiments, language, and religion over the centuries and having ultimately thrown out their conquerors from their heartland. It is a proud thing to survive domination and win freedom. This achievement, which raised Greek self-esteem and Greek preoccupation with their history, may account, to some degree, for their current attitude toward Turks, the psychological as well as the historical heirs to the Ottomans. It is essential to explore the story of the Greek *millet*, and Western support for it, if we are to understand the background of current Turkish-Greek relationships.

| 7 |

'Togetherness'

After the fall of Constantinople until the emergence of an independent Greece in the 1830s under the aegis of the Concert of Europe, the Greeks lived in a kind of 'togetherness' with the Ottoman Turks. There was much common blood—as well as bad blood—between them, but during most of the Ottoman period they co-operated more than they fought.[114] Leaving aside the many Ottomans of Greek origin who had been levied and educated through the *devşirme* process to hold high office in the Ottoman establishment, many Christian Greeks retained their religion while serving the Ottoman state. As an example, Greeks from the Phanar (Fener) area of Istanbul served as translators (*dragoman*) of the Porte, served in the Ottoman government, and were governors (*voivodes*) of Moldavia and Wallachia, especially in the eighteenth century. Such family names as Mavrocordatos, Ipsilanti, and Capodistrias are extremely familiar in the annals of Ottoman affairs.

Even when the disintegration of the Ottoman Empire was clearly apparent, many Greeks still maintained their varied relationships with members of the Ottoman elite. During the reign of Abdülhamit II (1876-1909), when the Ottoman Empire was well established as 'the sick man of Europe' in the minds of Europeans, a Greek, Alexander Caratheodory, represented the sultan at the Congress of Berlin. Also, a Greek physician, Dr. Mavroyeni, was politically influential in the same period until he fell out of favour, and Ottoman ambassadors to London, St. Petersburg, and Athens were of Greek origin, as was the governor of what is now southern Bulgaria. It would, however, be a mistake to consider the Greeks and the Ottoman Turks as brothers.[115]

Biological brotherhood between Greeks and Turks, however, has remained a topic of fascination for some Greeks. Vacalopoulas suggests that 'after successive conquests by the Seljuks and Ottomans, the purity of the Turkish race was itself broken down by an infusion of Greek blood, especially after whole populations in Asia Minor and the Balkans went over to Islam.'[116] Vacalopoulas believed, erroneously, that Turks originally had Mongol characteristics and became more like the people of southeastern Europe than those in Turkestan, and this must be due to Turks having acquired Greek blood. It is interesting that he does not suggest the reverse situation and attribute Turkish blood to Greeks. Voyatzidis calls these people 'Greco-Ottomans', and suggests that 'the Turks and Greeks of modern times are often the same stock'.[117]

Remarks regarding the common blood between the Turks and the Greeks can be found among the Greeks even at the present time. Dimitri Kichikis, a professor of history, stated in a journal of history in 1992 that 'Turks are the best kind of Hellenes'. He continued to say that the blood of the Turks is Greek blood. He proposed that a Greek-Turkish Federation in the part of Anatolia from the Aegean to Ankara should be heavily influenced by Hellenism.[118]

There can be no doubt that conquerors and conquered have mingled blood throughout history, but differences in ethnicity and nationality depend more on historical processes, chosen traumas, chosen glories, belief systems, and myths backed by a common psychology and shared emotions than on blood ties alone.

Turkokratia

Turkokratia, Greek for Ottoman rule over the Greeks, is usually spoken of by the Greek writers as a horror story, but it also refers to the symbiotic togetherness of Greeks and Turks and the comfort and suffering experienced by them which varied during the phases of Ottoman rule. *Turkokratia* 'covers a period of from four to six centuries, in some cases as early as the 1300s and as late as 1922, depending on which geographical area of Greece one has in mind'.[119] A more restricted version of this term can be applied to the period from 1453, when the Turks conquered Constantinople, to 1821, when the Greek War of Independence started. Under *Turkokratia*, Greekness was:

> At the popular level, a life-style practiced by Greek-speaking people, and, at the formal level, a corpus of learning conveyed in the Greek

language and preserved by the Christian Orthodox Church. Strictly speaking, it was the heritage of multi-ethnic Byzantium, a cultural category to which other ethnicities had contributed and in which they shared. Its hallmark, in theory at least, was its universalistic quality. If it was called 'Greek', it was in the sense of Greekness as a cultural treasure for equal access and benefit to all.[120]

This concept of Greekness was supported by the Ottoman *millet* system which, as indicated earlier, allowed the *dhimmis* [in this case, the *Rum* (Romans/Orthodox)] to retain their own language and religion and to conduct their own civil affairs. When the Ottomans conquered the Greek heartland, 'they inflicted no blow to Greek national pride, for no such thing existed. Indeed, the idea of a nation was as yet unconceived'.[121]

The images and ideas of ancient Greece had atrophied and were divorced from reality during the final centuries of the Roman Empire.[122] Greeks called themselves Romans. Under the Turks some adopted Islam, but they were not forced to do so. Turks 'had no desire to lose the heavy taxes Christians ceased to pay if they became Moslem'.[123] The Ottomans displayed tolerance toward the *dhimmis*, and the Greeks saw Turks as protectors of the Orthodox Church.[124]

According to Woodhouse, the Greek peasant of the fifteenth and sixteenth centuries was much better off than his counterpart in Europe.

> He had never been free in the nineteenth century sense of the word and therefore did not crave what he had not known. He had lived for a thousand years under a theocracy and to all intents and purposes still did.[125]

During *Turkokratia*, the conditions of Greek life never remained static nor was the reaction to the conquerors always the same. The Greeks had many different communities, and the life of the peasantry was quite different from that of urban Greeks. At the start of the Ottoman period, Greeks, in spite of their keeping the mental representation of the loss of Constantinople alive, felt Turkish rule to be an improvement in their lives as initially Ottoman taxation fell less heavily upon them than the traditional Byzantine system of the *meta*, or fifty-fifty division of the crops, and corvée labour dues exacted by the local lords. Turkish rule also brought in its wake better communications, thereby improving trade opportunities.

Life, as Raphaela Lewis has observed, continued along its traditional patterns.[126] Greek villages in Asia Minor and what later became known as Greece were usually in ethnic composition totally Greek. The Greeks practised their religious rituals, including paying their pre-Christian obeisance to their pagan Gods. Superstition characterized daily life, including belief in the evil eye which was shared by Turkish peasants as well. Greek girls, married at 12 or 13 years of age, did the farm work, spun and wove, and helped with the harvest. Greek men raised sheep, and those near the sea were sponge divers.

Vacalopoulas noted many obstacles to tracing the history of communities subject to protean influences of time, internal evolution, and external change.[127] Written documents are not always available, and the Turks, he claims, paid more attention to some communities than to others. For example, Zagora, Malakasi, and Agrafa in the Pindus enjoyed certain privileges perhaps because they had submitted to the Turks. Contrary to what the leading Ottoman historian, Halil İnalcık has demonstrated,[128] Vacalopoulos maintains that Christians did not benefit from the Ottoman seizures of monastic and manorial lands and the conversion of such labour services as road repair, harvesting, and maintenance of the lord's establishment into cash payments. He maintains that such may have been the case in the early stages of Ottoman conquest but that later on the peasantry's (*reaya*)'s position tended to become more onerous, and he details 'the profound humiliation to the proud and sensitive *raias* (he uses the term *reaya* to indicate the Christian peasantry) who were denied all means of retaliation'.[129]

> The weapons most commonly used to combat the conqueror were therefore equivocation, subterfuge, dissimulation and outright mendacity. Indeed, they were the only weapons which could ensure survival in this atmosphere of terror, torment and persecution. The spirit was shackled. It was an environment which bred a new sort of *graeculus*, the *raia*, a pitiful creature who trembled before the conqueror and who was always eager to serve, flatter or curry favor with him.[130]

It is true that with the economic decline of the empire, all ethnic groups (or *millets*) suffered. Turkish peasants were among them, but we know how important the shared feelings of a group can be and accept the Greek complaint of having been humiliated by the Turks, but the harsh Turkish stereotype in Greek writings should also be modified.

While it is true that the *dhimmis*, including the Greeks, were subject to sumptuary laws that limited what they could wear (they were intended for a dual purpose—both to remind the *dhimmis* of their inferior position and to prevent them from passing as Muslims, especially as Muslims of high rank), the Muslim peasantry, who also belonged to the *reaya*, suffered similar and other disabilities along with the *dhimmis*.[131] For example, neither group could ride horses or carry arms. It is also true that the *dhimmis* were restrained from building new places of worship; however, they could maintain old places in good repair. Christians could not ring their church bells. Islam punishes apostasy with death which rendered it difficult for non-Muslims to make converts among the Muslims, but Muslims were under no such prohibition in seeking to make converts among the *dhimmis*.[132]

On the subject of humiliation suffered by being made to feel a 'second class' member in a larger society and victimization by a harsh economic system, it is important to note that once the empire declined, ordinary Turks were often treated as shabbily as the *dhimmis*, and in some areas of life were worse off than their non-Muslim counterparts. Prior to the beginning of the nineteenth century when Western ideas of equality and 'rights' began to filter into the Ottoman Empire, it was the true Ottomans (those who served the religion and the state and who knew the Ottoman Way) who benefited the most from what the Ottoman society had to offer, and *everyone* else lagged behind. When the line between *askeri* and *reaya* was rigidly maintained, Christians had greater opportunity through the *devşirme* to enter the *askeri* group than did Muslim Turks of the *reaya*.

It is equally important to bear in mind that once the subjects of reform and 'equality' were broached within the empire, especially among the uppermost levels of the Ottoman elite, and were expressed in the two important reform documents of the *Tanzimat* (Restructure) era 1839-76 (the edicts of 1839 and 1856) the upper echelons of the Greek and Armenian Patriarchates were among the most vociferous opponents of the reform process. Reform threatened both their political and economic positions, causing them to resist change and especially the increasing pressure being mounted by lay elements within their respective *millets* who sought status and power commensurate with their growing economic wealth. Roderic Davison repeats the comment attributed to the Greek patriarch following the public reading of the reform edict of 1839 and the return of the document to its red satin pouch: 'God grant that it not be taken out of this bag again.'[133]

Turkish Life During the Ottoman Period

There was a gap between the Ottoman elite and most of the Turkish communities in Asia Minor and the other provinces. In respect to taxes, the Turks were better off than the Christians, but when the empire began to decline they, too, suffered from neglect and hardship at the hands of corrupt Ottoman officials. Officials, faced with the problem of recouping their investment in their tax farms and making a profit, found silver coins squeezed from Turkish peasants of the same value as those extracted from Christians. It was not so much ethnicity as the Ottoman system itself that bore a great deal of the responsibility for making their lives difficult.

Who suffered more at the hands of the classical Ottoman system that held *dhimmis* inferior to Muslims, but offered certain Christian *dhimmis* mobility into the coveted *askeri*/Ottoman status through the *devşirme* whilst closing that path off to ethnic Turks, is still an open question. The Ottoman Empire, like those others whose economies depended on agriculture, was initially organized for conquest. When geographical discoveries diverted the Eastern trade routes away from Ottoman territories to the oceans, the Ottomans' economy became depressed. By the end of the seventeenth century, the Ottoman world underwent social upheaval as the system proved less flexible than the times demanded, and all sectors of society suffered. Europe began to redress the military imbalance in its own favour against the Ottomans. Through the creation of the new monarchies, Europe was able to confront the Ottomans with new adversaries who were better equipped and structured and who possessed greater resources than the Ottomans had ever had to face.

It was not just in the areas of military hardware and tactics that the Ottomans were losing ground, but also in the realm of ideas. This multinational, multiethnic, multireligious empire was hard pressed to counter the twin incursions of nationalism and ethnicity. Reforms were embarked upon both as a necessity and as a sop to those Western powers who began to interfere in the internal affairs of the Ottoman Empire on behalf of client *millets*. Aware of the impact of the French Revolution on France and Europe, Sultan Selim III (1789-1807) sought to strengthen his empire through the creation of a new style army, the *Nizam-i Cedid*, itself supported by new taxes. His attempts at reform ultimately failed, and he was deposed and then killed. Mahmut II (1808-39) introduced a more thorough-going pattern of reform, including the destruction of the Janissaries in 1826, but it fell to his successor, Abdülmecit, to introduce the era of *Tanzimat*, which has the same meaning as *perestroika*. The reform edict of 1839 sought to guarantee the basic rights of life, honour, and property. As a result of these reforms and with the active support, protection, and intervention of the Western powers, the Christian subjects of the empire became more and more privileged. Meanwhile, the Muslims were impoverished by losing their young sons to war. The Christians began to look down upon the Muslims thinking that the latter's backwardness was an innate characteristic. The Turks, however, were not the only ones to have heard of the French Revolution. Encouraged by its message, the Greeks sought successfully to achieve their own independence, and the long togetherness of the Turks and the Greeks came to an end.

| 8 |

'Separateness'

Within the context of Turkish-Greek relations two major events of the nineteenth century were the Greek War of Independence (1821-1833) and the crystallization of modern Greek consciousness. They both shared many components of mass psychology. In studying these events, we seek links between observable real-world political, economic, legal, and military issues and unseen, but powerful, emotional motivations. It is doubtful whether we can speak of real history without consideration of shared emotions.

Petropulos suggests that 'Greek War of Independence' is a misnomer since the outcome of that war was independence only in a formal sense. 'In fact, Ottoman sovereignty was replaced by a kind of British-French-Russian protectorate, formalized by international treaty from 1832 until 1923.'[134] Petropulos would call it a 'war of liberation', although it liberated only some of the Greeks in the Ottoman Empire. What became today's Greece grew against the empire's territory in stages and came to include other Greeks as well. We agree, but choose to speak of 'independence'.

The Greeks revolted not only to form an independent nation. They had another vision as well: 'That vision was Hellas—the achievements of the ancient Greeks in knowledge, morality, and art, summed up in one evocative word.'[135] The word Hellas also stood for 'a generalized ideal, a symbol of cultural superiority'.[136] In trying to capture the vision of Hellas, Greeks had to deal with shifting perceptions, contradictory emotional investments, the division and merging of many emotional issues of identity, all of which deeply influenced their relationships with other folk, especially with the Turks. Before examining the psychologically pregnant processes involved, we present an overview of events occurring between 1821 and 1833, a period characterized by Hertzfeld as a period in which the 'most explosive' adventure of the nineteenth century took place.[137] It claimed thousands of lives and formally created a Greek nation-state that had never existed before as a sovereign entity.

While they achieved the status of a nation-state, the Greeks had not been the first group involved in a movement of emancipation from their Ottoman rulers during the last quarter of the eighteenth century and the first decades of the nineteenth century. Other peoples as well in the European half of the Ottoman Empire had begun to awaken to their national identities. The Serbs, in 1804, had been the first to initiate a movement for independence. With the Serbs having shown the way, the Greeks, under the leadership of two main groups, the elite Phanariot Greeks who had risen to power as associates of the Ottoman governing apparatus, and Greek merchants from the port cities and the Aegean islands. The story of their efforts to achieve independence is a complicated one.

Greek peasants began their uprising in the Morea (the Peloponnesus). There they massacred every Turk they could lay their hands on. Ottoman retaliation matched their violence, and as the revolt continued, the Ottoman sultan sought help from Mehmet Ali, his vassal in Egypt. In 1827, it appeared that Mehmet Ali's forces would capture the last rebel strongholds, but by that time the Greek War of Independence had become an emotional as well as a political issue for the western powers. Britain, France, and Russia intervened and sank the combined Turkish and Egyptian fleet anchored at Navarino in western Greece. With its fleet destroyed, the Ottomans were forced to sign the Treaty of Adrianople (Edirne) in 1829. By this treaty, territory which would ultimately become part of the new state of Romania became a virtual Russian protectorate, and the new small state of Greece was created. Many Greeks still remained within the Ottoman domains, and eventually some were gathered into the new Greek state that embarked on an expansionist policy, inspired by the *Megali Idea*.

Klephts, Armatoles, Phanariots, and Merchants

It is well known that the Ottoman Empire's retreat from Europe, commencing in 1699, resulted in a serious loss of manpower and tax revenue which in part caused a money shortage and economic decline. Thus, even before the start of the Greek independence war, the

Ottomans were threatened from within by a declining economy and the end of the almost moribund *devşirme* system,[138] and from without by threats to its territory from the Austrian push westward, the Russian impingement from the north, and the Persian pressure eastward. It can even be said that on the eve of the Greek War of Independence, the Ottoman Empire was no longer a unified state. In both Anatolia and Rumelia, the sultan's authority was encroached upon by both the *derebeys* (lords of the valley) and the *ayan* (notables) who exercised power in local areas. The *ayan* also began to emerge in the Fertile Crescent among the Arabs, especially in Syria. Both the leading *derebeys* and *ayan* had begun to establish their families as local dynasties. In the face of these continuing decentralization pressures, the central government embarked upon a series of reforms that were ineffectual in halting the downward spiral.

Meanwhile, the number of bandits and thieves in the countryside of the empire increased. The Greek bandits were known as *klephts*, and the Muslims as *çetes* or *hayduts*. In accordance with their traditional way of employing local forces to fight other local upstarts, the Ottomans used another group of Greek irregulars known as *armatoles* to fight the *klephts*. All these groups were common brigands who had roamed the countryside in lesser numbers long before the start of the Greek War of Independence, which saw the transformation of bandits on both sides into selfless, heroic 'freedom fighters' and defenders of Ottoman law and order. The war transformed the *klephts* and the *armatoles* in their own minds and in the minds of their fellow Greeks from brigands, who previously had no notion that they were engaged in national liberation,[139] into high-minded proponents of Greek statehood. Similarly, the Turkish brigands and the fighting forces under the control of the *derebeys* and the *ayan*, of whom there were many, saw themselves and were seen by others as defenders of the status quo embodied in the Ottoman state.

Yet, neither the *klephts* nor the *armatoles* launched the Greek War of Independence. That was the work primarily of the Phanariot Greeks who had risen to power in the period of 'togetherness' as translators of the Porte and administrators in the name of the Ottomans over the principalities of Moldavia and Walachia. These people were the successors of the noble Byzantine families who had died out in the course of the sixteenth century, and they claimed descent from those aristocratic families, a claim that was a myth at best.[140] The first

Phanariot to serve as Chief Translator (*Baş Tercüman*) of the Porte was Panayotis Nikousious (1613-73), the son of a petty tradesman. He was succeeded by Alexandros Mavrokordatos, who established a family dynasty devoted to Ottoman service that lasted until 1821. It was a Mavrokordatos who was appointed first Phanariot ruler in Moldavia in 1709.[141]

Phanariot administration of the principalities had been described, even by such historians as R. W. Seton-Watson, no supporter of the Ottomans, as a disaster.[142] They enriched themselves, their families, and friends at the expense of the local population. Even Greek historians have admitted the 'wickedness of their own regime'.[143] In the end, it was the scion of another Phanariot family, Alexander Ypsilantis, who is considered to be the initiator of the war of independence.

Ypsilantis did this in an area far removed from Greece. On 6 March 1821 he led an army of Greeks across the Pruth River into Moldavia. They had been propelled into activity through their association with a Greek clandestine organization, the *Philike Hetaeria* (Society of Friends) founded in the Crimea in 1814 to promote Greek independence. Ypsilantis was at the time a general in the Russian tsar's army. This military adventure was doomed to failure from the start. Ypsilantis was heavily dependent upon the local peoples' rising up and flocking to his banner, but they had too much previous experience with Phanariot misrule. They failed to react in a pro-Ypsilantis fashion and on 12 June 1821 the sultan's forces, who had entered Moldavia to meet this threat, defeated Yspilantis. Tsar Alexander I was infuriated when he heard the news of Ypsilantis' venture and dismissed him from the Russian army. After his defeat, Ypsilantis headed into Hungary. While this invasion did not result in Greek independence, it did result later in the birth of the national movement in the principalities that would ultimately result in the birth of Romania.

Controversy still hovers over the role played by the Phanariots in the achievement of Greek independence. Arnold Toynbee has suggested that the Phanariots sought to achieve for the Greeks within the Ottoman Empire what Joseph II had hoped to realize for the Germans within the Hapsburg monarchy.[144] Richard Clogg is unconvinced and considers the notion that 'the Phanariots were working to subvert the (Ottoman) Empire from within in the interest of the Greeks as a whole is scarcely tenable'.[145] In a similar vein, Mango comments:

> I do not believe that there ever existed a Phanariot master-plan for a settlement of the Eastern question. I am aware that some Phanariots became infected with liberal ideas, and that a few of them even won the crown of 'ethno-martyrdom'. But if we draw a conclusion, it is that the Phanariots, not by virtue of their descent, but by virtue of their position in the Ottoman Empire, the source of their wealth, and their close identification with the Church, represented a Byzantine tradition that was basically anti-national.[146]

It is generally assumed that besides the Phanariots, Greek merchants played a role in the Greek independence movement. Clogg wonders: 'How revolutionary in fact was this merchant class and what was its precise contribution to the movement for liberation?'[147] He states that the popular image of the merchants 'was unflattering'.[148] They were seen basically as unsympathetic to Greece's plight, more interested in profit than in independence. It is known that the merchants learned the language of Europe for the sake of trade and to link themselves to diaspora Greeks. The merchants were 'vehicles' to carry ideas from Europe to Ottoman Greeks[149] and go-betweens in making the Greek War of Independence ideologically a European/Western drive for an idealized reconstruction of the ancient Greek civilization. This fantastic emotional phenomenon should be taken into account, along with its implications in studying today's relations between Turks and Greeks.

The Morea was an ideal place in which to begin the Greek War of Independence; Greeks had a certain degree of autonomy there and owned a third of the land. In the Morea, Greek notables, called *Hocabaşıs*, were powerful; the Greek elite imitated the Turkish elite. Photakos Khyrsanthopoulos, a hero of the Greek War of Independence, states:

> The *Hocabaşı* imitated the Turk in everything, including dress, manners, and household. His notion of living in style was the same as the Turks', and the only difference between them was one of names: for instance, instead of being called Hasan the *Hocabaşı*, he would be called Yanni, and instead of going to the mosque, he would go to the church. This was the only distinction between the two.[150]

Meanwhile, the Greek Church was oppressive, holding heresy trials and burning offensive books.

The Morea revolt began as one against the Turks and against the

Greek elite and clergy. The Greek intellectual and literary development that led to a search for a new Greek nationalism was fuelled as Greeks fought against Turks and against Greeks who resembled them.

The Building of a Nation and the 'Megali' Idea

Zatos states that when the Turks came to Greece, Greeks called themselves Romans (*Romioi*), and even in 1821, a Greek executed by Turks would say, 'A Romios I was born, and a Romios I would die!'[151] But shortly after the beginning of the war, that same *Romios* was referring to himself as a Greek. Modern Greece was born from a dynamic process of nation-building rather than from any 'national awakening'.[152] As was true throughout the Balkans, Greek nation-building did not resemble the emergence of nation-states in Western Europe centuries earlier. Those movements rarely involved wars of liberation against foreign powers, but an evolution of culturally homogeneous peoples living in fairly well-defined territories with already existing state structures of their own. Their rebellion was against aristocracy and monarchy in the interests of political/economic rights and freedoms, and it represented a rising of the bourgeoisie on ideological and economic grounds influenced by the Enlightenment and its overthrow of feudal patterns. The power of the Church was greatly reduced in the process; countries established their own national churches, especially after the Reformation. Greeks, on the other hand, fought against an imperial country of which they had been part for centuries, and they had to redeem their ethnic brothers who stayed in Ottoman territory. Their aim was to create a nation and a state of their own, and it was an aim entertained also by Serbs, Romanians, Albanians, and other Balkan groups. There were exchanges of people and wars between newly independent countries in order to define the frontiers.[153]

With the economy of the Ottoman Empire stagnant at the time of their foundation, independent Balkan nation-states were launched under poor economic conditions. A further complication was the adherence of many Balkan Christians to the ecumenical Orthodox Church, which had political and judicial power over its people that transcended racial and ethnic differences. These factors influenced the Greek War of Independence. It was necessary for the new Greek state to build a nation gradually, and, according to Kitromilides, the process involved had two dimensions, the first being internal—the gradual development of a nation within the independent kingdom of Greece. The other was external and involved the orientation of the new Greek state towards Greeks living in the Ottoman Empire in places 'considered as integral parts of the historical patrimony of Hellenism'.[154] The dynamic interplay of these two processes was an essential part of the new Greek self-image, and with the crystallization of the new national identity came the channelling of the concept of Hellenism to Greek schools throughout the Ottoman Empire—'into the most remote areas of the Balkans and Asia Minor where Greek Orthodox Communities could be found'.[155] The University of Athens, a stronghold of the ideology behind the current Greek nationalism, disseminated the new Greekness outside the Greek state. In 1838, when the rector of the university reported on the first year of its operation, he indicated that students coming from outside the state were admitted with special leniency with respect to their qualifications. Also, in the 1830s and 1840s, one important function of Greek consulates and vice-consulates within the Ottoman Empire was 'the dispensation of official Greek citizenship to local Greeks who could prove or claim some form of participation in the Greek War of Independence'.[156] The main function of these offices, however, was to help communities evolve their own nationalism (Hellenism) and to articulate the claim that they could be incorporated within the Greek state. This activity had even reached Cyprus by the 1860s. The Greeks have developed an emotional and ideological network connecting internal and external communities around a major political force, the *Megali Idea*, the roots of which go back to the capture of Constantinople by the Turks, but which was basically a nineteenth-century phenomenon whose greatest achievement has been the national integration of all Greeks. 'Around this concept rallied all the conflicting, antagonistic groups, with contradictory objectives and goals.'[157] The *Megali Idea* supported the dream of a Greater Greece, and the new Greek state began to seek expansion almost immediately. The first serious manifestation of the impact of the *Megali Idea* occurred in Crete in 1866 when the Greek population revolted and demanded union with Greece. Athens supported the demand of the Cretans, but the powers refused to aid the Greek state. In the end, a conference held among the powers in Paris in January 1869 came down hard on Greece, requiring her to indemnify Turks on Crete for their losses in the revolt.

Greek aspirations, however, did not die on Crete. The Greeks tried to use the aftermath of the Congress of Berlin to be granted Crete, but that failed too. Greece had to be satisfied in 1881 with territorial frontier gains in Thessaly and Epirus. Matters on Crete boiled over again in 1896 and 1897. Again, the ineptitude of the Athens government demonstrated itself. An Ottoman occupation of Athens was narrowly avoided by the intervention of the powers, but the sultan's hold on the island was weakened, causing many of the Turks on Crete to emigrate. In 1908 Crete was finally joined to Greece.

Greece's next attempt at aggrandizement was ironically led by a Cretan-born politician, Eleutherios Venizelos, who by autumn, 1912, had engineered agreements with Bulgaria, Serbia, and Montenegro directed against the Ottoman Empire. War broke out on 8 October when Montenegro declared war. In a few days Serbia and Bulgaria joined in. The Balkan armies, revitalized over the past ten years, drove the Turks back on Istanbul with great success. An armistice in December 1912 brought the belligerents to the negotiation table, but a coup in Istanbul, directed against the Ottoman government's willingness to cede Edirne, brought Enver Pasha and his associates in the Committee of Union and Progress to power. The war was resumed in February 1913 with disastrous results for the Ottomans. By the peace arranged in May, the Ottomans ceded all their territory in Europe from Enos on the Aegean to Midia on the Black Sea. Albania received her independence, which caused the Balkan allies to fall out among themselves and led to the Second Balkan War. Serbia and Bulgaria began to fight each other on 30 June 1913 with Greece, Montenegro, and Romania ultimately joining in against Bulgaria. Thereupon, the Ottomans re-entered Thrace with Enver Pasha liberating Edirne. The Treaty of Bucharest in August brought an end to this war. Greek expansion, which had been going on the upswing, was halted temporarily, only to be restarted by World War I. The Ottoman Empire was unable to maintain itself in the face of the opposition of the Allies. The Greeks once again sought to realize the *Megali Idea* at the expense of the defeated Ottoman Empire, but the Turkish nation, as distinct from the Ottoman Empire, embarked upon its own war of independence about which we shall comment further.

Greek Nationalism
The Greeks had not made up a single nation since the Middle Ages.

While living as a *millet* under the Ottoman Empire they retained their own religion, customs, and language, and the 'Greeks became the most important non-Turkish element in the Ottoman Empire'.[158] Their religion, customs, and language provided a foundation for the new Greek mass consciousness, and the sense of nationality was derived from the *Megali Idea* which draws its inspiration in part from classical Greece and Byzantium.

How Greeks living with an identity called *Rum* (Roman) within the Ottoman Empire combined the ideologies and identities of classical Greece and Byzantium, which were not always compatible, is a fascinating story that exemplifies the great psychological forces they shared, the integration of old classical images with Byzantine images becoming necessary. The mending of opposing and contradictory investments, massive projection of those aspects of identity that threatened cohesion, a search for 'suitable targets'[159] of projections held in common, and the refinement of the new identity—all had to occur.

Veremis states that 'the umbilical cord connecting Greece's intelligentsia with its western European kin' was always present and through it passed Pan-Hellenism in the nineteenth century.[160] As Vacalopoulos and Xydis argued, the Greek cause can be traced back to the latter years of the Byzantine Empire.[161] We emphasize, however, that in the nineteenth century nationalistic philosophies of Western Europe were channelled into Greece through the political activity of the Russians as part of their anti-Ottoman campaign, and liberal political ideas entered through the works of British and French writers. Western perceptions of what Greece should be and what identity Greeks should have were highly influential, and the West so greatly admired ancient Greece that it emotionally identified Ottoman (Romeic) Greeks with ancient (Hellenic) Greeks. Greek independence was actively supported, sponsored, and even fought for by western European secular liberals in the aftermath of the French Revolution. Pro-Greek activists were the products of such movements as the Renaissance, the Reformation, and the Enlightenment. They were inspired also by the Romantic movement and fiercely opposed the Ottoman Empire which they saw as the symbol of Oriental Despotism. This attitude probably arose from unconsciously resented frustration of hopes entertained by proponents of liberty, equality, and fraternity following the French Revolution, their revolutionary zeal being displaced in both time and space. They now sought the liberation of Greece out of nostalgia for the restoration of the pre-Christian Hellenic civilization that had been in eclipse for some two thousand years. They confidently expected to see in contemporary Hellenes the characteristics of the time of Homer, in spite of the ebb and flow of history over a great reach of time.[162] Hopeful homage was paid to the past even in America, where James Monroe declared on 3 December 1822: 'The mention of Greece fills the mind with the utmost exalted sentiments and arouses in our bosoms the best feelings of which our nature is susceptible.' A few prominent Americans even went so far as to advocate the adoption of the Greek language in the United States.[163] European liberals, along with a few Americans who went to Greece to help were disappointed, even indignant, to discover little likeness between contemporary Greeks and the idealized Greeks that had such a hold on their imaginations from ancient history, and the many accounts of what was taking place in Greece that were published in America bore out the inaccuracy of their expectations.

Nonetheless, the idea of a Greek renaissance persisted, perpetuated and embellished by the romantic figure of Lord Byron and his coterie of poets and adventurers.[164] There were, indeed, many reasons for venerating the chosen glories of the pre-Christian past in what many thought of as the cradle of western civilization. A small group of elite Greeks who had been educated in Europe also longed for a return to the old Greece, but such aspirations played no part in the minds of the Greeks in the Morea, the Romeics of the Byzantine world, and the *Rums* of the Ottoman Empire, and it was they who were actually engaged in fighting for their independence with little affinity for the people from whom they were descended. Even they, however, came to realize that help from the Europeans, with their romantic notions, depended on the revival of a long-forgotten Hellenic identity and rejection of a Romeic one.

Massive Group Projections

It can be said, therefore, that to arise as an independent country the existing 'Greece' had to die psychologically and culturally. Current values, orientation, and ways of life had to be abandoned. It was as though a tremendous wave swept over the land and left behind a new sort of people. What the wave swept away was dropped on the shore of the Turks since the birth of the Greek nation-state was accompanied and even realized by massive group projections that were largely unconscious.

The involvement of a philhellenic western world led to (a) further crystallization of anti-Turk sentiment in the West and (b) confused identity among the Greeks. How far should the Greeks try to live up to their classical image? Greek intellectuals tried to narrow the gap between the reality of Greece and what the West wanted Greece to be, but rural populations were thoroughly confused:

> Some historians have argued that the rural folk preserved no knowledge or memory of the Classical past at all. The rural Greeks certainly seem to have been puzzled by the expectations which the philhellenes entertained of them, to judge from the accounts of those non-Greeks who returned to tell the tale. If this was the situation at the time of the War of Independence, it seems to have been substantially the same for several centuries before that.[165]

It was impossible to create Hellenism in the vacuum left by the wholesale projection of the existing Romeic identity unless only its unwanted aspects were projected. The Greek intellectuals had to unite what 'good' parts of the Romeic identity remained with the culture of ancient Greece and combine the glories of Byzantium with those of Classical Greece. This was not an easy task, and Herzfeld speaks of some of the problems: (1) The people in the new nation-state were told that they were identical to the long lost inhabitants of their land, and this was difficult to accept since most of the common people had no idea what the founders were asking them to be. (2) It was unacceptable for them to be 'Hellenes' in the old, pagan sense of the word since they strongly adhered to the Christian faith in their Orthodox church. (3) It was hard to be a Hellene while using the Romeic language, 'which was conceptually *opposed* to the ancient (Hellenic) tongue'.[166] Their leaders, and the foreigners on whom they depended, referred to their characteristics as 'barbarous' and 'oriental', therefore, the very antithesis of being Greek.[167] It was hard to include unlettered Greek peasants in the 'grand design' for there was no way they could be traced back to their supposed classical predecessors.

To deal with these difficulties, Greek intellectuals sought a continuum of Greek life from the idealized ancient civilization through Byzantium to the nineteenth century. They studied folk tales and dances, poetry, manners, lifestyle, and world views to substantiate their claims that *Romeika* was a derivative form of *Hellenika*, and that there was some evidence of a continuum in folklore and folk culture in general, even among Greeks living among Turks in the western part of Asia Minor.[168] The outstanding aspects of classical Greek culture, such as philosophy, theatre, and architecture, however, did not seem to have been inherited by modern Greeks but rather to have been kept alive by admirers in the West through the Renaissance and the Enlightenment. All this treatment from the past had to be recreated on Greek soil, and to accomplish this, all inappropriate traits, sentiments, and ideas had to be discarded (projected outward) to make room for a new identity and to establish a heritage of continuous superiority. The Turks were 'suitable targets' for receipt of what the Greeks discarded, not only because of their history, but more importantly, because of the past 'togetherness' of the two peoples. A target is a more effective storage place for projected elements if there are similarities between those who project and those who receive their projections.[169] According to Herzfeld, the new Greek nationhood depended on an intellectual and political article of faith the ethnological justification for which was set in motion *after* the establishment of the Greek state and had been virtually forced on the Greeks by the turn of events.[170]

Adamontios Koreas, struck with admiration for the goals of the French Revolution at the start of the nineteenth century, was an early advocate of Greek primacy, claiming that Europe owed a debt to modern Greeks because it was they who had preserved Greek classicism. He helped develop *katharevousa*, the neo-classical form of the modern Greek language that required the rejection of words used by Ottomans and which might be called a process of purification. Herzfeld reviews the writings of Spyridon Zambelios, Stamatis Valvis, Nikolaos Politis, and Dora d'Istria, the latter being a Romanian princess of Albanian extraction who was granted Hellenic nationality. They were all instrumental in the evolution and establishment of the new Greek mass consciousness and culture. Herzfeld demonstrates that, although Zambelios, Valvis, Politis, and d'Istria were not alike either in style or the content of their writings, they all helped relate current struggles to ancient glories. Ancient heroes were merged in the literature with the later *klephts*, though after independence was achieved they were debased into ordinary 'bandits' and 'brigands'. Since *klephts* were generally anti-government, it was easy to see them as partners in the struggle, and Hellenism saw a parallel between their feats and those of such Homeric figures as Ajax, Agamemnon, and Odysseus. Those ancients were all individualists, and although they were leaders in the Mycenean army, they were not members of a hierarchy, but played out their own ambitions in unruly ways while at the same time clinging to honour and friendship. While the *klephts* were also unruly, disobedient, and independent, they offered themselves in less lofty causes, being little more than thieves, whereas the classical fighters had fought to avenge wrongs.

The *klephts* attacked the Ottomans when they saw fit and abandoned their fight for reasons of their own. Basically lacking any cause but expediency, they engaged in what must be called criminal activity against both Turks (Muslims) and Greeks (Orthodox). By being extremely regressive and lacking in principle, they disqualified themselves as heroes. As is sometimes the case, however, the promotion of an idea for the sake of a group cohesion ignored reality, and with the continuing Ottoman decline and the territorial expansion of Greece, came confusion of *klephts* with the old heroes, and the establishment of something Koliopoulos calls a 'particular brand of politics' that saw outlaws as legitimate participants in the struggle for the Greek nation.[171] The effect of the *Klephtic* tradition on Greek political culture should not be underestimated. Koliopoulos reminds us that the Greek insurgents had never known a central government that was not foreign, distant, and hostile and could not grasp that the new Greek government might be different. Modernization and reformation was accordingly affected; their *klephtic* tradition, attitudes toward borders, and penchant for plundering 'diverted patriotic motives into self-defeating ventures and gave patriotism a suspect and sinister outlook ... it stood in the way of economic development and the establishment of public order and security'.[172] Lawlessness was favoured, but Western philhellenism persisted as 'a useful capital'.[173] The Greek way of thinking of nationalism changed, though original traditions that accompanied the emergence of the Greek nation-state did not disappear altogether but changed function, as can be seen in current relations between Turks and Greeks. Before we focus on this relationship, however, we shall describe in the next chapters the evolution of Turkish-Greek relationships since the Greek War of Independence.

| 9 |

The Last Century of the Ottoman Empire

Ideas imported into the Ottoman Balkans from the West led the Greeks in 1821 to embark upon their war of independence, but the Ottoman Empire, despite being deprived of its European provinces one by one, continued until 1923 when it gave way to the new Turkish Republic. We must review that intervening century in order to understand the conflicts that arose after World War I, when it was the Turks' turn to fight for their independence while the Greeks sought to realize their Great Idea and establish a Greek empire that would revive the chosen glories of their people.

Mahmut II vs. Mehmet Ali

In order to suppress the uprising that became the Greek War of Independence, the Ottoman government solicited help in 1823 from their powerful vassal, the Albanian-born pasha of Egypt, Mehmet Ali. He had come to Egypt in 1798 as part of the Ottoman forces sent to resist the invasion by Napoleon. Gradually rising in authority and power, in 1811 Mehmet Ali rid himself of his arch rivals, the Mamluk Beys, who had ruled Egypt prior to its conquest by the Ottomans in 1517 and who restored their dominant position in the seventeenth and eighteenth centuries. He became the semi-autonomous Ottoman vice-regent in Egypt, and embarked upon a policy of forced-draft modernization beginning with the military establishment. He built himself a powerful army and fleet and became a trusted vassal of the sultan who used him and his forces to pacify rebellious Muslims in Arabia in 1818-1820. Having ingratiated himself with the sultan earlier, he was called upon now to assist in putting the Greeks down.

Egyptian forces under the command of İbrahim Pasha, Mehmet Ali's son, were successful in pacifying this first phase of the Greek revolt. With his seventeen thousand troops İbrahim marched through the Morea and in 1823 moved his men to Crete which he also succeeded in bringing back under Ottoman control. İbrahim and his father were not being totally altruistic in this campaign, for Mehmet Ali had agreed to contribute his forces on the promise that he would be appointed governor of both the Morea and Crete, as well.

Sultan Mahmut II (1808-1839) needed the aid of Mehmet Ali because, following the example of his vassal, he had embarked upon his own policy of modernization in recognition of the fact that the Janissary Corps had become a toothless tiger, a worthless military force. Special attention needed to be paid as well to the naval forces which had also fallen on hard times. While Sultan Mahmut was busy with the Greek insurrection, he was also reasserting sultanic central control over areas of the empire in which local magnates had succeeded in establishing themselves as *derebeys*—lords of the valley—much the same sorts of people known as war lords in Chinese history.

Ottoman fortunes declined as Greek independence became a political reality, due in large part to the diplomatic and military intervention of Russia, France, and Great Britain, most notably at the Battle of Navarino (20 October 1827), in which a combined allied fleet destroyed most of the Ottoman-Egyptian fleet. With the Greeks firmly independent after 1830 under the umbrella of the support of the European states, Mahmut was subjected to further territorial losses when the French in July 1830 invaded Algeria and wrested it from Ottoman control. Especially galling was the invasion of the Fertile Crescent by Mehmet Ali's son İbrahim Pasha in 1831-1832 which brought with it the Egyptian occupation of Jaffa, Acre, Jerusalem, Haifa, and Damascus. Isolated from its British supporters by British problems at home and in Portugal, the Ottomans turned to Russia to save them from Mehmet Ali. The Treaty of Hünkar İskelesi (July 1833) provided the empire with a temporary reprieve but created ill feeling throughout the capitals of Europe as one great power after the other felt that Russia had achieved a position of superior influence in the Ottoman Empire. Despite attempts by the Russians to allay such fears, the British especially sought to befriend the Ottomans and thereby restore the old balance of power in the Near East. The British-Ottoman commercial agreement in 1838, which granted Britain most favoured nation status, was but one step in that direction.

Sultan Mahmut II used the lessening of international tensions to press on with the process of reform for his empire which effectively began with the destruction of the Janissaries (1826). Commencing in 1836, Mahmut restructured the bureaucracy, creating western type ministries of foreign affairs, the interior, and finance. Mahmut brought the *derebeys* to heel, reasserting central authority over Anatolia and Rumelia (*Rumeli*). He was, however, unable to control his own feelings of animosity towards Mehmet Ali and his desire to drive him out of Syria and back into Egypt. In 1834 Mahmut tried to use the pretext of revolts against İbrahim's policies of increased taxation, and conscription of non-Muslims into the military, to intervene, but the British and Russians restrained him. In 1838 Mehmet Ali sought to have the Ottoman sultan grant him hereditary rule over Egypt, Crete, and Syria, areas that had been granted to him on a yearly appointment in 1833 in return for an annual tribute of one hundred and fifty thousand pounds sterling. Mahmut II hoped that his military reforms had produced a fighting force capable of destroying his mighty foe, and he sent this fighting force into action in Syria. İbrahim Pasha routed them. It appeared that Mehmet Ali might soon reign in Istanbul rather than Cairo. This was not a prospect the British could tolerate, and they moved the Concert of Europe to restrain Mehmet Ali. Britain preferred to see the weak, dependent Ottoman sultan in Istanbul rather than the independent, reform-minded Mehmet Ali, especially since attempts to navigate the Tigris and Euphrates Rivers by steam had proven negative. Britain would still have to defend her routes to India.

'Tanzimat'

Mahmut II died without knowing that his troops had failed and that his empire was now dependent upon the support of Great Britain. Mahmut's successor, Abdülmecit, and the leading men of his government committed themselves to a policy of reform which became known as *tanzimat* (having the same meaning as *perestroika*) and represented in similar fashion a new way of thinking. The policy of greater emphasis on Turkification that had marked the career of Mahmut II gave way slowly to a more inclusive vision of society that would admit non-Muslims to coveted Ottoman status by opening careers in the military and bureaucracy to them. An imperial rescript (*hatt-i hümayun*) was issued in 1839 under the aegis of Mustafa Reşit Pasha, who was foreign minister at the time. As one of the leading statesmen of the *tanzimat*, he served as grand vizier six times and foreign minister three times before his death in 1858.

Tanzimat sought to guarantee all peoples living within the Ottoman domains their lives, property, and honour; promised to regularize tax assessment and collection; and to improve the conscription methods and training of the military. Also promised was greater participation in local government by minorities. This was bound to arouse feelings of hostility among the Muslims and non-Muslims. Nationalism had already brought changes in the Greeks' conception of their identity. Before the revolutionary movement began in earnest in Greece, Greek ballads spoke of identity in terms of being part of the eastern Roman empire. Vlachavas (d. 1809), the priest-*klepht* leader who rose against the Ottomans and was captured, was offered his life if he converted. He refused, declaiming his status as an eastern Roman:

> 'Priest! Wretch of a priest, you
> destroyed my province;

> Ali Pasha (of Janina) does not please you,
> the Sultan does not please you.

> And you raised up a standard, to become
> king yourself.'

> 'Do not blaspheme, Ali Pasha, do not
> blaspheme Vizier,

> I offended you, I fought you, I fell
> into your hands.'

> 'Become a Turk, priest, and I will
> forgive you all.'

> '*A Romneos I was born, a Romneos I will die.*'[174] [Italics added.]

Within a few years the Greek rebellion forged a new identification. In a ballad composed for Diakos, a *klepht* leader, Diakos rallies his forces against the Ottomans:

> 'Take heart my lads,' he says, 'fear not,
> Stand up boldly, like Hellenes and like Greeks.'

He is captured and sounded out about converting:

'Will you turn Turk, Diakos mine, change
your faith,

Make obeisance in the mosque and leave
the Church?'

But Diakos answered him, and spoke angrily;
'Go, you and your faith, you infidels,
to destruction!

I was born a Greek, and a Greek I will die![175] [Italics added.]

Within the empire, the Ottomans sought to gain the allegiance of all its subjects, but the minorities felt the sultan was dragging his heels on the promises contained in the imperial rescript of 1839. Objectively, there was a great deal of truth to support their contentions despite progress that was being made at the local level. It took another armed conflict to push the promises of *Tanzimat* to realities. This was the Crimean War, which broke out in 1853 between Russia and the Ottoman Empire (supported by France, Britain, and Sardinia). Fought in the Crimea, this was the first major European war since the peace instituted by the Congress of Vienna in 1815. Allied pressure and the understanding of the situation by leading Ottoman statesmen led to the sultan's promulgation of the second imperial decree in 1856 shortly before the belligerents met in Paris to negotiate a peace. The sultan's intention was to swing allied opinion to his side by offering guarantees of freedom of religion and participation in civil society to the non-Muslims, especially the Christians, living within the empire. This new attempt to halt the disintegration of the empire under the pressure of nationalism proved to be too little too late. An attempt to grant full citizenship to everyone living in the empire, which implied a complete change in what it had meant, for centuries, to be an Ottoman, failed to capture the allegiance of the non-Muslims now fully swept up in the current of nationalism.

Not only did the sultan have to contend with his own subjects, who were seeking to bring his empire down, the Russians also continued their inexorable push to extend their dominion over the northern littoral of the Black Sea, thereby undermining the status of that sea as an Ottoman lake, and to develop their own influence throughout the Balkans. Russia supported Slavs throughout the Balkans in their attempts either to break away from the Ottoman Empire or to expand their territories or privileges while still under the sultan's sway. This involved the Ottoman forces in almost continuous fighting in Montenegro, Bosnia, Herzegovina, and Serbia. While these events were taking place in the Balkans, the traditional Eastern Question was brought to the fore again as the leading powers in Europe jockeyed for position. Germany, under Bismarck, defeated Austria, and then in 1870 defeated France in the Franco-Prussian War. The tsar took advantage of that situation to renounce the Black Sea clauses of the Treaty of Paris (1856) which undermined Ottoman authority in the area. Britain sought to Europeanize this latest Russian power play and successfully brought the great powers to sign the Treaty of London (1871) by which the sultan could open the Straits to warships of friendly nations in peacetime.

Wanton Characterization

This was clearly a signal to the Russians to go slowly in their attempts to undo the Ottoman Empire, but it made little impression on them. Continuing unrest in Bosnia and Herzegovina, repression by Ottoman forces in Bulgaria in response to Bulgarian irregulars acting in similar fashion, and the outbreak of war between the Serbs and the Ottomans in July 1876 encouraged the Russians to take a more forward position with the Ottomans. This was especially so after Gladstone condemned the Ottomans for what he called the 'Bulgarian Atrocities'.[176] In his scurrilous pamphlet on the subject, Gladstone joined the ranks of the Turcophobes:

> Let me endeavour very briefly to sketch in the rudest outline, what the Turkish race was and what it is. It is not a creation of Mahometism compounded with the peculiar character of a race. They are not the mild Mahometans of India, and not the chivalrous Saladins of Syria, nor the cultured Moors of Spain. They are upon the whole, from the black day when they first entered Europe, the one great anti-human specimen of humanity. Wherever they went a broad line of blood marked the track behind them; and as far as their dominion reached, civilization disappeared from view.[177]

Gladstone is only one of many, before and after his time, who conceptualized 'the terrible Turk', his own term being 'the unspeakable Turk'. In this view the Turks were without any virtue, devoted solely to rape and rapine, driven by their religion to wanton violence. It was clear that Gladstone's interest was not so much to support the Bulgarians but rather to embarrass the prime minister, Disraeli, in order to bring his government down and himself to the prime ministership. Nevertheless, the damage was done, and the Turks have suffered for over a century through this wanton characterization.[178]

In the Balkans, far from the halls of Westminster, matters were degenerating rapidly. From September 1876 the Ottomans and the Serbs were engaged in heavy fighting, with the Ottomans gaining the upper hand. The Russians threatened the Ottomans with intervention on the Serbian side, a manoeuvre that forced the Ottomans to withdraw their troops from Serbia. The European powers called a conference in Istanbul to meet in December to settle the matter. Ottoman statesmen decided that they would pre-empt the conference through the promulgation of a constitution that would be the culmination of the *Tanzimat*, making it unnecessary for the foreign powers to intervene on the side of Ottoman minorities. A new sultan, Abdülhamit II, was brought to the throne to replace Murat V, who was deposed as incompetent. Abdülhamit was ambitious and promised Midhat Pasha, the leader of the *Tanzimat*-minded Ottoman statesmen, that he would approve the constitution that was in the process of being drawn up and that he would act with the advice of his ministers, thus converting the sultanate into a parliamentary form of government. The constitution was proclaimed on 23 December 1876 as the Istanbul conference got underway. It soon became obvious that the conference was superfluous, and it broke up a month later having accomplished nothing.

Undeterred, Russia pushed on with plans to attack the Ottoman Empire, declaring war on 24 April 1877. The Ottomans were unable to raise any support from the European powers and were left to face the Russians alone. It was a complete route, except for the heroic resistance of the city of Plevna under Osman Pasha, with the Russians advancing all the way to the walls of Istanbul—to the town of San Stefano which today is Yeşilköy, the location of Istanbul's airport. On 3 March 1878 the Treaty of San Stefano ended the hostilities, but the terms of the treaty were too harsh, allowing for an enlarged Serbia, an autonomous Bulgaria extending from the Black Sea to the Aegean, and an independent Romania. The European reaction to Russian aggrandizement was immediate. A congress was called to convene in Berlin to review the San Stefano agreement. There, under the brokerage of Bismarck, the Russian gains were modified especially with respect to Bulgaria. British support for the sultan was repaid by allowing Britain to occupy and administer Cyprus. Austria was satisfied with the permission to annex Bosnia and Herzegovina. Greece had come to the congress with great expectations of territorial aggrandizement, but while some territory was granted, the main objective was unrealized. The Congress of Berlin concluded on 13 July 1878, leaving the Ottoman Empire deprived of one-fifth of its population and two-fifths of its territory in Europe. 'The sick man of Europe', as the Ottoman Empire had become known, since the Crimean War was now on the verge of settling into his death bed.

Crete

Crete was one area in which the Ottoman Empire emerged from the Berlin Congress with its sovereignty still intact. The island had been conquered by the Ottomans from the Venetians over a period of seventy years, from the Ottoman's initial invasion in 1645 until the last Venetian stronghold surrendered in 1715. Crete was not an easy possession for the Ottomans to govern. A succession of revolts, starting in 1770, marked the history of the island for the next century and a quarter. In 1821 it needed Mehmet Ali to subdue a Cretan revolt. For a short period until 1840 the island was administered by the Pasha of Egypt when it again came under Ottoman control. Unrest was fed by the slowness shown by Ottoman officials on the island in applying the reforms guaranteed in the imperial rescripts of 1839 and 1856. Another revolt, fuelled by aid from the Greek mainland, broke out in 1866 and witnessed massacres carried out by Greeks and Turks alike. The Ottomans, aided by the inability of the European powers to agree among themselves on what pressure to bring to bear upon the Turks, put the revolt down. Ali Pasha, one of the leaders of the second generation of *Tanzimat* reformers and a future grand vizier, was sent to the island to formulate a more lasting policy. He introduced many *Tanzimat* reforms (February 1868), including local government, mixed law courts, a new cadastral survey to assist in more equitable tax collection, and Christians were exempt from payment of tax in lieu of conscription. Greece was unhappy about these developments and tried to stir up the revolt anew by sending 'volunteers' to Crete, but the powers intervened, forcing Greece to back down. In 1878 Greece again promoted trouble, hoping to take advantage of the exhausted state of the Ottomans after their war with Russia. Britain mediated the insurrection which ended with a Pasha of Greek origin being appointed as governor of the island.

Ethnic strife continued on the island due especially to the declining financial situation. Another major revolt broke out in 1897 under the auspices of a Greek secret society that sought to provoke a war with the Ottoman government in order to acquire Macedonia. In February, a Greek force landed on the island. The landing incited the Christian population to massacre the Muslim peasants wherever they found them. The powers intervened to stop the killing. Crete was given an autonomous status on 20 March, with the Greek soldiers leaving on 9 May 1898, and the Ottoman troops on 14 November. Another round of insurrections followed. Eleutherios Venizelos, who would eventually become Greek prime minister, led an insurrection in 1905 which ultimately united Crete with Greece in 1913 after much of the Muslim population had migrated from the island.

Capitulations

Another indication of the impending demise of the Ottoman Empire, in addition to the loss of territory, was the last phase in the story of the Ottoman capitulatory regime. Capitulations, which were concessions granted to Western merchants in the interest of fostering trade, pre-dated the Ottoman regime. For example, one of Sultan Selim's first acts after defeating the Mamluks in 1517 was to reconfirm the capitulation which the Mamluks had in effect with the French trading in the Fertile Crescent. In 1536 Sultan Süleyman the Magnificent granted the French a capitulation covering the entire Ottoman Empire as a means of cementing his new alliance with the French.[179] In addition to arrangements about customs duties, French subjects trading within the Ottoman domains would be under the authority of their own consuls and their ambassador in Istanbul. This privileged position became sought after by other nations trading with the Ottomans. English merchants were successful in obtaining their capitulation in 1580 to the dismay of the French. As Ottoman power waned, these capitulations were changed from concessions granted by a powerful sultan to illustrate his power and authority to elements of special status wrung from sultans unable to resist these demands by European states. They constituted a serious infringement on Ottoman sovereignty. In the late nineteenth century, almost every European state had its own post office in the Ottoman domains and other concessions, such as educational institutions, and the capacity to grant their citizenship to Ottoman subjects who worked for them in consular capacities. These privileges had been woven into a pattern that became known as the capitulatory regime. While Europe sought to trade on evermore favourable terms, the image of the Turk as 'lazy/terrible' was still maintained in the public mind.

Abdülhamit II and the Young Turks

Abdülhamit II (1876-1909) was a paradoxical, unappealing man, ruling over an unhappy country. Increasingly fanatical concerning religion and politics as his people began to rebel, he was inconsistent in his attitude toward modernization. While he suppressed the Ottoman Parliament, he also expanded the military and the educational systems. The restive Armenian minority sought European intervention and engaged in one assault after another, including the raid on the Ottoman bank in Istanbul.

> Thousands, even tens of thousands are said to have perished and the Armenian revolutionaries share with the Sultan the culpability for their deaths. There may have been cases when, by their avarice and treachery, the Armenians deserved the hatred of their Turkish neighbours, but once the fanatical passions of the mob had unleashed, there was no discontinuity between the innocent and the guilty.[180]

The group known as the Young Turks, which had been secretly organized by four students in the School of Military Medicine in Istanbul, and which then made contact with liberal Turkish exiles in Paris, opposed Abdülhamit II. A former member of the parliament that had been put down by the sultan, began publishing from Paris an inflammatory journal known as *La Jeune Turquie*, thereby giving a name to the group that envisaged a union under which all races and creeds would live in order and would progress together. When the Young Turks did gain power, however, they 'could not envision the empire without the sultan at its head, and they lacked the experience of high administrative office. Therefore, they agreed to co-operate with the sultan and his government'.[181]

A remarkable Turkish woman, Halide Edib (Adıvar), has written of the hopeful early days of Young Turk ascendency, when Muslim holy men, Christian priests, and Jewish rabbis marched arm-in-arm through the streets of Istanbul to celebrate the arrival of brotherhood and unity. She tells of calls from minarets mingling with the sound of church bells, as though announcing a new era of 'togetherness'.[182]

Abdülhamit was eventually exiled to Salonika and was replaced by a new sultan. Enver Pasha, a leader of the Young Turks, then assumed great power in the Ottoman government. He was a charismatic man with an obsessional narcissistic character.[183] A fine horseman who paid much attention to his appearance, he seemed at first to the Young Turks a dashing and romantic leader, and he took the fancy of Europeans as well. However, old habits die hard, and the honeymoon of the Young Turks with the European powers soon came to an end with the Italian assault on the Ottoman territories of Benghazi, Tripoli, and Libya. Then came the Balkan Wars in 1912 and 1913, when the Young Turks were still in power.

In the first Balkan War, Ottoman strongholds were attacked by Greeks, Bulgarians, and Serbians; the Greeks, Bulgarians, and Serbians won. Among the cities lost were Salonika (Thessalonika) and Edirne (Adrianople). When Salonika fell (it was the birthplace of Mustafa Kemal, who was to play a stellar role in the story of Turkey before long) the old sultan returned from exile to Istanbul, where he eventually died. The second Balkan War liberated Edirne and made Enver Pasha the hero of the day. These wars turned out to be the prelude to the First World War (1914-1918), and Enver joined alongside the Germans.

The Ottoman Empire at that period included people of twenty-two races, there being about ten million each of subjects who spoke Turkish and Arabic, respectively.[184] Twenty per cent of the rest of the population were still Christians, and this included Greeks. The Allies prevailed over the Ottoman world and partitioned their gains. In control of all European Ottoman areas, they entered Istanbul. When the truce was signed with the Allies, in October 1918, Prince Vahdettin, who became Mehmet IV, was the thirty-sixth and last ruler of the ten-centuries-old Ottoman dynasty, and he dissolved the organization of the Young Turks. Enver Pasha escaped to Turkistan, where eventually he was shot fighting against the Communists' Red Army. Characteristically, he had gone into battle wearing all his medals and decorations and was clad in the uniform of a general. On 10 August 1920 Mehmet IV authorized his representatives to sign the Treaty of Sèvres, which left Turkey about one hundred and twenty thousand square miles of almost barren steppes. What had once been one of the most proud and powerful empires on earth had been virtually wiped out.

The Voyage of the 'Bandırma'

A year before the signing of the Treaty of Sèvres, Mustafa Kemal, one of the two Turkish commanders who did not lose a battle during World War I, obtained a document from the Ottoman government in Istanbul authorizing him to restore law and order in Anatolia, the Turkish heartland, and to ferret out the causes of the disquieting disturbances there. He began, accordingly, to make plans for a hasty departure from Istanbul lest he be detained by the Allies.

On 15 May 1919 twenty thousand Greeks landed at Izmir and began their invasion of Anatolia.

> The Greek landing was carried out under the auspices of the Allies. Lloyd George, out of a mixture of motives that included pro-Hellenic and anti-Turkish sentiments as well as political considerations that saw Greece as a possible bastion in the Mediterrean, backed the claim of the Greek premier, Eleutherios Venizelos, that Greece had the right to occupy Izmir. Convincing Woodrow Wilson and Clemenceau that support for Greece was the best policy, Lloyd George garnered the approval necessary to launch Venizelos's grand scheme for the resurrection of a Greek empire. Self-determination, one of Wilson's Fourteen Points, was going to be denied the Turks.[185]

On 16 May, as Greeks continued to arrive at Izmir, Mustafa Kemal and his men boarded the *Bandırma* at Istanbul's Galata Bridge. The *Bandırma* was a cargo ship, built in England and purchased from a Greek. Alhough it was scarcely seaworthy, Mustafa Kemal succeeded in landing at Samsun, a small port on the Black Sea, on 19 May. He was to see his landing at Samsun as his birth as a saviour of a grieving and devastated nation and the beginning of the Turkish struggle for liberation. Since he was, in fact, ignorant of the exact date of his birth, he would say for the rest of his life that he was born on 19 May.

| 10 |

The Turkish War of Independence

Although the Turkish War of Independence was fought mainly against the invading Greeks, it had elements of a civil war as well, since the movement for liberation also opposed Turks who still supported the Ottoman sultan and his government in occupied Istanbul. The Greek War of Independence, fought a hundred years earlier, had not turned up a single super-hero. The Turks had one in Mustafa Kemal and rallied around him. He was to be known later, after his many successes, as Atatürk—the Father Turk.

There were British soldiers at Samsun, and Mustafa Kemal and his men went inland for safety's sake, moving quickly toward the heart of Anatolia. Atatürk had authority over the situation there and was bent on saving his country. He began at once to form political and military alliances with other patriots in Anatolia. Within a month, however, the Ottoman government stripped him of his authority and ordered his arrest. Against incredible odds, he determined as a civilian to organize political resistance and find a political group that would grant him new authority. The invasion of Anatolia by the Greeks may have helped galvanize local groups to the point where the broken-down, war-weary, and grieving nation could summon up new energy and rally around him.

When his three-car caravan entered the dusty little city of Ankara in the middle of Anatolia, the provincial newspaper reported that:

> The dawn of the daylight-creating sun took place in Erzurum. Glistening in Sivas, it illuminated the nation.[186]

Every place opened its heart and soul to that sun of reality. The

Turkish world was turned entirely into a single mass of radiance.[187]

This clearly indicates that the grieving Anatolians, including many Kurds, who had lived with the Turks for about one thousand years, saw Mustafa Kemal as ushering in the dawn of a new day. A charismatic leader *par excellence*, he was again and again referred to symbolically as the warming sun.[188]

Ankara became the nationalist centre; it eventually became the capital of modern Turkey. While Mustafa Kemal and his men were adjusting to life in Ankara, the Allies were busy dividing the Ottoman lands, including areas of the Turkish heartland. One Allied misconception was that Mustafa Kemal's nationalist movement had been supported by the Ottoman government in Istanbul. Despite a wish to reduce the harshness of the Treaty of Sèvres, differences among England's most powerful politicians slowed the development of a unified Near East policy. Lloyd George was totally committed to promoting the *Megali Idea* of the Greeks, but Lord Curzon feared any extension of Greek rule into Asia Minor. Politicians representing British interests in India were concerned that harsh treatment of Muslim Turks might be resented by Indian Muslims.

The Italians, who were promised the Dodecanese Islands and a large part of Anatolia from the Aegean Sea coastal zone south of Izmir to Adana, disapproved of the Greek influence in the Aegean and the Mediterranean. The territory from Adana to the end of the Italian zone at Sivas was under the French, but the French were also concerned with Syria and suspicious of the British. An independent Armenia was envisaged; its borders were to be determined later by the United States. The autonomy of the Kurds was recognized, and the Ottoman Empire was stripped of all its Arab lands, Iraq being placed in the British zone. Eastern Thrace, including Edirne, was assigned to the Greeks, who were allowed to land at Izmir and move into the heart of Anatolia. In spite of disagreements among the Allies, Mustafa Kemal and his nationalist followers clearly had their hands full, and at last it seemed that no more would be heard of 'the terrible Turks'. The Greeks moved further and further inland, expressing both consciously and unconsciously their centuries-old dislike of Turks and forgetting the comfortable times of 'togetherness'. The unconscious 'togetherness' the two peoples had once experienced had to be extirpated if the Greeks were to find even a newer identity in forming a new Greek empire.

Many issues had to be dealt with before Mustafa Kemal could undertake a major war to drive the Greeks from Anatolia. They had to put down a revolt of Armenian revolutionaries and make the Russians, who were preoccupied with the Bolshevik Revolution, accept a new Turkish-Russian border and surrender the districts of Kars and Ardahan, according to the Treaty of Gümrü (3 December 1920). Although the Bolsheviks subsequently helped Mustafa Kemal in his struggle for independence, he never adopted communist views.

After settling the border with the Soviets, Turkish forces gained the districts of Malatya, Diyarbakır, and Van; put down a Kurdish revolt; and compelled Iran to acknowledge a new Turkish-Iranian border. Mustafa Kemal then went south to recapture Urfa, Gaziantep, and Adana, coming face to face with French forces on their way to occupy Cilicia. The French chose to relinquish their share of the spoils and signed the Franklin Bouillon Treaty on 10 October 1921. Mustafa Kemal forced the Italians out of Konya in February 1922. While all this was taking place, he faced the Greeks on Anatolian soil but refrained from initiating a major offensive.

Facing the Greeks
After landing at Izmir in May 1919, the Greeks had met with little resistance as they pushed inland; the Turkish troops fell back to Bursa, the first substantial Ottoman capital. Panic gripped Ankara when Bursa fell and an outcry rose against Mustafa Kemal's leadership. Addressing the nationalistic Grand National Assembly from a rostrum draped in black as a sign of mourning, he stated that since the Turkish people were not prepared it was inadvisable to mount an offensive to recapture Bursa at that time. With telling oratory, he stressed the main aim of defending Anatolia.

Meanwhile, the political situation in Greece was undergoing drastic changes. Venizelos, who had been called 'the new Agamemnon', was driven from power by losing an election, no doubt in popular reaction to massive military mobilization that had accomplished so little in the way of permanent territorial expansion. In October 1920, King Alexander died suddenly from the consequences of a pet monkey's bite. In an election during the following month, the Royalists defeated the Liberals, and a plebiscite restored Constantine to the throne. He had few friends among the Allies, but he purged the officer corps of its pro-Venizelos elements and began to prepare for further offensive action in Anatolia.

When the Greeks had commenced their struggle for liberation a hundred years earlier, they had depended on *klephts*, whom the *çetes* of Anatolia resembled. Mustafa Kemal, a graduate of an Ottoman military school, wanted nothing to do with *çetes* and got rid of them. Therefore, when the Greeks began a new offensive on 21 March 1921, they clashed at İnönü with a regular Turkish army and lost the battle. This was the second Turkish success at the same place, under the command of İsmet, who would later adopt the name of İnönü and become the new Turkey's second president following Atatürk's death.

Turkish jubilation over the victory was matched by the determination of the Greeks and their preoccupation with their *Megali Idea*. When Constantine went to Asia Minor, he was the first Christian ruler to appear there since the Crusades, and he decided to go after Ankara. As the Greek forces moved on Ankara, Greeks who had been living in Turkish territory for centuries were caught up in a frenzy of patriotic fervour for their original homeland and, exploding with hatred for their erstwhile neighbours, committed atrocities against them. To keep his army together and to draw the Greeks farther away from their main base of supplies, Mustafa Kemal ordered a systematic retreat. The Turks crossed the Sakarya River, the last natural obstacle between Ankara and the enemy. The resulting confrontation, in which the Turks were led by Mustafa Kemal himself, ended in a disastrous rout of the invading Greeks.

It took another year for the Turks to complete their preparation for a major offensive. Mustafa Kemal predicted that the 'real saviour sun of the Turks would shine down on the morning of the attack in all its splendour'.[189] The attack that began on 26 August 1922, was followed by a day in which everything seemed to be over for the Greeks and their hope of reversing a history of one thousand years by re-establishing a Greek Empire that would include Asia Minor. The operational commander of the Greek front was captured, and without a leader the Greeks began retreating toward Izmir with the Turks in hot pursuit.

Lord Curzon, the British Foreign Secretary, was informed by Sir Horace Rumbold, then High Commissioner in still occupied Istanbul, that the Greeks 'went to pieces altogether', leaving behind 'a sickening record of bestiality and barbarity'.[190] The Turkish writer Halide Edib, who was following the Turkish army, was stunned by what she saw.

Describing Alaşehir, a small city not far from Izmir, she wrote:

> Neither Greeks nor our people had found time to bury the dead, the
> Turkish army running at top speed to save Turkish cities from being
> burned. The Greek army in escaping from the fires it started and from
> atrocities. But each side shows no mercy to the other ... Women
> mindlessly try to dig the ground with their fingers. It is as though
> hell had come to earth.[191]

When the Turkish army reached Izmir, the city was full of Greek
refugees from the interior. A large contingent of the Greek army had
been evacuated just before the arrival of the Turkish army. However,
some Greek troops had been left behind, and these, along with the
thousands of refugees, were in a state of confusion. Some jumped into
the water in an effort to reach Allied warships that were still in the
harbour.

Mustafa Kemal entered Izmir on 10 September 1922 as the hero of
the Turks, who made available to him the house in which King
Constantine had stayed and where he had trampled the Turkish flag as
he entered. A Greek flag was spread out on the marble entrance steps
of the house, and Mustafa Kemal was expected to walk on it. He
objected, however, saying that a country's honour should not be
trodden upon and that he did not propose to follow the erroneous
example of Constantine.[192]

Soon Izmir was engulfed in flames; the Turks blamed the fire on
the Greeks and the Armenians, who, in turn, blamed the Turks. No
one seeing the conflagration could have guessed that, within a few
years, Mustafa Kemal and Eleutherios Venizelos, once more returned
to power, would make peace.

| 11 |

Atatürk and Modern
Turkish Nationalism

Sigmund Freud, in his exchange with Albert Einstein, stated that all human beings are either leaders or followers.[193] Obviously, the latter comprise, by far, the majority. A political leader deals with political, economic, legal, and military issues on a conscious level. On an unconscious level, however, he (or she) must also devote energy to trying to uphold the rituals of his group in interactions with other groups. The leader's role is to preserve the stability of his or her group's identity.[194]

Influential leaders who are able to transform their followers are usually regarded as charismatic: they are experienced by their followers as a 'total parent', as both mother and father.[195] As such they can be reparative, destructive, or both.[196] They are reparative if they attempt to uplift their followers to higher levels, without the destruction of 'others'. Some transforming leaders, however, try to raise the status of their followers by destroying a rival group. Charismatic leaders, such as Atatürk, usually appear during a time of crisis, suggesting that the followers' needs have created an atmosphere for a certain type of leader.[197] The leader-follower relationship, even when a leader is charismatic, is a two-way street, and the movement of traffic may become congested (can be regressed or become a vehicle for progressive change) depending on the psychological make-up of the leader and/or the forces that influence his followers.[198]

When Atatürk assumed the leadership of the Turks, the Ottoman Empire had been defeated; people were tired of war. Many people and many sons had been killed. In short, people were in an emotionally 'regressed' state responding to many traumas. Atatürk's personality make-up included strong unconscious and conscious motivations to become a repairer and saviour. A 'fit' occurred in a dramatic fashion between the leader and his followers, and this led, together with the influence of world events, to the creation of modern Turkey and a new Turkish nationalism. An examination of Atatürk's personality is essential for an understanding of modern Turkish nationalism.

We believe that Atatürk's case is an excellent illustration of the exchange of influences between an individual's inner and outer worlds as well as the interactions between a leader and his followers. These exchanges and interactions led to momentous historical events and cultural revolutions.

Here we present some details of our findings pertaining to Atatürk and his times. Those readers who are interested in examining this topic in depth are referred to our book, *The Immortal Atatürk: A Pyschobiography*.[199]

Early Childhood

The child of a minor customs official married to a wife twenty years his junior, Atatürk was born, probably in 1881, in Salonika. This Macedonian city, then within the borders of Ottoman Turkey, was divided into three sections inhabited by the Turkish, Greek, and Jewish communities, as well as small groups of Slavs and Albanians. Atatürk's parents had recently come there from the customs outpost on the Turkish-Greek border near Mount Olympus, a harsh environment. Earlier they had three children—two boys and a girl—and lost them one after another, the oldest only reaching the age of seven. One son's body had been buried on the sandy shore, and according to a family story, it had been uncovered by rising water and then torn by jackals. Whether or not the tale is accurate in all its grim detail, it provides a poignant reflection of parental anguish and a life of hardship.[200] The birth of the fourth child, Mustafa, who would later be known as Atatürk, came during an all-too-brief interval of family prosperity and confidence. The move to Salonika took place because a wealthy lumber merchant had taken the father into partnership on account of his knowledge of the forests gained while on Mount Olympus. Mustafa is said to have been born in a house that is now an Atatürk museum; it was a step up from anything the family had known, and prospects were bright.

Mustafa's mother had been beautiful as a child bride, a fair-skinned peasant with blue eyes and amber hair, uneducated but bright. Her husband called her his 'dream girl' and his 'heavenly rose'. She bore him two more daughters after Mustafa's birth, but Mustafa and a younger sister were the only children to survive into adulthood. The mother had them to care for when she became a widow at twenty-seven. Her husband had lost his partnership when Greek bandits burned the forests for which he was responsible, and he lapsed into drink and despair, dying when his son was seven.

Mustafa was thus born into a house of death and found himself in the care of a grieving mother whose life had been, save for a brief respite, one of hardship and melancholy. He even bore the name of a an infant uncle who had died in the accidental overturning of his crib for which Mustafa's father was responsible.[201] It is likely that his childhood world was full of fearful images. Not only did death stalk the household, but memories of the harsh life at the Ottoman-Greek border and of the sombre, bandit-ridden forest cast a shadow over it. The father's stories of bandit border raids and their threats remained for many years in the memory of Mustafa's sister.[202] In spite of having been born during the family's brief flirtation with prosperity, at a time when they had been able to employ a wet nurse for Mustafa as well as a black housemaid, he wrote an essay in 1930 reflecting a far from happy early home life. His preoccupation with freedom seems to have risen as much from a need for personal freedom (individuation) as from a political concern that his country should be free. This 1930 essay on freedom opens with a discussion of the relationship between man and nature.

> Man does not decide whether or not to be born. At the moment of his birth he is at the mercy of nature and a host of creatures other than himself. He needs to be protected, to be fed, to be looked after, to be helped to grow.[203]

Reference to his dead siblings and to the concern that both he and his mother felt about safety can be seen here. He saw man born at the mercy of nature and its creatures. He further wrote of primitive people, who were probably representative of his childhood, living in fear of the thunder, the darkness of the night, floods, wild animals, and even one another. This echoes the story of the jackals tearing at a child's body.

It is likely that Mustafa's mother turned more and more to God as she ultimately lost her four doomed children and, finally, her husband. Living in the Muslim style, she left her house only to visit other women, neighbours, or relatives. The fastidiousness of her appearance was to be reflected later in her son's emphasis on personal elegance. Her hair was dressed with curls and jewels; she wore lace-trimmed blouses and colourful long skirts. Although she was excessively religious and was later called a *Molla* (a religious person seeking mystic union with God and his power), she was headstrong and unconventional, known to substitute an abrupt departure from any home she visited for the leisurely leave-taking required by Muslim custom.

It was common to speak of tragedies, such as those that overtook Mustafa's family, as being due to the will of God, and the idea of the God his mother acknowledged frightened little Mustafa, who may have seen his mother as His agent. Atatürk's 1930 essay notes that the fear of one's parents becomes the fear of God, thus creating many prohibitions and restrictive traditions militating against the freedom of the individual. 'Those who are heads of communities ... run the communities in the name of God.' For Atatürk, such pious people seemed to represent his religious mother.[204]

Just before Mustafa's father died, he had directed that his son should have a modern elementary school education instead of enrolling in the religious school preferred by the child's mother. At that time, Turkish parents living in large cities of the Ottoman Empire, including Salonika, could select either kind of training for their children. His mother wanted Mustafa to make religion his career. Atatürk's earliest memory was of the strong disagreement between his parents over his schooling. He recalled how skilfully his father worked out a solution. First, the child entered the religious school with the traditional ceremony in which hymns were sung and requisite garb worn. 'Thus my mother's broken heart was made good,' he noted. But a few days later he left this school and was registered by his father in a modern one. 'Soon after this my father died.'[205]

The name of the headmaster of Mustafa's new school was Şemsi, which means 'sun'. We believe that when Mustafa lost his father, first to an ailment and then to death, he idealized Şemsi instead, and assimilated the teacher's influence toward modernization. His father, who took him away from his mother's grasp by placing him in Şemsi's school, and the teacher who taught him modern thoughts later became his role models in his cultural revolutions. In fact, there are many examples in Atatürk's life in which he first pays his respects to a 'mother figure' and religious customs, and then he flees from such situations and embarks upon activities of modernization and lessening heavy religious influences. The meaning of Şemsi (sun), we believe, also appears in Atatürk's and his followers' perceptions as well as in descriptions of the leader's actions. As we mentioned in the previous chapter, he and his followers perceived the leader's activities as sunshine triumphing over darkness (grieving mother/nation).

After the father's death, his widow and her children had to seek the support of a relative who lived on a farm. Mustafa, however, was then returned to Salonika to live with an aunt while he completed his schooling.[206] Without consulting his mother, he took and passed the entrance examinations for a military secondary school. Such schools then offered an education closer to the western model. Mustafa entered this environment at puberty.

His mother then remarried. Mustafa was now on his own. Because he excelled in mathematics, his teacher called him 'Kemal', which means 'perfect', and thus he became 'Mustafa Kemal'—the perfect one. The name, 'the perfect one', fits his personality make-up. Our research shows that he had responded to the traumas in his early environment (the loss of his siblings and his father, having a grieving mother, and being exposed to a teacher's physical punishment) with a premature maturation by holding on to a self-concept of sufficiency and 'number one-ness', a feeling of superiority and being above hurts. His personality make-up denied and/or repressed his dependency needs; thus, he was the 'perfect one'. His later preoccupation with power, leadership, virility, personal appearance,and beauty were due mostly to his internal adaptations to a harsh childhood.

From Mustafa Kemal to Atatürk
Continuing his military education, Mustafa Kemal then went to the War College and, later, to the Staff College in Istanbul. There he was a great success with women, but he made no emotional commitment in any of his liaisons. While Atatürk was a military student, the Ottoman Empire was already collapsing. At the War College and, later, at the Staff College, young Mustafa Kemal began suggesting a special vision for the country. Those around him may have thought he was joking when he spoke of plans for grandiose deeds; in retrospect it is evident

that he was completely serious. He gathered friends about him who shared his self-ascribed mission to save the country and assigned them key positions in the government or military that he planned for the future. In his schemes, he pictured himself as the undisputed and rightful leader.

Mustafa Kemal was introduced to the world of Turkish and French literature while in military school where he developed the powers of oratory that later brought him great fame. The poet who fed Mustafa Kemal's passion for nationalism was Namık Kemal, one of whose best-known verses tells how:

> The enemy put his knife at the throat of the country—
> There is no one to save the mother from her black fate.

Mustafa Kemal was later to paraphrase this, substituting for the second line:

> There is someone to save the mother from her black fate.

In our psychobiographical study we show how Atatürk had an (unconscious) fantasy to repair his grieving mother (she was represented by the grieving nation) so that he would have a better childhood and erase his hurts. In his developing self concept he could 'cure' himself by 'curing' the grief-stricken woman/nation.

Mustafa Kemal, charged with disapproved political activity, was sent into exile for two years. Shortly after he finished Staff College with the rank of lieutenant, the sultan's government ordered him to Syria, which was then still part of the Ottoman domain. He was unable to carve out a prominent place for himself in the Young Turk Revolution that was already underway in his homeland, Macedonia. Then came the Balkan Wars and World War I.[207] Just before World War I Atatürk was sent to Sophia to be the Turkish military attaché to Bulgaria. There he was impressed by what westernization had done for Bulgaria.[208] With the outbreak of World War I he returned to Ottoman territory. Despite both his belief that he was unique and his efforts to gain recognition, he was in his mid-thirties and still only a divisional commander. However, he became a hero in World War I, demonstrating uncanny military ability in the defence of Gallipoli against the British and their allies. An incident at Gallipoli had a deep psychological effect on him. He was struck over the heart by a bit of shrapnel as he recklessly stood in the line of fire, but the shot shattered the watch in his breast pocket without injuring him. We believe that this incident unconsciously crystallized his belief in his uniqueness, superiority, and immortality.

Although Mustafa Kemal was successful in battle on the Russian and Arab fronts, the Ottoman Empire's ultimate defeat in the war in 1918 pushed the empire towards disaster. The Allied Fleet entered the harbour of Istanbul, and the Turkish Parliament was dissolved. The British, acting with the French and Italians, prepared to partition Turkey, and Greek forces landed later in Anatolia. After the defeat of the Ottoman Empire, Mustafa Kemal found himself in occupied Istanbul, virtually a prisoner in spite of his status as a high-ranking general. He managed to 'escape' to Anatolia on the steamship *Bandırma*. (See Chapter 9).

Mustafa Kemal's mother died early in 1923, and fifteen days later her son married a young, westernized Turkish girl. His new wife was as much her husband's junior as his mother had been at the time of her first marriage. Atatürk's marriage ended in 1925.

Mustafa Kemal became the first President of the Turkish Republic, which was proclaimed in 1923. With the collapse of the Ottoman Empire there emerged from the ruins of that spacious, multinational, multireligious, and multilingual land a considerably smaller, but unitary nation-state. After Mustafa Kemal abandoned his military career to become his country's civil head, he began his cultural revolution, generally called 'westernization'.

In 1934, four years before Atatürk's death, when a new law required that the Turks use surnames, the Grand National Assembly granted him the one that means 'Father Turk'. The process of change and the struggles it involves still continue in the Turkey of today, almost sixty years after his death at the age of fifty-seven. Before he succumbed to cirrhosis of the liver, most likely caused by his habitual drinking accompanied by nutritional deficiencies, he was already a legend, a virtual deity. The Turks could not bring themselves to inter him, but kept the body preserved for fifteen years awaiting the construction of a mausoleum in Ankara. Now he lies in this mausoleum.

Atatürk's Personality Organization and his Westernization Efforts
Atatürk was a highly intelligent and handsome man, but he also had a sense of grandeur which served him well as a leader.[209] Unlike the average individual with this type of character, however, he was very

successful since he was capable of changing his environment to conform to high demands coming from within. Furthermore, he was a reparative leader, as we described the concept earlier.[210]

In the interest of achieving a thorough-going reform process, Atatürk had the fledgling Turkish Grand National Assembly separate the caliphate from the sultanate on 1 November 1922. The sultanate was abolished, and the caliphate was vested in the person of an Ottoman prince chosen by the Grand National Assembly. Then, the governmental form of the new Turkey was declared a republic on 29 October 1923. The following year the caliphate, too, was abolished. Mustafa Kemal refused the title of either sultan or caliph.

One of the most influential changes on the road to westernization was the language reform which rid Turkey of its Arabic script, substituting a Latin alphabet for the Arabic in which the Ottoman language had been written. Virtually overnight, Turks woke up to the necessity of learning the new script. The language reform was a great tool in the hands of the government in its war on illiteracy. Turkey has since gone from a country in which perhaps five per cent of the population (the Ottomans) were literate to a country in which eighty per cent of the people can read and write, one of the best records in the Middle East.

When Turks began to leave Central Asia in the tenth century, as described earlier, they filled the vacuum the Arab Empire had left, assimilating the Islamic culture of the vanquished Arabs and Persians. Religion coloured daily life in the Ottoman Empire[211], affecting laws, customs, medicine, etc. Atatürk proscribed education based on the sacred values and symbols of the Koran and the laws of Islam, replacing them with westernized education, the Swiss Civil Code, the Italian Penal Code, and German commercial law. The state launched the process of creating new commercial ventures in textiles, mining, and shipping among others. He discouraged veils for women, who within a few years, were given rights equal to men's. He introduced western dress for men, banishing the fez. He patterned Ankara, the new capital city, which in 1920 was little more than a dusty town, after European cities, and introduced all manner of entertainment and worldliness there. He was striving to transform the 'house of death' he had known as a child into a 'house of life'.[212]

Rustow writes:

> The criticism sometimes levelled at Kemal's reforms—that they dealt

with surface trivia as headgear, letters, and family names—does not stand up under closer examination. Kemal ... cared far more deeply about cultural matters than about social and economic problems as these are commonly defined in the post-Marxian world. But culture consists of a set of symbols, and in the context of his time and place externals had profound symbolic meaning ... That Hat Law meant an ostentatious break with Islam, which required the faithful to touch his covered head to the ground in his daily prayers. The alphabet change produced its intended effect by cutting off later generations from most of their pre-1928 literary heritage.[213]

Furthermore, at that time Atatürk's Turkey was the only non-western nation attempting an about-turn in its mode of life in order to be accepted by the western world as a western nation. The emotional climate of the West was less than generous toward this aspiration as Nazism and Fascism gripped Europe. In the face of this intolerance, it was Atatürk who opened the doors of the new Turkey to Jewish scholars escaping from Nazi Germany. Many of these remained in Turkey for years, helping with its westernization.

In ordinary circumstances, Atatürk disliked the sight of blood, although he spent so much of his life engaged in bloody battles and ordered his men to die at Gallipoli in order to defend the peninsula. Rustow (1970) states that:

Readers of a generation inured to the mass murders of a Hitler and a Stalin ... should at once be reminded that in an average day those regimes killed off more victims than the Kemalist regime did in all its two decades. Although the exact arithmetic is hard to establish, it is clear that those who lost their lives for political reasons in Turkey in the twenties and thirties numbered several dozen, at most a few hundred.[214]

It appears that immortality was included in Atatürk's early self-concept and persisted into his later years. His survival after being struck by shrapnel in battle helped maintain such a belief. After an attempted assassination when he was president, he made a speech in which he exclaimed that although his own insignificant body would one day become dust, the Turkish nation would live forever.[215] Atatürk's immortality was eventually perceived by the Turkish nation. When he died the nation refused to 'kill' him, preserving his body for fifteen years and, even after it was duly placed in the huge mausoleum built for the purpose, maintaining his mental representation as immortal, exciting their admiration.

Kemalism

Atatürk's personality, what drove him internally, and the psychology of his followers dovetailed in the creation of a new concept of Turkishness. Intellectualized principles of this new Turkishness became known as Kemalism and eventually were included in the constitution of the new Turkey.

Kemalism was divided into six ideological principles which formed the six-arrow symbol of Atatürk's political party, the People's Party:

1. Republicanism: This principle emphasized the elimination of the Ottoman Dynasty. The new Turkey was designed to be a nation-state with defined borders where sovereignty belonged to the nation and would be republican in form.

2. Nationalism: Considering the events which led to the establishment of the Turkish Republic, nationalism was an essential element in Kemalism. Ottomanism, a multicultural and multinational phenomenon, was transformed into Turkish nationalism, a more restricted, but more cohesive, phenomenon. In 1927, the census studies showed that 97.3 per cent of the people in the new Turkey were Muslims. Kemalism, however, aimed to treat the population according to their ethnic, instead of their religious, identity. Nationalism was in the service of establishing a homogeneous group of people living as a nation within the state's borders. While the ethnic differences of the Kurds and others were acknowledged, nationalism attempted to put every citizen under the umbrella of the new Turkishness. It also meant that, Turkey had no irredentist claims on territory outside its borders.

3. Populism: This was another principle indicating that power had passed into the hands of the people, but supported the second principle by saying that, 'The people of Turkey, regardless of religion and race, are Turks as regards citizenship.'[216] Equal rights were extended to all citizens, and they were given freedom to practise their own religion.

4. Etatism: Due to the poor international and domestic economic situation at the time the Turkish Republic was established, Etatism was accepted as a principle wherein the state would assist private enterprise to develop Turkey's economic future.

5. Secularism: This principle also sharply differentiated the new Turkey from Ottoman times. State and religion were separated, and each citizen was free to seek his own path to salvation.

6. Revolutionism: This principle refers to the on-going, continued process of reform to prepare the nation for changes and to help the Turks adopt a new life-style.

Kemalism is a good example of how the internal processes of a charismatic leader and the ideology governing the external environment dovetail. Mustafa Kemal, by taking the name of Atatürk (Father Turk), gave an indication that he had identified with an ideal father figure while he drastically separated himself from 'bad' fathers, the sultan or the caliph. He rejected a royal role for himself. Furthermore, as a 'good' mother figure, he wanted to spare the new nation from a 'grieving mother' figure who had to turn to religion for inner comfort.

The new nation would not be a continuation of Ottomanism. It would have a cohesive identity and would depend on itself. While there were 'real world' reasons for turning Turkey towards westernization, the revolutionary attempts and the principles of Kemalism, modelled after Atatürk's personality organization, were rather self-reliant and self-centred. Dependency on others was minimized, while new Turkishness was over-emphasized. Thus, Atatürk's phrases such as, 'One Turk is equal to the world', or 'Turk! Be proud! Work and trust!' started to be heard among the population. Earlier we wrote:

> Kemalism was peculiarly Turkish and unlike any system espoused by any other contemporary world leader. What was appropriate for Turkey in that particular period of her history was not easily adoptable by any other nation, although many developing nations, especially in the East, regarded Atatürk's Turkey with awe and wished to emulate his example. Kemalism required nothing from any other nation except peaceful co-existence.[217]

Atatürk's own heightened self-esteem and the grandiose self-esteem of the new Turkey, we believe, served an important purpose during the initial period of the Turkish republic. The population could 'adjust' to the drastic changes and postpone mourning over losing an empire and their old identity as Ottoman Turks since their gains (i.e., who they had as their leader and what they created) outweighed their losses. Thus, the new Turkey was full of excitement and people, in general, followed their leader in accomplishing a miraculous change from Ottomanism to Turkishness and in accepting drastic revolutions. Because of its nature, it was very different from the Greekness that was created after the Greek War of Independence about a century earlier. (In the last chapter, we shall compare the two nationalisms in detail.)

The principle of Kemalism, the population's centring itself around a great reparative leader and new Turkey's self-esteem, made the Turks less preoccupied with their neighbours,[218] including Greece. In 1930 Atatürk's government, in fact, genuinely sought peaceful co-existence with Greece.

As we stated earlier, attempts at westernization among the Turks had begun in the Ottoman period, before Atatürk's time. The late sociologist Niyazi Berkes, a well-known Cypriot-Turk, states:

> Throughout [Turkey's] history, in respect to its economy and politics, it has been more western then eastern. The dominant direction of Ottoman history has tilted more toward the west than toward the east. But its adherence to an eastern cultural reference has prevented Turkey's inclusion in the western world ... Europe has never considered itself as including Turkey, and if we think the contrary, no one but ourselves believe it.[219]

What Atatürk did was to push westernization as a state policy from the top. The Turks followed their beloved leader. Of course, as expected, there were conscious and unconscious resistances against change. Human beings always resist change. It takes time to adopt new ideals, new symbols, and new social and political institutions. Initially, the adaptation to changes included denial of certain aspects of past Turkish history. But since Atatürk had 'chosen' westernization as a goal, the western world, which had been the enemy, did not become a target for Turkish projections of their unwanted aspects. Turks were 'forced' to modify internally the concept of themselves without massive projections of their unwanted parts. However, there was a distancing from the Arab world, brothers during the Ottoman period, since Turks now perceived themselves as more 'westernized.' But this too did not lead to malignant proportions. In fact, many in the Arab world wanted to follow in Turkey's footsteps.[220]

After Atatürk

Atatürk was one of the truly reparative, charismatic leaders in known history, and when he died, his idealized representation, merged with the ideal of Turkishness he had helped create, lived on, and could not be 'killed'. The Turks' inability to reduce Atatürk's representation to realistic proportions, even almost sixty years after his death, has made it difficult for them to complete their mourning for him. Eventually, however, this mourning began to take place (see Chapter 17).

Having established a cohesive new Turkey, Atatürk and his followers attempted to remain faithful to his direction of the new Turkey's international policy, 'peace at home, peace abroad'. However, Turks and Greeks would have further difficulties and one more war. This war was fought on the island of Cyprus.

| 12 |

The Peace Disappears

In 1930 an agreement was reached between Turkey and Greece inaugurating a new era of peace and co-operation between these two historic adversaries. This rapprochement was based on the status quo that emerged in the wake of the Turkish War of Independence following the defeat of the Ottoman Empire in World War I. In the independence war the Turks resisted the invading Greek armies from the mainland and drove them out of Anatolia. Kemal Atatürk, who was the founder of modern Turkey and was born in the Greek city of Salonika when it was part of the Ottoman Empire, and Eleutherios Venizelos, the Greek Prime Minister, who was born on the Ottoman island of Crete (which in time became Greek), demonstrated both creativity and clairvoyance in reaching an understanding over the principle of separation.

In this case, separation was defined as the division of land and people according to the Treaty of Lausanne, which had been signed seven years earlier. It was the treaty of Lausanne that officially sealed the demise of the Ottoman Empire and left Greece and modern Turkey as inheritors of large portions of the former empire stretching from Thrace to the Fertile Crescent. While the old territories in the western part of the Ottoman domains had successfully filtered out of the empire as nation states by the close of World War I, the territories in the east, the Arab lands, would emerge as mandates, thereby continuing the imperialist struggle under a new guise.[221] Not all the outstanding territorial problems between Greece and Turkey were laid to rest in 1923. Cyprus, where Turks and Greeks lived, and which was under British rule in 1923, remained under the Union Jack, and issues of territorial coastal waters, continental shelf, and airspace that would insinuate themselves into the relations between the two states much later, were non-existent at the time.

With respect to people, the Lausanne Treaty incorporated an exchange of populations between Greece and Turkey embodying the transfer of approximately one million Greeks from Anatolia to Thrace, and some four hundred thousand Turks from within Greece to Turkey. This wide-ranging exchange of populations may have helped to prevent large-scale ethnic disputes, which could easily have erupted in the years that followed. As a result, both Turks and Greeks hoped that peace and tranquility would come as they lived side by side as neighbouring countries instead of as neighbouring households.

Separation of the Turks and Greeks at that time along an accepted border between them was psychologically sound. During the Balkan Wars, World War I, and the Turkish War of Independence previously existing borders had been breached. This caused profound emotional impact on the identities of both parties.[222] Under stress, the physical borders become more psychologized, as a tear in the physical border is perceived as a wound in the group's identity, and, therefore, in the identities of the individuals within that group. The re-establishment of new and agreed borders is similar to the healing process of a person's skin. A crust develops over the wound which may require continued attention until a full healing occurs and a new layer of skin is formed. But the 1930 friendship agreement left a vulnerable scab as about one hundred thousand Greeks remained in Istanbul[223] and some one hundred and twenty thousand Turks remained in Thrace.[224] As a result of staying behind, these two groups would suffer in the future. For the time being, however, the 1930 agreement had settled most of the major disputes concerning population exchanges and the value of properties left behind by those who were repatriated. Thus, a relatively peaceful era between the Turks and the Greeks was ushered in.

Borders formed between modern Turkey and Greece after Lausanne, and the acceptance of these borders by the two nations, appeared to render the ethnic tents (see Chapter 1) more stable on both sides. In part, this was due to both sides no longer feeling 'under attack'. We use the word 'appeared' because, in reality, the Greeks continued to perceive the Turks as the storm raging outside their tent, and the Turks did not forget the recent devastation wreaked by the Greeks in Anatolia during the Turkish War of Independence. In so doing, they focused on the memories of ill feelings, creating a dichotomy between their own identity and their neighbour's identity. This served to strengthen identities as each group's border became clearer in their minds.

Conducive to a more peaceful environment as the Lausanne and 1930 treaties were, however, they did not resolve all outstanding issues. One was that of the previously mentioned minorities left 'on the other side' in Istanbul and Thrace; these hot spots could always be fanned into open flames. This has been especially true in more recent times with the new emphasis on minority rights that goes beyond the protections provided by existing treaties. This new ethos has served to bring into sharper focus the minority rights of the Turks in Western (Greek) Thrace and the Greeks in Turkey.

Another issue stemmed from the inability of the peacemakers to foresee the future importance of the Aegean Sea's waters, airspace, and continental shelf, and the rivalry over the resources that would be produced. From the late fifteenth century until the emergence of modern Greece, the Aegean Sea had been little more than an Ottoman lake. Today, however, modern Turkey and Greece not only touch each other in Thrace, but are also linked in the Aegean where Greek islands are sprinkled on the water like salt over a meal. In fact, some of the islands are rather close to the Turkish mainland and are visible from Turkey's shore. This proximity constitutes a grievance that can always be elevated into a political confrontation.

Of a far more inflammatory nature, however, was Cyprus, an island forty miles south of Turkey containing a Greek community of about eighty per cent and a Turkish community of close to twenty per cent. In 1923 as well as in 1930, Cyprus was under British rule. Today, however, this island embodies all of the problems inherent in Turco-Greek relations.

After the 1930s

This chapter reviews how relations between Turkey and Greece have gone sour since 1930. The first step away from the trend of bilateral co-operation came in 1931 as the Greeks extended their airspace to ten miles off their coasts (this was done by 'royal decree', therefore, unilaterally). Later, in 1936, the Greeks extended their territorial waters from three to six miles. Turkey did not act to extend its own territorial waters until after World War II. These activities, however, did not prevent the two governments from signing a Friendship Pact in

1933. The excitement of the time led the Turkish Foreign Minister, Tevfik Rüştü Aras, to declare that the two nations 'have almost become one country'.[225]

During this period of its history, Turkey was led by a strong charismatic leader, Atatürk. In loving Atatürk the Turks, in general, had joined hands in identifying with one another. The situation closely resembled Freud's description of mass psychology.[226] Ataürk was involved in the accomplishment of one cultural revolution after another as he moved Turkey out of the moribund Ottoman mentality into a modernist world view characterized by enforced westernization. The new Turkey would be secular, populist, republican, statist, nationalist, and reformist, thereby differentiating it from the Muslim, Ottomanist, sultanic-caliphal, capitulatory, multi-national, and traditionalist Ottoman Empire.

The Turks used the image of their beloved leader to develop a feeling that their wounds from the Balkan Wars, World War I, and the Turkish War of Independence had healed, and their self-esteem was enhanced regardless of what outsiders thought of them. They considered that all their suffering had been justified, as was their faith in following such a charismatic leader. With all Turkey's internal changes, there was little room for the people to be preoccupied with outside groups, including, most notably the Greeks. The time, energy, and commitment that was required to change the face of Turkey totally was almost all consuming as a new constitution was enacted; a republican form of government put in place; women emancipated; the Turkish language reformed; industries created; the school system revamped; the legal system overhauled; relations with the leading nations of the world regulated; internal dissent quieted; and a national infrastructure of roads, railroads, seaports, and airports instituted. The Greeks did not weigh heavily on the Turkish consciousness.

On the other hand, the Greeks had been the losers in their latest encounter with the Turks. Although their country's physical borders *per se* had not been violated, the Greeks suffered a blow to their historical aspirations in Anatolia, and their wounds ran extremely deep. Their humiliation with respect to the defeat and the fact that they did not have a leader as charismatic as Atatürk (nor as great a need for one), might make them more prone to projecting some unwanted aspects of themselves on to the Turks, depicting them in a stereotypical manner. Despite their sense of injury, however, the

Greek people continued to support Venizelos' policy of *détente* with Turkey, especially due to the emerging threat from Mussolini's Italy.

After Atatürk's death in 1938, his image was immortalized.[227] His staunchest ally, the negotiator of the Lausanne treaty, İsmet İnönü, became the new Turkish leader and pursued friendly relations with Greece while he and his government kept Turkey neutral until the waning days of World War II. Greece, on the other hand, had become deeply involved in World War II and suffered greatly under German occupation. Their historical wounds had been re-opened by non-Turks. As is sometimes true, the images of the new enemy became contaminated with those of the old. The Greeks developed a new set of grievances against the Turks whom they accused of not assisting them against Hitler and Mussolini.[228]

After World War II both countries shared certain benefits, concerns, and activities.[229] In 1947, Turkey and Greece were joint beneficiaries of the Truman Doctrine as well as the Marshall Plan. Along with other nations, they were both members of the Organization for European Economic Co-operation (in 1960 the OEEC became the Organization for Economic Co-operation and Development). In 1950, they became joint members of the Council of Europe, and in that same year each contributed military contingents to the Korean conflict. Two years later, they were admitted as members of NATO. In 1954, Turkey and Greece signed the Balkan Defence Pact. Each signed the European Economic Community (EEC)'s association agreements in the hopes of becoming full members. In most of these activities Turkey followed Greece's lead. Greece became an associate of the EEC in 1962 and a full member in 1981. Turkey succeeded in gaining associate membership in the EEC in 1964, but she still has not been accepted as a full member. Responsibility for this failure is placed by Turkey at the doorstep of Greece, since the Greeks publicly have opposed Turkey's application.

Though Europeans may have had multiple reasons for hesitating to allow Turkey's integration into the EC (now the EU), such as fear of Turkish immigration into Europe, at the present time the Turkish-Greek conflict is used as an excuse for the non-examination of those other reasons. In addition to the immigration issue, there is a psychological one—would a Christian Europe be comfortable with a Muslim Turkey?[230]

After World War II, Turkey and Greece shared a common,

powerful enemy in the USSR. Assistance to the Greek communists was coupled with demands on Turkey for a revision of the 1925 Russian-Turkish non-aggression pact, claims on Turkish territory in the northeast of the country, and insistence on the USSR's right to participate in the defence of the Straits (the Bosphorus and the Dardanelles). With the disappearance of the Soviet threat, the new world condition, especially events in places previously known as Yugoslavia, has led Greece to develop other worries. They are warranted by real world conditions. But Greece also worries about other developments. For example, most of the new republics of central Asia, as well as Azerbaijan in the Caucasus, are inhabited mainly by Turkic peoples. As soon as these republics were established, Turkey began to assist them, to establish communications systems, and to provide scholarships for undergraduate students. While the Turkish government in Ankara has been careful not to foster feelings of pan-Turkic nationalism, the spectre of pan-Turanism (the union of all Turks)[231] led by Turkey causes anxiety in Athens.

Cyprus

Conflict origins are often difficult to isolate, but in the case of Turkey and Greece, the issue of Cyprus heads the list. Strategically important to Britain with respect to her position in the eastern Mediterranean and proximity to the Suez Canal, Cyprus came into Britain's possession following the Congress of Berlin. Britain agreed to support the Ottoman Empire, owner of Cyprus, in its claim for the restoration by Russia of three of her eastern provinces in what was referred to at the time as Asiatic Turkey. In return, Britain was allowed to occupy and administer Cyprus. The island was formally annexed by the British at the outset of World War I. In 1915, they offered the island to Greece as inducement to enter the war against Germany on the Allied side, but the offer was rejected. In the Lausanne Treaty, both Greece and Turkey recognized British sovereignty over the island which became a Crown colony in March 1925.

In addition to this political history of the island, there exists the story of the island's population. Wresting Cyprus from Venetian control in 1570-1571, the Ottoman government then proceeded to populate the island with Turks forcibly relocated there through the practice of *sürgün* (forced relocation), the means by which the Ottomans created a Turkish presence along sensitive frontiers and in other areas of strategic importance. Since that time there has been a substantial Turkish population on the island.

In the 1950s, the Cypriot Greeks began a struggle for independence from British rule with the hope of eventually uniting the island of Cyprus with Greece, a movement that came to be know as *Enosis*. While this issue has become the backbone and the symbol of the present Turkish-Greek estrangement, it is a case of 'the chicken and the egg dilemma'. The Cyprus conflict became deadly and killed any hope of friendship between the Turks and the Greeks because of the feelings and perceptions between the two groups that had existed for a rather long time. In turn, the Cyprus problem rekindled the flames of a smouldering fire (chosen traumas and chosen glories) that had been hidden under the ashes of time. As Bahcheli states: 'Past memories of injustice, grievances and mistrust have provided a crucial context for modern Greek-Turkish disputes.'[232]

For the Cypriot Greeks, 'self-determination' meant elimination of the Turkish community from the island and eventual union with Greece. The Cypriot Turkish community maintained that 'self-determination' could not be applied to the island as a whole, for that would mean neo-colonization and their removal from the island. 'Self-determination' would have to be applied separately to both communities, and that could best be achieved through the establishment of a federated state of Cyprus. This was, in effect, accomplished through the Zurich and London agreements of 1959 signed by Greece, Turkey, the United Kingdom, and the representatives of the Greek and Turkish communities on the island. The Republic of Cyprus was created in 1960 but with the fatal flaw of an 'unworkable constitution'.[233] While a new state had been formed with some significant limitations on its sovereignty, there was no Cypriot nation. One was still either a Greek or a Turk (or a member of another very small minority that included Maronites and Armenians), not a Cypriot.

Illustrative of the limitations imposed by this mentality is the story regarding the creation of a flag for the new republic. Dr. Volkan's brother-in-law, the well-known Cypriot Turkish artist, İsmet V. Güney, was invited to help design that flag. He was told that he could use white, which appears on both the Turkish and the Greek flags, but he must avoid using the red of the Turkish flag and the blue of the Greek flag. Accordingly, in addition to white, yellow was used along with green since none of those colours appeared on the flags in question. This yellow-green-white banner is still the 'official' flag of Cyprus, but in name only. After the establishment of the republic, the Cypriot Turks continued to fly the red and white colours of Turkey while the Cypriot Greeks responded with the blue and white of Greece. Raised in only a few places where the law required it, the 'official flag' flew primarily over Archbishop Makarios' presidential palace as an 'ornament'. The story of the flag illustrates the peculiarities of ethnic arithmetic on Cyprus, as elsewhere, where two communities do not add up to one nation. *Realpolitik* never found an echo in the psyche of the Cypriot Turk or Cypriot Greek. The Cyprus constitution allowed for political power to be shared by the Greek and the Turkish communities, but the former never gave up the dream of *Enosis*. They saw the establishment of the Republic of Cyprus merely as a stepping stone in that direction.

Beginning in December 1963, the Cypriot Turks were forced by the Greek Cypriots to live in enclaves. Ultimately, a military operation by Turkey in 1974 led to a division of Cyprus into a northern Turkish sector and a southern Greek sector. The Cypriot Turks declared their own independent republic in 1983, calling themselves the Turkish Republic of Northern Cyprus (TRNC) and flying their own flag, which now appears all over the northern sector of the island alongside the flag of Turkey. Currently, a search for a settlement in Cyprus is in the centre of the present Turkish-Greek conflict.

The Aegean Sea
Almost contemporaneously with the escalation of the Cyprus conflict, there developed new attitudes in international law with respect to the seas. The first dealt with the demand for the extension of territorial waters and the second with the definition of rights in respect to sea-beds as new technologies made possible the economic exploitation of those hitherto untouched riches. This new perspective only served to deepen the dispute between Turkey and Greece over the delineation of sovereign rights in the Aegean Sea. With its complex coastal configurations, the Aegean became an inheritance to be squabbled over by Turkey and Greece. Added to those problems were the questions of a redefinition of sovereign airspace and the remilitarization, starting in the 1960s, of the islands of the eastern Aegean by Greece, which is claimed by the Turks to be in violation of the provisions of the

Lausanne Treaty and the Montreux Convention (1936). Following the Turkish military action on Cyprus in 1974, the Greeks began to fortify those eastern islands more heavily. The atmosphere became more threatening, and in 1987, Turkey and Greece almost went to war over their disagreements on the Aegean. This new crisis stemmed from a Greek attempt to drill for oil in the Aegean in an area outside its territorial limit of six miles. Turkey insisted, according to the decision of the International Court of Justice at the Hague, that the Aegean Sea beyond the respective territorial waters is a disputed area until a solution is reached by the parties. In response, Turkey decided to send an oil research vessel into the contested area. Greece then made it known that they would confront this vessel. Under heavy pressure from NATO and the United States, both sides stopped short of hostilities, resulting in a continuation of the status quo in the Aegean.

| 13 |

The Latest Encounter
The Cyprus Conflict

The Cyprus Republic could be called the 'Humpty Dumpty Republic'. After its establishment in 1960, it 'had a great fall', and it came apart. All the United Nation's horses and all the United Nation's men are still trying to put Cyprus together again. The fact is that, when the Cypriots' psychology is considered, it is difficult to apply the Humpty Dumpty analogy. When the Cyprus Republic sat on a wall from 1960 to 1963, it was not a cohesive and integrated unit; it was already cracked. When it fell, it simply returned to its original state.

The Cyprus issue is not an isolated Turkish-Greek problem having it's own 'private' life; rather it is a significant part of the larger Turkish-Greek issue with a thousand-year history. The island simply became the stage of the latest encounter between the Turks and the Greeks. Both sides brought their chosen traumas and glories, their past griefs and hopes, and their past aggressions and ideals to the Cyprus problem.

Rothman puts the Cyprus conflict among a 'new class of conflicts in the world'. He states that these conflicts are not new, rather they are newly noticed:

> These conflicts are the ethnically rooted ones that rage primarily within states but also transcend their borders... They stretch conventional ways of analyzing and addressing international conflicts; in fact, they pose important challenges to concepts about what constitutes 'international'. In the sense that they are contained within single states, or at least occur in situations in which two separate sovereign states are not yet clearly defined, they may be called domestic disputes—and many are thus beyond the mandate of the

United Nations. Yet, they are clearly about discord between contending nations, even if not embodied in sovereign states, seeking to perpetuate or change the status quo of the single state in which their conflict occurs.[234]

The History of Cyprus before the Ottoman Conquest

The strategic location of this island, smaller in size than the state of Connecticut, has made it a hotly contested prize throughout history and, since Neolithic times, a stage for the unfolding of human drama. One conqueror after another has claimed it.

Cyprus was well populated during the late Neolithic (or New Stone) Age (4,000 to 3,000 BC). In the Bronze Age, Mycenean settlers came, to be followed by Phoenician penetration in the eighth century BC. There are villages in Northern Cyprus today whose occupants consider themselves the descendants of Phoenicians. The year 709 BC marks the island's submission to the Assyrian King, Sargon. A hundred years of independence followed the end of Assyrian domination. Arriving about 560 BC, the Egyptians allowed the Cypriot kings and kingdoms to remain in place. When Egypt was annexed to Persia in 520 BC, the island fell under Persian domination, only to come under Macedonian rule in 332 BC. It passed after the death of Alexander the Great to the Egypt of the Ptolemies, and in 58 BC it was annexed by Rome.

Cyprus underwent a dramatic religious conversion as a province of the Roman Empire, and Christianity replaced the many religious cults. In AD 395 the division of the Roman Empire made Cyprus part of the Eastern Roman (Byzantine) Empire. Greek became the official language, and Byzantine culture prevailed. The emperor Zeno made the Cypriot ecclesiastical province autocephalous; that is, he exempted it from direct jurisdictional, though not spiritual, dependence on the Patriarch of Constantinople.

For eight centuries Byzantine rule was unchallenged save for intermittent invasion by the Arabs. In 1191, Richard Lion Heart seized Cyprus after hostility had been shown there to the English crusaders. He then gave it to Guy de Lusignan, who had been dispossessed as king of Jerusalem. Guy de Lusignan founded a feudal monarchy under a court French in language and culture, and this monarchy lasted into the Middle Ages. With the growing maritime supremacy of the Italians, particularly the Genoese and Venetians, Cyprus, so crucial to Mediterranean trade, became part of the Venetian Empire in the fifteenth century and so remained until its conquest by the Ottoman Turks in 1570-1571.

The Ottoman Period

To win Cyprus it was necessary for the Ottoman Turks not only to overcome the Venetians but to oppose also the combined forces of the Catholic states with interests in the Mediterranean. As Turkish casualties mounted into tens of thousands, 'it was a fact of history that they [the Turks] risked the fate of the Empire' in order to conquer the island.[235] Under the Venetians the island's population had dwindled to little more than two hundred thousand. After the Ottomans' triumph, the original Turkish settlers were drawn from among the soldiers; they were given fiefs (*timars*) on the island by Sultan Selim II. The sultan also issued an imperial order for certain towns in Anatolia to send one family out of each ten engaged there in any given trade. Tailors, shoemakers, cooks, candle makers, carpenters, stone masons, jewellers, and so on were relocated. The imperial order to colonize acknowledged the devastation on the island but emphasized the suitability of the land for agriculture. Farmers chosen to go carried their own farm implements and seed with them. The settlers were guaranteed protection and forgiven their taxes for two years. This 'forced exile' (*sürgün*) method was taken so seriously that the imperial order included the recording of detailed descriptions of all those ordered to Cyprus so that officials there could make sure that all had complied. Muslims frowned on making any representation of a human being, so identification depended on written descriptions.

Approximately thirty thousand Turks settled in Cyprus by the end of the seventeenth century, and this method of colonization was used until the middle of the eighteenth century. The Turks who became Cypriots introduced a new but cohesive cultural influence to the island. The Turks of Cyprus today are the descendants of these settlers and have been living on the island over four hundred years, twice the length of time that has passed since the establishment of the United States.[236]

Interestingly enough it was the appearance of the Ottomans on the scene that provided a strong sense of cohesiveness among the Greek-speaking Orthodox Christians, adherents of the Church of Cyprus. During the Venetian period the Greek Orthodox Church was suppressed, and attempts were made to impose Roman Catholicism on the people. In taking over the island, the Ottoman government liquidated the Latin church in Cyprus and restored the autocephalous Orthodox archbishopric, thus re-establishing the religious and political leadership of the Greek-speaking community and assuring its cultural autonomy and survival.

The local population was included in the *millet* system. As members of a *millet* they constituted a semi-autonomous unit in charge of its own churches, schools, cemeteries, and clerical discipline, with jurisdiction in cases involving marriage, dowries, divorce, and so on. Thus, the local population enjoyed more freedom than before and organized themselves around their church. The head of the Orthodox church also became the *de facto* political chief.[237] He became the ethnarch, the political and national representative of his people in its relations with the Ottoman government. Sir Harry Luke states that the Archbishop of Cyprus, whose office was created by the Turks after lying dormant for three hundred years, became the supreme power and authority over the island. He had greater influence than the Turkish Pasha (governor) himself because of his control of Cyprus finances.[238] During the Ottoman period, Greek was accepted as an official language together with Turkish, and the Greek Cypriots were not obliged to learn Turkish or use it to correspond with government and officials. Furthermore, the names of streets, squares, public places, and offices were displayed in both the Turkish and Greek languages.[239]

As the Ottoman Empire began to decline, the island fell into economic hardship; the situation became worse due to earthquakes and locust infestations. There was famine between 1859-1861 when supplies of biscuits were distributed by the Ottoman government. It was the burden of taxes, however, that led to uprisings by Greek and some Turkish segments. The Ottomans gradually became the enemy in the eyes of the Cypriot Greeks. But a dual system and balanced administration remained intact. Writing in 1879, W. H. Hepworth Dixon described how on the one side of this dual system was the Turkish Pasha (Governor) ruling from his *Konak* (mansion), and on the other side was the Greek Archbishop of St. John's Cathedral. The Turkish governor and the Greek religious/political leader came to terms, not by articles and treaties, but by consent.[240]

When the Greek War of Independence started in 1821 the Ottomans were anxious lest the Cypriot Greeks might also rebel. Turkish historians accuse Archbishop Kyprianos of Cyprus of plotting against the Ottoman government, while Greek historians, in general, speak of his innocence and humane qualities. Kyprianos and other priests and laymen were executed by the Ottomans on 9 July 1821, in the heat of the Greek War of Independence. The Cypriot Turkish writer Ahmet Gazioğlu (1990), who examined the events leading to these executions, states:

> This was the only incident during the entire 308 years of Turkish rule which resulted in politically motivated executions. Although regrettable, they have to be seen within the generally accepted terms of similar uprisings in the world at that time. It is sad that such executions still take place even today in some parts of the world.[241]

The executions became a chosen trauma for the Cypriot Greeks. A few years later the new archbishop's authority was restored in religious matters, but his political powers in dealing with the Ottomans were curtailed. This, paradoxically, increased his political prestige among his followers.

In the nineteenth century the idea of *Enosis* (the idea of uniting Cyprus with Greece) was implanted, but the island Greeks had no power to initiate a military process. Increased demands and agitation for *Enosis* would wait for British rule over the island.

British Rule

Russia declared war on the Ottoman Empire in April, 1877; this war ended with the Treaty of San Stefano and for the practical purposes it gave control of the Dardanelles to the Russians (see Chapter 9). The British and the other European powers were alarmed, and they refused to accept the Treaty of San Stefano. Instead, they insisted that certain matters pertaining to the Ottomans be discussed at a six-power conference in Berlin. The Berlin Conference took place in June 1878.

In order to protect British interest in the region, Disraeli's government carried on clandestine negotiations with the Ottoman sultan's government which were concluded on 8 June 1878. Accordingly, the Ottoman sultan consented 'to assign the island of Cyprus to be occupied and administered by England'. But an 'annual fixed payment' should be paid by Britain to the Ottomans. This proviso enabled the Ottomans to assert that they did not surrender the island to the British, but only temporarily turned over administration. Because of this 'leasing', Cyprus remained nominally Ottoman territory until 1914.

When World War I began in 1914, the Ottomans joined forces with the Central powers. Thereupon, the British annexed Cyprus. This annexation was not recognized by the Ottoman government. In 1915 the British offered the island to Greece if the latter entered the war on the side of the Allies. But at that time Greece favoured a policy of neutrality and declined the offer. After the demise of the Ottoman Empire, Atatürk's new Turkish government recognized the annexation of Cyprus by Britain. The island became a crown colony in March 1925, and the British high commissioner became governor.

In 1931 Cypriot Greeks rioted, and expressed their sentiments for *Enosis*; incidents occurred in some two hundred out of five hundred and ninety-eight villages. What precipitated the riots was a claim for debt charges. When the British 'leased' the land they collected monies from each Cypriot in order to pay a 'rent' to the Ottomans. In fact, the money was never paid to the Turks; instead, it was deposited in the Bank of England to pay off Ottoman Crimean War loans. The rioting Cypriot Greeks also claimed that debt charge payments were illegal after 1914 since the British annexed the island at that time.

The British reaction to the riots was harsh. Alongside the Cypriot Greeks, the Cypriot Turks, who were referred to by the British as Muslims instead of Turks, also suffered since the measures which the British adopted applied to both ethnic groups. The teaching of Greek and Turkish history was curtailed; the ethnic groups could not publically display portraits of their heroes, nor could they fly their nations' flags. Gatherings of more than five people required permission, and interference with the internal affairs of the Cypriot Greek Church occurred. The British, who had offered the island to Greece in 1915, were now causing hardships and humiliation for Cypriot Greeks (as well as for Cypriot Turks). For practical purposes the *Enosis* movement had to go underground. Cyprus was not seriously effected by World War II. It was after this war was over that the British liberalized their colonial administration.

Makarios III and Colonel Grivas
In 1950, a thirty-seven year old bishop took office as the youngest archbishop in the history of the Church of Cyprus and took the name Makarios III. He was born Mikael Christodoulos Mouskos in the village of Ano Panayia, not far from the port city of Paphos.[242] He

was the first-born child, and his parents owned a small piece of land and goats. His mother Eleni gave birth to Mikael's brother when Mikael was five years old. She died a few months after giving birth to Mikael's sister when Mikael was ten years old. A few months later his father remarried. The stepmother, as we learn from all accounts, was a good woman who bore another son for Mikael's father.

At the age of thirteen Mikael was taken to Kykko Monastery as a novice. This monastery dates from 1100; 'it ranks in prestige in the Orthodox world with St. Catherine's in Sinai and the monasteries of Mt. Athos.'[243] All indications are that a motherless bright boy in the midst of the adolescent passage, searching for idealized images, found Hellenism, along with Orthodox Christianity, as targets of idealization.[244] Makarios' biographer Stanley Mayes writes: 'If the immediate purpose of the school at Kykko was to prepare young Cypriots [Greek] for the life of a priest or monk, its overriding mission—like that of the monastery itself and of the whole Church of Cyprus—was to keep alive the flame of Hellenism.'[245]

In 1931 Mikael was still a novice at Kykko when the Cypriot Greek riots against British rule occurred. The eighteen-year old Mikael wrote on a wall in the monks' kitchen: *Zito i Enosis* (Long live Union [with Greece]), and added his initials.[246] Mikael eventually went to Athens where he studied theology and where he witnessed the brutality of the Nazi occupation, which we believe also shaped his personality as a tough politician.

We should mention another Cypriot-born Greek, George Grivas, who would also play a large role in the island's history. In 1898 George Grivas was born in a Cypriot village, Trikomu, which is not far from Famagusta. While Famagusta is an eastern port, Paphos, which is near to Mikael's birthplace, is a western port. George's father was a prosperous villager, a corn-merchant. George was rather short, and as an adult, because of his moustache, he resembled Groucho Marx.

Grivas, older than Makarios, grew up during the Balkan Wars, went to Greece in 1916, and entered the Greek Military Academy. As a young officer he was filled with the *Megali Idea*, and he participated in the Turkish-Greek War (1920-1922) in Anatolia. In 1940, when Italy invaded Greece, Grivas was posted as chief of staff to the Second Army Division which was defeated. In war, Grivas was humiliated twice.

When Greece was under the Nazi occupation in 1943, Grivas formed a secret organization called by the Greek letter 'X' (*xkhi*) and attempted to harass Nazis and also 'be ready to neutralise the main Greek resistance movement, the Communist-led EAM, when the Germans left'.[247] After Greece was liberated from the Nazis, Grivas' 'X' became a paramilitary terrorist organization, composed of 'fascist thugs who brutally tried to impose their own kind of order on the Greek countryside'.[248]

Makarios and Grivas first met in Greece during the last year Makarios resided there. In 1951 Colonel Grivas came to Cyprus, (his first visit in twenty years) and made his ideas to achieve *Enosis* known; it could be achieved through terrorism and guerrilla uprising. Makarios, who apparently developed a dislike for Grivas, had misgivings about Grivas's extremism from their very first meeting. A year later in Athens another discussion took place on how to reunite the island with Greece. Both men were present, and once more they disagreed on tactics to achieve *Enosis*. It can be assumed that Makarios, while a tough politician who would not rule out violence in achieving political aims, had identified with the idealized aspects of Hellenism. Meanwhile, Grivas identified himself with the *klephts*.

In August 1954 Greece's United Nations' representative formally requested that the subject of self-determination pertaining to the people of Cyprus be included on the agenda of the General Assembly's next meeting. Archbishop Makarios seconded this formal request by a petition to the United Nations. Meanwhile, anxiety among the Cypriot Turks arose and their identification with the Turks in Turkey grew even stronger. In turn, the Turkish government became increasingly involved in the Cyprus issue.

EOKA and Volkan

When the UN General Assembly decided that it did 'not appear appropriate to adopt a resolution on the question of Cyprus', the Cypriot Greek leaders called for a general strike, and violence broke out. Makarios returned from New York where he was attending the United Nations' meetings. Once more he met with Grivas to plan their next move. With Makarios' blessing, the National Organization of Cypriot Fighters (Ethniki Organosis Kyrion Agoniston-EOKA) became the official name of the Greek terrorist organization.

The whole Greek world was obsessed with *Enosis*; it was the latest call to express 'a dream shared by Greeks' that the Byzantine Empire would one day be restored. Markides, a Greek sociologist born in Cyprus, wrote that *Enosis* originated 'in the *minds* of intellectuals in their attempt to revise Greek-Byzantine civilization. However, being the most central and powerful of institutions, the church contributed immensely to its development.'[249] Cypriot Turks declared that they favoured *Taksim* (partition), a division of the island between Greeks and Turks and formed their own underground political organization called Volkan (volcano) which supported TMT (Türk Mukavemet Teşkilatı - Turkish Resistance Organization). This organization was no match for EOKA.

In 1955 Britain made a major policy decision. Until then the British government considered colonial domestic affairs to be internal matters; now, they invited representatives of the Greek and the Turkish governments to London to discuss Cyprus. This meeting did not accomplish much. In September 1955 as the British, Greek, and Turkish foreign ministers were discussing the Cyprus issue in London, a bomb exploded in the yard of the Turkish Consulate General in Salonica near the house marking the birthplace of Mustafa Kemal Atatürk. That evening (September 6th) anti-Greek riots erupted in various parts of Turkey. Istanbul, the only Turkish city with a sizeable Greek population against whom the Turks could vent their anger, was especially hard hit. The Greeks later accused a Turk of planting the bomb in Salonica. After the explosion in Greece and the riots in Turkey, the Turkish people also began to share an emotional obsession with the Cyprus problem.

In 1956 the British exiled Makarios to the Seychelles after charging him with complicity in EOKA. This left Grivas, who was never caught by the British, 'alone' on the island. He and his people brought waves of terror to Cyprus mostly directed against the British. But, when they began to kill Cypriot Turkish members of the police, one could see the shape of things to come: a bloody intercommunal struggle. During the EOKA revolt, between 1955 and 1958, Turkish Cypriots were in a very vulnerable position. Hundreds of Turkish Cypriots were killed or wounded and six thousand Cypriot Turks became refugees as thirty-three villages were destroyed by EOKA.

Makarios was allowed to leave the Seychelles in 1957 but could not return to the island. He received a hero's welcome in Athens. Soon after this, in Zurich in February 1959, the Republic of Cyprus was 'designed' by representatives of the Greek and Turkish governments after consultation with the leaders of both communities. The Zurich agreements were later confirmed by the London conference. The Republic of Cyprus came into existence in 1960.

The Republic of Cyprus

The British, Greek, and Turkish participants of the Zurich and London meetings reached a compromise; they rejected the idea of *Enosis* or *Taksim*, and instead 'created' an independent Cyprus (56 square kilometres remained under the British as two air bases.) This Republic was the result of *Realpolitik* in spite of the observable presence of a situation in which psychology was a compelling factor. According to Glen Camp, *Realpolitik*, or a policy of realism can be described as follows.

> Such a policy assumes that the role of diplomacy is to develop solutions to international problems that ratify an existing distribution of power rather than solutions that would change that distribution in the direction of greater equity. The statesman is thus a realist seeking a settlement based upon the existing balance of power, not an idealist seeking to rectify passionately felt injustices.[250]

He added: 'Nationalist movements in Cyprus, both Greek and Turkish, were and are relevant actors in the same sense that states are: they have the capacity to impose or subvert stability.'[251] When Makarios became the president, Dr. Fazıl Küçük, a Cypriot Turkish physician, became the vice-president. Grivas and his followers received full immunity from prosecution, and Grivas went to Athens, receiving a hero's welcome and a promotion to the rank of lieutenant-general. One group's terrorist is another group's hero!

The Greeks never relinquished their aim and plan, determined by the *Megali Idea*, to unite the island with Greece. An independent Cyprus was only a stepping stone towards their goal. Makarios, upon being elected president of Cyprus in December 1959, declared that for the first time in eight centuries the government of the island would pass into Greek hands. He did not say 'into Cypriot hands'. In September 1962, Makarios declared in a speech given at his home village, Ano Panayia, 'Until this small Turkish community that forms part of the Turkish race which has been the terrible enemy of Hellenism is expelled, the duty of the EOKA cannot be considered as terminated.' Later, in 1964, he spoke of his ambition to link his name with the union of Cyprus and Greece. And he added: 'This is my ambition, for the realization of which I shall continue to struggle till death.'[252] The above statements are samples of dozens which the new president of the independent Cyprus made. For Makarios and many other Greek leaders, to unite Cyprus with Greece would bring the *Megali Idea* to reality; for this Grivas' and EOKA's terror was sanctioned. Makarios said:

> Either the whole of Cyprus is to be united with Greece or become a holocaust... The road to the fulfillment of national aspirations may be full of difficulties but we shall reach our goal—which is *Enosis*—alive or dead.[253]

The 'End' of The Republic of Cyprus

While one may consider the Republic of Cyprus as an 'ideal' creation in that two ethnic groups might function in legalized harmony, the chosen traumas and the chosen glories of both sides dictated the nature of their 'togetherness'. Since the Cypriot Greeks were in the majority, their aim could be pushed forward. Their aim was *Enosis*, and to achieve this a criminal plan called 'the Akritas Plan' came into existence. The plan was to destroy the partnership government by suppressing any resistance from Cypriot Turks in the shortest possible time, 'within a day or two, before outside intervention would be possible, probable, or justifiable'. At one point the plan reveals the following:

> It is obvious that today the international opinion is against any form of oppression, and especially against oppression of minorities. The Turks have so far been able to convince world public opinion that the union of Cyprus with Greece will amount to their enslavement. Under these circumstances we stand a good chance of success in influencing world public opinion if we base our struggle not on *Enosis* but on self-determination.[254]

In 1963 Makarios offered thirteen proposals to amend the constitution.[255] These proposals, if accepted, would give all the power to the majority Greeks. For example, Makarios' proposals included the revocation of the veto rights of both the president and the vice-president (the latter still to be a Turk) the abolition of their separate election by each group's representatives and the unification of municipalities. If this unification occurred, the Turks feared that they would not get their share of municipal services. The Turks refused to accept the proposals. Tensions increased. On 21 December 1963 two Turks were killed and five wounded. Turks called this outbreak and the events of the following days 'the bloody Christmas massacre'. By 23 December Nicosia, the capital of Cyprus, became an inter-communal battleground. Since it was physically impossible for Cypriot Turkish ministers and members of the House of Representatives to attend meetings of the Parliament, which met in the Greek sector, they were effectively excluded.

Eventually the Cypriot Turks were forced to live in enclaves in overcrowded slum conditions. Eighteen per cent of the population, the Turks, were forced to live on three per cent of the land. (At the time of the establishment of the Republic of Cyprus they had owned thirty-five percent of the land.) About thirty thousand Turks had become refugees. It was the Cypriot Turks' turn in world history to suffer greatly.

In March 1964, the United Nations' Security Council authorized the provision of an international peacekeeping force in Cyprus, and United Nations' troops took command before the last of that month. The UN troops still remain on the island until today. In June 1964 Grivas, on the invitation of Makarios, returned to the island and assumed the leadership of the newly founded National Guard (all Greeks). At the same time a large number of Greek regular troops from Greece were clandestinely infiltrated into the island. Since the Turks on the island were in great peril, Turkey prepared to intervene but was stopped by the United States.[256] However, Turkish planes bombed Greek positions in support of Cypriot Turks who were under attack, bringing the 'hot' phase of the conflict to a temporary halt.

In October 1967, Rauf R. Denktaş, the first president of the Turkish Communal Chamber and exiled since January 1964, returned secretly to Cyprus, only to be captured by the Greeks. His capture precipitated still another crisis, but political pressure from Turkey brought about his release. Soon after this Grivas' men precipitated another crisis by attacking a Turkish village and massacring twenty-six villagers. Once more Turkey exerted pressure and demanded that Grivas and all Greek military who came to the island clandestinely be removed from the island. Grivas left the island two days after the Turkish ultimatum and fifteen thousand Greek soldiers were sent back to Greece, but Greece left about two thousand officers behind. Later these officers or their replacements would plan to overthrow

Makarios.

In January 1968, elections were held among the Greek Cypriots and Makarios was re-elected by an overwhelming victory. While Makarios' only opponent, Takis Evdokas, had run on a straight *Enosis* platform, Makarios publicly supported an independent Cyprus. Turks, who did not believe that *Enosis* sentiments were dead, held their own election according to the Republic's original constitution, and Dr. Fazıl Küçük became president of the Turkish administration. Later he would be replaced by Rauf R. Denktaş.

The Birds of Cyprus

Anna Freud is reported to have said in an informal exchange with another psychoanalyst, Joseph Sandler, that 'We know that with persecuted minorities, against whom atrocities are committed, the atrocities are preceded by a withdrawal of the feeling of sameness' (by the victimizer). She identified this as a sort of dehumanizing process that is applied to the victim—in this case to the minority about to be persecuted. She added that 'without this preliminary withdrawal of boundary setting what happens afterwards could not happen, because of the feeling of sympathy and empathy, of sameness, which has to be done away with'.[257] Cypriot Turks suffered because they were, to a high degree, dehumanized in the eyes of Greek Cypriots.

At the time of the establishment of the Republic of Cyprus (1960) the island contained one hundred and fourteen mixed, three hundred and ninety-two all-Greek, and one hundred and twenty-three all-Turkish villages or towns. Between December 1963 and the following summer about thirty thousand Cypriot Turks became refugees. They were forced to live with other dislocated Turks in enclaves which comprised, as has been noted, only three per cent of the island. The Cypriot Turks were to experience a chosen trauma the effects of which were palpable in the minds of the population for decades to come and were to pass from one generation to the next.

The period of confinement in the enclaves can be divided into two periods; in the first, which lasted five years until 1968, the people were virtually prisoners. In the second, the six years that followed, the Greek soldiers were no longer stationed in positions encircling the enclaves, and the Turks were allowed to enter the Greek sectors 'freely' and to visit other enclaves. But for all practical purposes, they were treated outside their own enclaves as second-class citizens. The

Greek sectors glittered with a prosperity that contrasted sadly with the shabby enclaves. The Turks had to be submissive when entering a Greek sector. Their humiliation was great and their self-esteem sadly reduced, as was apparent during the six years of 'open' enclaves. Many people were hypochondriacal, and most habitually used antidepressive or tranquilizing drugs, which could be obtained without prescription. The society had become orally-dependent on sedation. One could hear the lament: 'We'll all die off! Within fifteen years no Turks will be left on Cyprus!' This was the situation when, in the summer of 1974, war erupted. Troops from mainland Turkey, liberating the Turkish enclaves in the north, divided the island in two. New adjustments were then required.

Cypriot Turks tolerated the period of total confinement in the enclaves between 1963 and 1968 by developing a mass hobby: raising parakeets in cages. Parakeets are not native birds of Cyprus. It seems that some people had them, and as this mass hobby evolved, the parakeets multiplied by thousands. They were found in the houses, markets, and public places; one had to step over cages to buy a loaf of bread in a grocery. No one saw this bizarre preoccupation with the birds as out of the ordinary, and we are reminded of a Turkish proverb that fish living in the water do not know what water is. In 1967 and 1968 the bird hobby peaked, and it was still there in the summer of 1968 soon after the borders of the ghettos were 'opened'. When the Cypriot Turks began to be more mobile, the caged birds quickly disappeared.

The birds were raised as extended families. When Dr. Volkan visited Nicosia in the summer of 1968, there were dozens of birds in three cages in a relative's house where, also, three families had to live together. The original pair of parakeets—the 'mother' and 'father'— were pointed out to him, along with a 'bride' who had just been moved into a new 'home'. It should be remembered that the confinement had forced the Cypriot Turks to re-establish something very like the traditional extended family, which modernization had generally modified in the direction of smaller kinship units. Many family members, and even friends, were obliged to live together in crowded houses and even in caves.

The birds represented Cypriot Turks' vision of themselves as needy, and as they cared for them they identified with an abstract saviour. Raised in families that represented the Turkish extended family, the birds helped their owners accept the denial of their needy selves which were externalized on to the birds. When the birds sang, they were felt to be joyously extolling their caretakers. People confined in enclaves felt free compared to birds living in small cages. As long as they could maintain the illusion of being self-sufficient by controlling the saviour and the saved (in the small, simple world of their birds) the people could tolerate their imprisonment.[258]

Sampson

Greece had been governed by a military junta since Spring 1967, and the junta saw Makarios as an obstacle to attaining *Enosis*. In 1971 George Grivas, after publicly calling Makarios a traitor, returned secretly to the island and began rebuilding his terrorist organization under the name EOKA B, and Turkish anxieties soared. Makarios began flirting with the Soviets in order to maintain the support of the Cypriot Greek communist party. In 1972 three bishops (from Kition, Kyrenia, and Paphos) publicly joined the anti-Makarios groups. When Grivas died in January 1974 from a heart attack, Makarios did not attend his funeral, but one hundred thousand Greeks did, and they listened to a fiery speech by one Nikos Sampson (born Yeoryiadis) condemning Makarios. Nikos Sampson, who was thirty-nine years old at that time, was a known terrorist who bragged openly of killing at least a dozen men and had been tried and sentenced to death for carrying firearms before the Republic of Cyprus was founded. A general amnesty declared in 1959 just before recognition of the independence of Cyprus had spared him.

Stanley Mayes describes how young Sampson was the first reported on the scene of some bloody event against the British. His timely presence was not due to any prescient alertness; 'he or one of his team had made the killing'.[259] When EOKA turned its attention to Cypriot Turks, Sampson symbolized Greek aggression. 'Sampson had the ingenious idea of using a bulldozer with its excavator raised as an improvised tank',[260]—for killing, evacuating, or taking Turks as hostages. On several occasions he had his photograph taken with one foot resting on the corpse of a fallen Turk as though he were a hunter who had just killed a deer.[261]

After Grivas' death, Athens began to direct Sampson and EOKA B. In mid-July 1974 Makarios barely escaped death in an attack by the (all Greek) Cypriot National Guard. Greeks were fighting against

Greeks. A detachment of Soviet-built T-54 tanks pounded Makarios' presidential palace. But Makarios managed to be driven to Paphos; the opposition simply failed to control a small road at the back of the Palace. The next day the British came to Makarios' help and managed to take him to London. Meanwhile, Sampson was declared President, and this signalled to the Cypriot Turks that soon their end would come.

Summer 1974

After the *coup d'état* in Nicosia, Turkish Prime Minister, Bülent Ecevit, flew to London to seek a peaceful solution, but he was not successful. The original Treaty of Guarantee, drawn up at the birth of the Republic of Cyprus, established the right of guarantor powers, whether Britain, Greece, or Turkey, to intervene unilaterally should territorial integrity be breached. Under Sampson's 'presidency' the union of Cyprus with Greece would certainly have taken place, bringing the Akritas Plan to a successful end. Using the 'permission' provided by the treaty, Turkey landed troops on the island on 20 July 1974. The Turkish troops parachuted down from airplanes and landed from the sea. The opposing side was no match for a regular military force, though the clash of arms was severe. Soon the Turkish military secured a northern position on the island. Three days after the beginning of the Turkish military operation the Greek junta in Athens collapsed and Sampson in Nicosia to resign. Democracy returned to Greece. Constantine Karamanlis, who was in exile in France, came back to Athens to restart a democratic government. In Cyprus, Glafkos Clerides, an intelligent Cypriot Greek patriot, was sworn in as acting president of the Republic of Cyprus. He remained the head of the Cypriot Greeks until the return of Makarios, after five months of absence from the island. In 1975 Sampson was arrested by the Makarios government and was given a twenty-year sentence.

In August 1974 the Turkish troops took more territory and on 16 August 1974, after taking about thirty-seven per cent of the island, they stopped their movement. As has been mentioned, when the Republic of Cyprus was born, the Cypriot Turks owned thirty-five per cent of the land. They had been forced to live in three per cent of the land during their horrible ordeal; now, after the war, the Turkish military provided a little more for them than they had originally owned. For practical purposes, the island was divided into northern

(Turkish) and southern (Greek) sections. *Taksim* (this division), once thought of as a political opinion, became a fact of life through military force.

|14|

Cyprus After 1974

The events of 1974 brought the inevitable personal and social tragedies that are part of every war. About one hundred and sixty thousand Cypriot Greeks became refugees. Under the psychological principle termed by John E. Mack as 'the egoism of victimization', the Cypriot Turks had very little empathy for the Cypriot Greeks' suffering. The egoism of victimization is described by Mack as a tendency, 'which severe hurt and grief seem inevitably to bring about, to direct all investment, all empathy and love, toward those of one's immediate circle of fellow sufferers, defined generally in no broader terms than oneself and one's own afflicted people. Conversely any investment of caring in the other side is withdrawn'.[262]

The Cypriot Turks did not experience conscious guilt about the changes on the island; they had suffered, and now their adversaries would suffer in turn. Furthermore, the Turks state that the figure of one hundred and sixty thousand Greek refugees needs closer examination since many Greeks were living on Turkish-owned land when the Turks were 'imprisoned' on three per cent of the island.

Sixty-five thousand Cypriot Turks also became refugees. They voluntarily escaped from their southern enclaves to the Turkish-held territory of the north. Out of sixty-five thousand persons, only one hundred and seventeen Cypriot Turks chose to stay in the Greek area.[263]

The Greeks claimed six thousand dead and three thousand missing in action. To this day, the Turks insist that this toll includes Greeks killed by their compatriots from EOKA B during Sampson's takeover and rampage. The Turks reported their losses as one thousand five hundred dead and two thousand wounded.

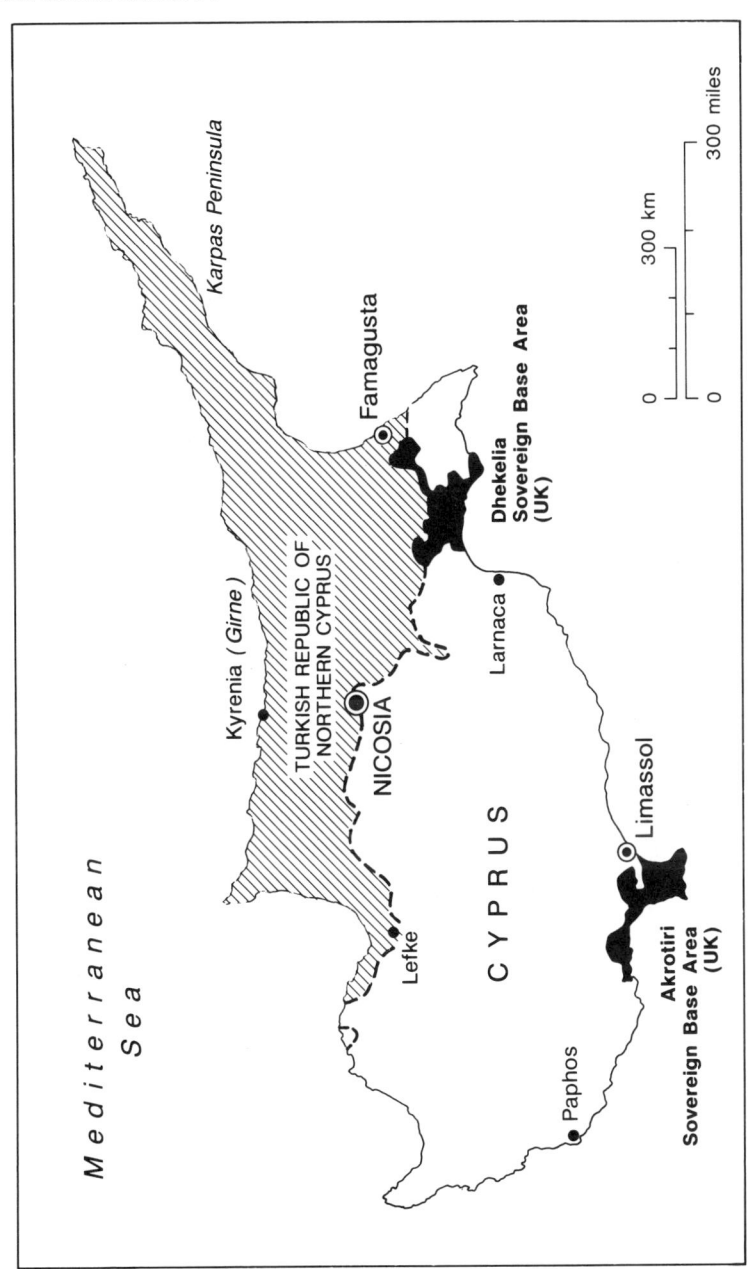

Map 4: Present Day Cyprus

We can say that after the summer of 1974, there was a 'forced' population exchange on the island which led to the creation of a *de facto* partition. Volkan has studied in detail Cypriot Turks' mourning over the loss of their previously imprisoned selves and adaptation to their newly found free selves.[264] All indications are that the Cypriot Greeks, the losers, could not grieve as effectively as the Turks and adjust to the new reality. Their pain, suffering, and humiliation made 1974 their newest chosen trauma. This war and the *de facto taksim* was also another devastating blow to the *Megali Idea*.

Denktaş - Makarios Guidelines

After the summer of 1974, the powerful Greek lobby in the United States demanded an American embargo on military aid to Turkey and got a positive result. In turn, Turkey retaliated by closing American military bases in Turkey, exempting only those involved in the NATO Joint Defence System. During its forty-two months of existence, until late September 1978, the embargo did not facilitate a quick settlement on the island.

In February 1975, the Turkish Cypriot administration, under the leadership of Rauf Raif Denktaş decided to change the status of the island's government. They proclaimed a Federal Republic in anticipation of the union of a Turkish Federal State within the framework of a federation based on two geographical regions. The Greeks, not surprisingly, refused to accept such a plan, and continued to enjoy international recognition as the only government of Cyprus.

Rauf Denktaş, for some years now, has become the key figure in Cypriot Turkish history. He was born in January 1924 in Paphos, not far from Makarios' birthplace. He was the youngest of four children and lost his mother during his early childhood. Denktaş, who studied law in London and later worked on the island as a lawyer and a judge, had begun to be involved in the Cypriot Turkish community's affairs even before he had gone to London. As a young man, he had begun writing about Turkish affairs in a Cypriot Turkish daily. Denktaş, a very intelligent and effective leader, is known to use humour and his long-time hobby, photography, as a means of relaxation as he deals with 'crises' which are daily occurrences.

As the status quo continued on the island, Denktaş wrote a letter on 9 January 1977 to Makarios offering to meet with the Archbishop and discuss all aspects of the Cyprus problem. Makarios accepted the invitation. The two leaders met and agreed on four items as guidelines for the interlocutors as a basis for future negotiations. These guidelines were:

1. We are seeking an independent, non-aligned, bi-communal Federal Republic.

2. The territory under the administration of each community should be discussed in the light of economic viability or productivity and land ownership.

3. Questions of principle, like freedom of movement, freedom of settlement, the right of property and other specific matters, are open for discussion, taking into consideration the fundamental basis of a bi-communal federal system and certain practical difficulties which may arise for the Turkish Cypriot Community.

4. The powers and functions of the Central Federal Government will be such as to safeguard the unity of the country, having regard to the bi-communal character of the State.[265]

It is difficult to know if Makarios, a believer in the *Megali Idea* and *Enosis*, would have had a change of heart and would have joined Denktaş in finding a solution to the Cyprus Conflict. We believe that it was impossible, emotionally, for Makarios, in the long run, to give up his long-held beliefs. To give them up would be like changing his identity.

Shortly afterwards Makarios died (3 August 1977) from a cardiac crisis ten days short of his sixty-fourth birthday. His death created a shock reaction in the Greek world. A few days later, on 8 August, after a splendid funeral service in Nicosia, his body was carried from Nicosia to high above Kykko Monastery where he was buried. He had chosen this location as the site of his tomb and ordered its unusual design. On that summer day, an unusual thing happened on the island. The sky was covered by clouds, and it rained fiercely. The Cypriot Greeks declared that the Gods were crying over their leader's death; Dr. Volkan, who happened to be visiting Northern Cyprus on that day, heard the Cypriot Turks' interpretation of the unusual summer rain as the Gods' wish to wash away Makarios' sins which were committed against them in the service of the *Megali Idea*.[266]

The Turkish Republic of Northern Cyprus
There was no heir-apparent at the time Makarios died. Later, the

Archbishop was be subject to some harsh Cypriot Greek criticism and was described as a megalomaniac, a power-hungry tyrant who believed in his own immortality.[267] Initially, Makarios had favoured Glafkos Clerides as his successor. Clerides and Denktaş knew each other since 1959 when the former was Defence Advocate for EOKA criminals and the Turkish leader was a Crown Prosecutor. But, before his death, Makarios considered Clerides as soft in dealing with the Turks. Spyros Kyprianou was another important Cypriot Greek. The Archbishop did not like Kyprianou's obsessional personality. But, when Makarios died, Kyprianou, as the president of the House of Representatives (of the Greek side), automatically became the acting president. After an election, he became the president and claimed that he was the president of the entire island despite the fact that he did not have *de facto* control over thirty-seven per cent of its area. The Cypriot Turks refused to recognize Kyprianou as their President. But the world, ignoring the Cypriot Turks' plight, and on the basis of the continuity of states, accepted Kyprianou as the representative of the island.

Makarios was an authoritarian leader. The vacuum created by his death encouraged further disturbances among the Greek Cypriots. EOKA B showed its face once more; this time they kidnapped Kyprianou's oldest son in December 1977 during the height of the election campaign. Kyprianou refused to negotiate, and his son was released. These events led to a 'formal' dissolution of EOKA B. In a 1993 conversation with Rauf Denktaş, Volkan learned that there is another side to this kidnapping story. According to Denktaş, Clerides confirmed in a private conversation that the 'kidnapping' was an arranged event in order to force him out of the election race—which, in fact, happened. In protest to this 'kidnapping' and to prove his non-involvement, Clerides resigned and Kyprianou was, thus, elected unopposed. Whatever the truth, since mid-1979 we can say that there has been no systematic Cypriot Greek terrorism on the island. The Cyprus conflict became a matter of political process.

On 15 November 1983 the Cypriot Turks established the Turkish Republic of Northern Cyprus. Rauf Raif Denktaş was elected its first president. Turkey recognized the new Republic, but no other country followed Turkey's lead.

Legal Opinions, 'Real World' Politics and Life on a Divided Island
Legal opinions, both for and against, have been stated regarding many issues, decisions and events which have taken place on the island during the last three decades. When the Turkish military forces came to the island in July 1974 their actions had followed a *coup d'état* on the island. The Turks declared that they acted according to an international agreement. But when they increased the percentage of Cyprus under their control in August 1974, were they acting according to the Guarantee Treaty of 1960? Could they justify that their actions in August 1974 were according to *clausala rebus sic stantibus* (doctrine of fundamentally changed circumstances)? As expected, the Turkish and Greek interpretations of international law are different. When the Cypriot Turks offered various legal opinions to support their establishment of the Federated State and then the Turkish Republic of Northern Cyprus, Greek legal opinions were the exact opposite. The Cypriot Turkish position is that since the Bloody Christmas of 1963, there has not been a single Cypriot Turkish member of the 'House of Representatives of the Republic of Cyprus'. This house is under the monopoly of the Cypriot Greeks, and the partnership government has collapsed because of the aggression of the Cypriot Greeks.

It is beyond this chapter and our expertise to mention the details of every legal and political development and attempt to find a solution to the Cyprus conflict.[268] Above and beyond the legal, political, economic, and military issues, the history of the Turkish-Greek relationship and the mental representations and affects attached to these representations are the 'unseen' power to maintain the 'separateness' of the Turks and the Greeks on the island. Legal and political opinions, the American Greek lobby, traditional diplomacy, the need to keep a balance of power, economic gains, and many other 'real world' issues are certainly present in the Cyprus Conflict. It is also, however, true that the dictates of these 'real world' issues do not 'fit' the emotional refusal of the Turks and the Greeks to enjoy 'togetherness'. Conscious, and more importantly, unconscious forces in the relationship of large group neighbours need to be analysed, understood, and considered, along with the 'real world' issues if we wish to be creative in finding a solution on the island.

Cypriot Turks and Cypriot Greeks have been physically separated for thirty years now, living in their own sections under democratic regimes. The new generation of Cypriot Turks and Cypriot Greeks have not seen each other and have had neither peaceful nor aggressive actual relationships. While the Greek side has taken great steps in economic growth, the Turkish side does not match them, one of the reasons being the economic embargo imposed as a result of non-recognition by the world community. The people in Northern Cyprus have been living as if they do not legally exist! But the Turkish Republic of Northern Cyprus has made adaptations peculiar to their situation. For example, one cannot send a letter to the Turkish Republic of Northern Cyprus from the United States because the American government does not recognize the Turkish Republic of Northern Cyprus. Therefore, on the envelope, Americans write the Cypriot address, but underneath this, the city shown on the envelope is Mersin. Mersin is a city in Turkey which functions as the point where the mail for Northern Cyprus is gathered. The added zip code, 10, is an indication that this mail is intended for the Turkish Republic of Cyprus, and it is forwarded.

A person can fly with Turkish Airlines from London to Izmir. The plane lands and takes off again with the same pilot, stewardesses, and the passengers. But, now, on its way from this Turkish city to a Northern Cyprus airport, the plane is identified as belonging to the Kıbrıs Türk Hava Yolları (Cyprus Turkish Air Lines). The Cypriot Turks complain that their 'passports' are not recognized by other countries outside Turkey. Yet, one can see Cypriot Turkish businessmen, tourists, or students in Washington, in London, in Moscow, in Tokyo, and anywhere else. The American embassy in Cyprus has its official headquarters in the Greek section but has a summer house in the Turkish section. American diplomats, as well as those from other countries, go through certain routines and rituals, which appear rather silly to an outside observer, in order to comply with the political/legal positions of their country. For example, when they visit Denktaş at his office, they refrain from calling him 'Mr. President', but for practical purposes, they behave as they would in front of an official head of state.

Since 1974, many Cypriot Turks have tasted the pleasure of being bosses in business ventures. In the old days, no Turkish company could successfully compete with a Greek company. They could not easily survive in a hostile Greek-dominated atmosphere. Now, there are Cypriot Turks who are executives in companies, such as those dealing with European or Japanese auto imports, certain manufactured goods from the United States, baby carriages from England, and so on. Others have their own export companies or factories. One of the biggest fears the Cypriot Turks have of a future 'togetherness' is the fear of losing such freedom as owning and running one's own business.

One of the lesser known facts about Cyprus is that, on both the Greek and the Turkish sides, populations are highly educated. The joke in the Turkish Republic of Northern Cyprus is that there are so many physicians on a certain street that some of them serve petrol at service stations in order to make money. Because of the high level of education, there are unending discussions and analyses of every wrinkle of the 'Cyprus Conflict' by the politicians and the news media. But, to an outside observer, at least in Northern Cyprus, the average person does not seem to be living in conflict; the 'emotional divorce' from the Cypriot Greeks is striking. The solution to a historical problem is, for the average Cypriot Turk, what the world calls the Cyprus Conflict. A 'wall' (both physical and psychological) divides the Turkish and Greek sections of Nicosia. Living in a house at the border, the family members behave as if one part of the city, seen from their windows and belonging to the opposing side, is like a large vacuum. It is understood, however, that the situation on the Greek side is different. Since 1974 humiliated them, the acceptance of the new reality is difficult, if not impossible. So, among the Cypriot Greeks, the link to the north and the wish to regain it remain as an emotional force.

Any Solution?
There has been no inter-communal aggression on the island since 1974 because the Cypriot Turks and Cypriot Greeks are physically separated. On both sides of the island, the leaders and the governments are democratic and civilized, the populations lead normal day-to-day lives. Furthermore, generally on both sides the people are active, healthy, and appear happy; they are friendly towards foreigners. Because of the above factors, many think that it would be easy to make the political situation on the island stable. When the Cypriot Turks and the Cypriot Greeks got together for negotiations, inevitably the Turks refer to their chosen trauma—the period between 1963 and 1974 when they were, like their birds, restricted physically and felt imprisoned. The Turks' remarks fall on the Greeks' deaf ears

since the Greeks have 'repressed' the pre-1974 period and are busy focusing on their chosen trauma, which begins with 1974. In such gatherings, sometimes individual Turks and Greeks become friends and can experience empathy for the opposing side's dilemma, because in personal relationships, reality testing and other psychological phenomena can tame the malignant projections and counter-projections. But, once they are out of actual interaction and go back to their groups, the psychology of the group process becomes dominant over individual opinions. There are certainly people on both sides who consider one or another type of future 'togetherness'. Most Cypriot Turks express such sentiments in the expectation of a better economic future or in the hope that they would be able to strengthen their positions within the political opposition. Some are simply humanists and idealistic. Again, our observation is that such remarks about a future 'togetherness' come to a standstill when the individuals inevitably realize that the dominant group wish for the Greek side is still 'owning' the whole island, and the dominant group wish on the Turkish side is still not to be a minority but a separate community which should have all the legal, political, and economic privileges the Greeks have.

Since Cypriot Turks and Cypriot Greeks (however physically separated during the last thirty years) live in a location which is surrounded by the sea, they eventually have to find a 'solution' so that they do not fear each other and are free to move around the whole island while maintaining their own identities and respecting each other's human rights. It has been very difficult for the United Nations to deal with the Cyprus Conflict while the Republic of Cyprus, which in reality only lasted three years, continues to be perceived as a political entity by the United Nations. To consider Cyprus as one state fits neither the 'reality' on the island nor the 'reality' of the Turkish and Greek group psychologies. The legal and political processes being followed lead to unending obsessionalism and not to creative thinking. For example, no one now speaks of *double Enosis*—the division of the island between Turkey and Greece, with the 'border' which exists between the Cypriot Turks and the Cypriot Greeks becoming an extension of the general Turkish-Greek border. Such a statement is not politically acceptable! It does not fit the agenda of global politics. Furthermore, it creates emotional problems for the Greek Cypriots, who still harbour a wish to 'own' the whole island, and the Cypriot

Turks, because they have thirty years' experience in running their own lives in a democratic atmosphere (however, with the continuous help of Turkey) and have crystallized their own identity as Cypriot Turks.

Still another solution which is not politically acceptable in the 'real world' atmosphere of the United Nations is to consider the present status quo as a solution and call the present situation on the island, with some adjustment in the percentage of the area that Turks can have, the 'Cyprus Solution' instead of the 'Cyprus Conflict'. There are variations on this theme. One is to legalize two separate republics on the island; the other one is to have two states federated under a 'weak' central government. While the Cypriot Turks might find such solutions preferable, emotional attitudes, especially of the Cypriot Greeks, as we mentioned earlier, constitute obstacles. Besides, Cypriot Greeks fear the maintenance of the Turkish military on the island. They think that the Turks, one day, may conquer the whole island. On the other hand, the Cypriot Turks fear that, without the Turkish military and guarantee of protection, they will be once more swallowed up by the Cypriot Greeks who, at the present, have armed themselves with modern weaponry. If a federation is to be accepted, the Greeks want a 'strong' central government dominated by Greeks.

Taking into consideration the history of the Turkish-Greek relationship and the shared mental representations attached to it, we conclude that a political solution, under the existing reality on the island, should be psychologically sound. A 'forced' togetherness may again bring bloodshed. Both sides should have a 'border' in order to deal with their anxiety about identity and physical and psychological security. In this way, we think that what Cypriot Turks prefer is the psychologically sound solution. In spite of this, the legal/political idea that one Cyprus exists won new support with the election of Boutros Boutros-Ghali as the Secretary General of the United Nations. When Javier Perez de Cuellar was the Secretary General of the United Nations, he and other United Nations officials were very involved with the Cyprus situation. They were frustrated in their efforts and concerned with the expense of keeping a United Nations force on the island year after year. However, Javier Perez de Cuellar seemed to understand well the complexities between the 'real world' and psychological issues. Boutros Boutros-Ghali seems to believe that his office may play a more direct, forceful, and personal role in the world issues. When he became the Secretary General, he wanted to utilize power politics and exert pressure on both George Vassiliou, the president of Cyprus (in reality, the Greek side) and Rauf Denktaş, the president of the Turkish side. A map was presented to them showing how the island should be divided between the Greeks and the Turks. This map was known as a 'non-map', since it was originally discussed in an unofficial way. According to this map, the Cypriot Turks were asked to make significant concessions on the issue of territory and displaced persons. The Greeks had an emotional desire to return to their homes. But, the Turks felt that the territorial and displaced person issues were the outcome and symptoms of the conflict of 'togetherness'; they were not the primary issues under consideration but the secondary ones.

Boutros Boutros-Ghali's ill treatment of President Denktaş in the autumn of 1992 at the United Nations is no longer a secret. Boutros Boutros-Ghali stated that his personal feelings would not deter him from behaving in a politically appropriate manner. His power politics, however, were based on a solution which considered Cyprus, as a member of the United Nations, as a single entity. The United Nations had to protect its child, Cyprus, and bring the island back, as much as possible, to a situation which existed at the time of the 'Republic of Cyprus' birth in 1960. Accordingly, Boutros Boutros-Ghali supported Resolution No. 789 through the Security Council in November of 1992. This created a shock reaction among the Turks. Denktaş declared that he could not go along with such a resolution (which *inter alia* stressed single sovereignty and single citizenship within the Republic of Cyprus, territorial changes, and freedom for Cypriot Greeks to return to the North) and the Turkish government led by Süleyman Demirel, publicly supported Denktaş, It looked like another crisis was in the making. In early 1993, however, Vassiliou, who had campaigned feverishly for years in Europe, the United States, and elsewhere to reverse the situation on Cyprus, lost the election on the Greek side by about two thousand votes to Glafkos Clerides. Clerides, under the influence of the Rightist elements, refused to recognize Resolution 789. Principally the Right wanted absolute recognition of the Greek Cypriots' rights to return to their home, to own property and to move freely between the two communities. They also wanted the return of Turkish settlers to the North and the withdrawal of Turkish troops.

One of the first to congratulate Clerides was Denktaş. He informed

Clerides that he was ready to meet with him and 'work very hard to see whether there is any base on which a joint future Cyprus can be established'. The world waits to see if two 'old friends', Clerides and Denktaş, can develop a creative solution for the Cyprus problem.

We have presented the Cyprus problem not as an isolated issue, but as part of the general Turkish-Greek relationship. A workable 'togetherness' on the island can be an ideal model for the future interactions between Turkey and Greece. As the world began to change drastically in the late 1980s, parallel to the negotiations between Cypriot Turks and Cypriot Greeks, there were increased discussions and political activities between the leaders of Turkey and Greece, which we discuss in the next chapter.

|15|

Davos and Beyond

Aghast at the possibility that minor confrontations in the Aegean and concerns over Cyprus might have led to war, both the Turks and the Greeks were motivated to try to improve relations. In January 1988 the then Turkish Prime Minister, Turgut Özal, and the then Greek Prime Minister, George Papandreou, met in Davos, Switzerland. They met again in March 1988. In May of the same year Özal visited Greece, the first time a Turkish Prime Minister had done so in thirty-five years. Davos became a symbolic term for a process in which the dispute between the Turks and the Greeks had, for the first time, been taken up over an extended period. Along with two summit meetings between the Turkish and Greek leaders, there were minister-level committee gatherings as well.

During his visit to Greece, Özal delivered a psychologically-informed speech. He spoke of the history of the two nations, their historical grievances, and the era of co-operation under Atatürk and Venizelos. Özal said:

> Both nations have a millenium-long common history. We have had good and bad times. Alongside our cultural differences have emerged profound common characteristics rising out of a long interactive process. Our relationship has been passionate and volatile, and this has had as much to do with the founding of lasting friendship on the grounds of common cultural aspects and common memories of peaceful times as with hostile relations based on cultural differences and dark periods. Our disappointments can be as influential as our mutual affection, and can lead our two countries to extreme reactions. The mutual sympathy we feel in times of peace can become enmity because of some insignificant incident. We can fly over the peak of euphoria out of the abyss of struggle. It is not very easy to establish

stable relationships on this sort of historical past.

The Turkish Prime Minister also stated his feeling that both the Turks and the Greeks share the ideal of creating a new Turkey and a new Greece which have solved their problems and done away with the anomaly of being friends as individuals and enemies as states. Özal's speech was intended to extend an olive branch to Greece.

The Davos process constituted an unconventional approach to conflict resolution by attempting to solve legal and political issues in an atmosphere of mutual trust. In this sense their dialogue can be characterized as a form of *track two diplomacy* even though the participants were official diplomats.[269] In the initial stages this process resembled the Camp David meetings engaged in by Jimmy Carter, Anwar Sadat, and Menachem Begin, but it only issued a series of meetings rather than an accord.

Initially, the Davos process promised some success. For example, Turkey released property assets of Greek nationals who had left Istanbul during the Cyprus crises, and Greece recognized the association agreement between Turkey and the EC. In the long run, however, this process did not bring about the hoped-for results. Beyond the real world issues, the Turks believe that Davos failed because Greek enmity towards them, consciously and unconsciously, had already been adopted by every segment of the Greek population and had become an autonomous psychological force.

On their part, the Turks saw in the Davos process a three-pronged attack by the Greeks. First, influential sections of the Greek Foreign Ministry objected to, and still object to, any agreement that concerns the continental shelf, a dispute which should be referred to the International Court of Justice in the Hague. Second, in their view, until Turkey consented to and accepted the basic tenets of the Greek position with regard to Cyprus, co-operation with Turkey in other fields was not only futile but harmful as well. In this regard, the Greek political opposition criticized the fact that the Davos process did not include the Cyprus problem. Third, the Greek press was critical of the government for agreeing to the initial dialogue without getting anything in return. The Greek government had set a precondition to any talks—that Turkish troops must either withdraw unconditionally from Cyprus or that a meaningful gesture should be made by allowing the return of Cypriot Greeks to the currently uninhabited Varosha district of Famagusta. This gesture had to be made prior to a solution of the Cyprus problem and before any dialogue would be entertained. This implied that the Greeks demanded that a 'solution' to the Cyprus problem be found before an agreement could be reached on any other outstanding bilateral issues or a programme of economic co-operation. For the Turks, making such a gesture meant that they accepted the view that the Greeks were right, and they were wrong. Furthermore, it was not certain whether the Greeks, once having acknowledged this gesture, would then request further gestures with respect to other problems.

Eventually, the attitudes attributed to the Greeks by the Turks came to dominate the Greek position in the Davos process. Three committees had been organized to facilitate the discussions—the political, co-operation, and military-civilian committees. Two meetings of the political committee failed to define the problems besetting the Turkish-Greek relationship. The Greek side retreated from the position it had held in Davos and insisted on the existence of only one problem—the continental shelf. In a Catch-22 situation the co-operation committee did not make any progress, for it awaited the outcome of the work of the political committee. The only successful result was achieved by the military-civilian committee, which proposed and adopted confidence-building measures confined mostly to military exercises. They would be conducted during tourist off-seasons.

Subsequently, Papandreou became ill and underwent surgery in the second half of 1988. This resulted in the loss of momentum despite a hasty visit by Özal to Athens in June. Three consecutive general election campaigns in Greece led to the virtual abandonment of the Davos process.

After a period of stagnation in the process that lasted a year and a half, the new government formed in Athens by Constantine Mitsotakis in April 1990 gave top priority to improving relations with the United States and the EC. It also established *de jure* relations with Israel and signed a Defense Co-operation Agreement with the United States, thus putting an end to the uncertainties over the future of the American bases in Greece. Mr. Mitsotakis travelled extensively in the EC countries and bolstered Greece's image as a good member.

In addition, he embarked on an important programme to stabilize Greece's finances aimed at the reduction of inflation, the re-establishment of growth by means of the transformation of the economy on a free market basis, and the re-establishment of discipline in the labour force. In these efforts he enjoyed both the moral and material support of the EC.

While Greece was waging this public relations campaign, Europe entered a phase of euphoria brought about by the collapse of the Berlin Wall and the subsequent disintegration of Communism in eastern Europe and in the Baltic republics. The Soviet Union fell into disarray as democracy won the day. The necessity for NATO was being questioned, and western European public opinion began to express doubts about the strategic importance of Turkey in this changing geopolitical environment.

At this juncture, the Greek government altered its position on dialogue with Turkey. At first Mitsotakis declared that Greece would be ready to take up all questions with Turkey, while giving Cyprus priority. The Turks did not understand that this was, in reality, an impediment. Later on, the Greek position underwent further changes, and Cyprus became a precondition to dialogue. In the meantime, Mitsotakis had succeeded in linking progress on the Cyprus problem with the issue of Turkey's entry into the EC.[270] In almost all the forums of western Europe there was an increase in the critical tone being expressed about Turkey's 'intransigence' over the Cyprus issue. Gradually the agenda for dialogue between Greece and Turkey was reduced to this single issue. In reaction, Turkey began to take a more active interest in the conditions of the Turkish minority in western Thrace which emerged as a deepening problem after 29 January 1990 when Greek mobs physically attacked some forty Turks and destroyed two hundred shops in front of the Greek police, who had turned the other way.

The Gulf War
Assistance in breaking the downward spiral in Turkey's external relations came from an unexpected source, Iraq. With Iraq's invasion of Kuwait on 2 August 1990 the importance of Turkey was rediscovered by the West. Turgut Özal, who had made the transition from prime minister to president, resolutely aligned Turkey with the West, an act that was more appreciated abroad, especially in the United States, than at home. Pressure on Turkey with respect to Cyprus withered. This time it was Greece's turn to feel discomfited in the face of Turkey's growing influence and prestige.

Desert Storm wrote a swift ending to Iraq's adventure in Kuwait. Özal's victories in foreign affairs did not shield him, however, from internal discontent. His party was turned out in the next election largely on its failure to achieve the economic miracles it had promised. While Özal remained president, the government was transferred to a new coalition headed by the new Prime Minister, Süleyman Demirel.

Turkic Republics

This successor government was faced with another challenge, the creation of five independent Turkic republics in former Soviet Central Asia and the Caucasus. Republican Turkish foreign policy had been based on non-involvement in the affairs of Turks outside the boundaries of the Turkish state. This now gave way, in the face of the interests and needs of these new republics for closer ties with Turkey. They look upon Turkey as a model for successful reform that has eventuated in democracy, secularism, and a free market economy. A spree of exchanges at all levels began to take place between Turkey and the five republics. Turkish television began to beam its broadcasts to Azerbaijan and Central Asia to serve as a window on to the external world for them. Turkey also granted ten thousand scholarships to students in the republics for study at university level in Turkey.

One of the major underlying issues in all this activity is the future of Iranian-style fundamentalism in this new arena. The West, Turkey, the Central Asian Republics, and Azerbaijan see Turkish-style secularism as a strong bulwark against the spread of fundamentalism. Islamic fundamentalism as a concept bids fair to become the 'new enemy' of the West, replacing the void left by Communism's collapse. As Volkan has demonstrated, the need to have enemies and allies is compelling, almost inherent.[271] Turkey's emergence as a strong factor in Central Asia, together with her active role in seeking a settlement to the Armenian-Azerbaijani conflicts has led to a re-evaluation of Turkey's importance in, and to, the West. Russia's recent revival of interest in the former republics of the Soviet Union characterized as the 'Near Abroad' indicates that it will not be as easy a matter as originally thought for Turkey to insinuate herself into the affairs of those republics. Nevertheless, Turkey continues to be a vital part of western thinking in the global context.

Recent Problems

After the collapse of Communism and the Gulf War, the new

Süleyman Demirel-Erdal İnönü (the son of the late İsmet İnönü) coalition government moved towards positioning Turkey as a leader in that part of the world. But one big issue had to be faced. The Gulf War and the events in Iraq following this war brought international attention to the plight of the Iraqi Kurds as Turkey was instrumental in helping the Kurds in northern Iraq. However, there is a large Kurdish ethnic group living in Turkey. The Kurdish Workers' Party (PKK) which wages a terrorist war aims at independence for the Kurds in Turkey. Since Turks and Kurds have lived 'together' for nine hundred years, sorting out the separatist movement will be extremely difficult. It has already evolved into a major problem which will preoccupy Turkey for years to come.

Meanwhile, events in the former Yugoslavia have begun to worry the Greeks as they perceive a Slavic plot against them. Because of this, the Greeks have a new obsession, Macedonia. The Macedonia that Tito created for Yugoslavia in 1944 does not have the same location as the Kingdom of Macedonia of the fourth century BC. After the disintegration of Yugoslavia, all the new republics were recognized by EC members except Macedonia. The Greeks (according to the polls, ninety-eight per cent of them) wish to block the recognition of Macedonia on the grounds that the very name of this republic constitutes a territorial threat to the region of Greece which bears the same name. This has become such an emotional issue that Greece has rebuffed other members of the European Community.

In light of all these happenings, the United Nations has once again taken up the Cyprus issue, seeking to bring the Cypriot Turks and Cypriot Greeks together to find a solution to the Cyprus problem. There is much diplomatic activity, but even if the Cypriots find a solution, the other Turkish-Greek conflicts will not simply evaporate, in spite of Mitsotakis' proclamation in the summer of 1992 that clouds are massing on Greece's northern borders and that 'we do not face a threat from the East'. It has been over three decades since the Turks and Greeks first began to live with the problems concerning Cyprus and the Aegean. Going from one crisis to another has been a recent, real-world history of these two countries. Despite serving as NATO members, they have come to the brink of war four times over Cyprus (1963, 1964, 1967, and 1974) and once more in 1987 over the Aegean. Their military aircraft encounter each other often in Aegean airspace, as they train, patrol, identify, intercept, and even engage in dry-run dogfights.

The Turkish president, Turgut Özal died suddenly in April 1993. More than anyone, he had moved Turkey more and more away from the economic philosophy of state interventionism of the earlier republican period and brought her name forcefully into the international arena during the Gulf War. A month before Özal's death, at a meeting in Ankara, each Turkic republic (Azerbaijan, Kazakhstan, Kirghizia, Turkmenistan, and Uzbekistan) agreed to prepare the replacement of their Cyrillic alphabet with a new Turkish alphabet of thirty-four letters. It is estimated that Turkish, spoken in different dialects, is the fifth most widely used language in the world. The Turkic republics, and Turkey also, decided to establish a permanent 'Alphabet-Spelling Expert Working Group' to solve problems and confusion that might emerge from different spellings among dialects. Özal was instrumental in evolving a destiny for Turkey as a mentor for the Turkic republics. Süleyman Demirel is now the new president of Turkey. Although no drastic changes are expected in Turkey's international politics, in June, 1993, Tansu Çiller, a United States' educated former economics professor, became the country's first female prime minister and declared that this event has changed Turkey's history. Change there has been, but not necessarily for the better. Inflation continued to run rampant and the Turkish lira lost more than half its value in a few months, declining from 16,000 to the dollar in December, 1993 to over 40,000 in February, 1994. Çiller sought new loans hurriedly from the World Bank and in Washington to shore up the lira, but her political fortunes, already shaken by terrorism in southeastern Turkey, appear threatened. She was not helped by the unexpected return to power in Greece of Andreas Papandreou in October, 1993. He had been driven from office while Prime Minister by a combination of financial and sexual scandals in 1989. Faced by a sudden decline in political support, the Conservative Party Prime Minister Constantine Mitsatakis called for new elections to be held on 10 October 1993. Papandreou's Socialist Party scored a stunning victory. Since his return to power Papandreou has sought to further his popularity by stirring up the ingrained fears of Turkey in relation to the troubles in the Balkans and the creation of the new republic of Macedonia which seceded from Yugoslavia. Both Papandreou and Çiller continue to be faced by many internal and external problems.

| 16 |

Symptoms of Obsession

In the winter of 1992 at a meeting in the United States, Dr. Volkan met a Greek psychoanalytic colleague whom he had not seen for some years. Both men had been interested in similar clinical topics and had, in the past, participated in professional discussions. Upon greeting this colleague, Dr. Volkan asked how life in Athens had been. The Greek quickly responded: 'We are awaiting an invasion by the Turks, but we will continue to keep them out of the EC.' Dr. Volkan, expecting the usual social response to his question, was stunned with a sudden understanding that his Greek colleague was deadly serious in his remarks. The Athenian, in this unexpected encounter with another psychoanalyst whom he knew to be of Turkish origin, gave a clue to his preoccupation with the Turks, as if experiencing a slip of the tongue. What we want to illustrate in this chapter is that the Greek psychoanalyst's remarks about the Turks are not just the reflection of one individual's personal concerns. He expressed a *shared* group phenomenon. It appears to us that sometimes this group phenomenon reaches almost bizarre proportions.

In this instance an expectation of invasion by the Turks is openly discussed by a Greek. The Foundation for Defence and Foreign Policy, a Greek think-tank partly funded by the government, is staffed with experts who see and monitor sinister Turkish designs on Greece. In late March 1992 when the Turkish government had its hands full with PKK terrorism and the Azerbaijani-Armenian conflict, Greek Foreign Minister Andonis Samaras was quick to speak of the premeditated Turkish pressures on Greece through the encirclement of his country by the Muslims in the Balkans, in Bosnia-Herzegovina, Albania, Macedonia, Kosova, Bavaria, as well as western Thrace

(Greece). In a similar vein Thanos Veremis, the director of the think-tank, stated: 'Turkey plans to annex Western Thrace in the long run.'[272] The average Greek citizen, who may not be aware of the intricacies of international law, tends to take for granted the concept, put forward by his own governmental representatives, of Turkey's expansionist desires. This fantasy of a deep-seated Turkish desire for expansion is widely held throughout the Greek government. Since Turkey's 1974 military intervention in Cyprus and the threat of force in case Greece unilaterally extends the breath of its continental shelf from six to twelve miles—which would virtually turn the Aegean Sea into a Greek lake—Greek public opinion is more and more inclined towards accepting Turkey's expansionist designs. Greece's allocation of funds for its military before the events in the former Yugoslavia is ten to eleven per cent of its total budget. This is one of the highest among all nations. The Turkish military only allocates five to seven per cent to its military despite the fact that extremely volatile and unstable Middle East and Caucasian regions are Turkey's neighbours.

It appears that, in recent years, Greeks await, seemingly daily, a pre-emptive Turkish military attack. This is reflected in such public pronouncements as that made by Alekos Filippopoulos:

> Turgut Özal wishes to make the city Istanbul a province as it was during the Ottoman Empire. Consequently, its boundaries will reach Greece.

> We pursued a policy of saints against Turkey. It has failed. Let us make demands. Let us forbid hesitations on our frontiers.

> The future of this homeland is apparently difficult ... If Greeks accepted abandoning lands of their forefathers without reaction, and if politicians concealed from the people the gravity of the danger ... it would mean that the bells of history were ringing for the last time ... The only way out is to elabourate a dynamic, serious national strategy. If we fail in this national task, it would be difficult to belie those who emphasize that our national existence is crumbling.[273]

People in Greece claim that at times false alarms trigger a rush to the shops for war-time provisions, especially when tension runs high in bilateral relations. Even tourists who visit Greece are constantly reminded of the past, present, and future evil deeds of 'bad Turks'. While this shared mood in Greece is known to Turkish diplomats who work in the field of Turkish-Greek relations, the average Turk has no idea about it, and he, in turn, is *not* obsessed with the Greeks. The

Turks' preoccupation with the Greeks remains pale in comparison to that of Greeks with the Turks.

The Media

Content analysis research commissioned by the Aegean Foundation in 1987 on reports and editorials in the Greek press on Turkey, in general, and on Turkish-Greek relations, in particular, indicated that such material appeared in the Greek press more frequently than any other topic. In Turkey, on the other hand, such material on Turkish-Greek relations ranked only *sixteenth* in the Turkish press.

Two years later another survey, sponsored this time by the Turkish government, had similar findings. Between 1 September and 31 December 1989 twelve major Greek newspapers with ties to various political parties were examined with respect to their contents. The nature of their contents was then compared with the news items in major Turkish newspapers published in the same time frame. This investigation demonstrated that the 'preoccupation' of the Turkish press with Greece was one-third the magnitude of that observable in the Greek press on Turkish matters. Furthermore, when the length of all the news items about Turkey in the Greek press was compared to that about Greece in the Turkish press, the Greek press devoted six times more space than did their Turkish counterparts.

Polls were also used to measure this sense of 'preoccupation'. In November 1989 PIAR and ICAP, two major public relations firms from Turkey and Greece, respectively, carried out a joint poll. They found, just as one might expect, that both sides mistrust each other, with eighty-one per cent of the Greeks and seventy-three per cent of the Turks suspicious of the other. Zatos mentions that Greeks, in general, dismiss statistics.[274] Most likely, statistics change according to the last shared emotional event to which people respond. What is more interesting than the results of the polls, therefore, is the analysis of the content of Greek and Turkish news media, including books and newspapers.

Embodied in the Greek news media is the image of Turkey as the enemy *par excellence*. Turkey is described as a large, undemocratic, aggressive power disrespectful of human rights. Turkey is inclined to torture and genocide and, is now, as in the past, barbaric and uncivilized. In short, Turkey is the source of almost all the evil in the world. Greece, on the other hand, is described as totally antithetical to

Turkey. The Greeks are characterized as being small, innocent, and victims who are brave and civilized Christians.

Several typical examples will convey the flavour of the Greek press' reporting on Turkey. K. Kolmer, writing in the Greek daily *Mesimvrini* said: 'Turkey is an economically backward, Asiatic, Moslem country which has no Western characteristics. In other words, she lacks Greco-Roman culture, Christian traditions, and is alien to democratic ideology of the West. For example, the Turkish male is superior to the Turkish female. Moreover, the army plays an important role in the country's politics ... Turgut Özal has been trying to introduce a Western way of life into the country. But this goes beyond the capacity of the Turkish people.'[275]

About a week later the headline in *Kathimerini* for an article by Akis Kosonas blared: 'Expansionist Recklessness of the Neighbouring Country (Turkey)'. The text suggested that Greece should militarize the Aegean islands against the Turks. According to Akis Kosanas, Turks consider Greeks' good intentions as concessions.[276] On 7 January 1991 State Minister Miltiadis Evert, in an interview given to Radio Sky, likened Muslims to snakes. As it was reported in *Ta Nea*, of 8 January, Miltiadis said: 'As I pointed out before on our northern frontiers, a snake is growing. It is Islam, encouraged by Pan-Turkism.' Later, on 29 April 1991, in *Apoyematini* Titos Athanasiadis, commenting on the scene in the Balkans, called Islam a 'viper'.[277] He was followed on 22 May 1991 by Hristos Panayiotopoulos who wrote an article in the Greek weekly *ENA* under the title 'The Empire of Hallucinations', saying: 'Under the pretext of protecting the Muslim populations in the region (the Balkans) the hallucination of the Ottoman Empire is being revived.'[278] *Rizospastis*, on 11 March 1991 referred to a statement by Özal, in which the Turkish president had stated that Turks and Greeks had lived together for four hundred years in harmony, and commented: 'Turkey imagines the resurrection of the Ottoman Empire. Özal is the best representative of this Turkish "*Megali Idea*".'

It should also be noted that while the Turks are portrayed in the Greek press as barbaric, there is a tendency to see Turkey as 'father' (or male) and Greece as 'mother' (or female).[279] For example, on 4-5 June 1989 in the *Athens News* this identification process was in full view. 'The Davos spirit is growing old, but it has not yet died. *Mother Greece* is gently taking care of it, while *Father Turkey* is doing all to exterminate it ' [italics added].[280]

In the above example, Father Turkey is charged with trying to kill off the Davos spirit. The Greeks usually accuse Father Turkey of raping Mother Greece—the echo of the perception of what Mehmet the Conqueror did in 1453 is still heard. The mental representation of the fall of Constantinople, we believe, explains certain seemingly bizarre incidents. For example, during the October 1989 World Conference of Psychiatry which was held in Athens, a high-level Turkish political figure received a postcard from two Greek women attending this conference. The postcard depicted a rape scene; on it the women wrote: 'The Greek people gave you this pleasure (of rape) in 1897, 1922, and 1974. ... We hope, however, that you will ... appreciate the eternal existence of the Greek nation and her contributions to civilization and will never again claim our land or continental shelf.' Ambassador Duntas epitomized this perspective in a comment at a conference held at the University of Dimokritos in Komotini on 14 March 1991: 'I do not say that warplanes of the Turkish Air Force violate our airspace. I say they rape it. And I use this word deliberately.'

Often the Greek press reports some fantastic commentaries on Turks or Turkey. For example, they report how Greek young men were taken off Cyprus after Turkey's intervention there in 1974 and are kept in mainland Turkey by force. These young men were married off to Turkish women. In addition, the Greek press often employs the first person plural, 'we', 'our side', etc., in talking about Greece's problems with Turkey, indicating thereby its total identification with the Greek nation and people. Furthermore, the Greek press refers to the other side as a monolithic element, 'the Turks' and 'Turkey'. Another feature of the Greek press is the fact that all elements within it take similar stands on what they call 'national themes', regardless of the political leanings of the particular paper. Moderate treatment of the Turks and any criticism of the Greek government's foreign policy may result in an accusation of high treason, which has occurred in the past. Even such a famous personality as composer and Minister without Portfolio Mikis Theodorakis has been accused of high treason for weakening Greek positions on 'national themes'. Greek journalists Lianni Kanelli and Andreas Politakis (president of the Abdi İpekçi Prize named after the Turkish journalist who promoted Turco-Greek friendship but who was assassinated in the mid-1970s for his liberal views) have been accused by the Greek press of high treason for treating the Turks with moderation. Journalistic criticism of the Greek government, therefore, is largely confined to such areas as the government's lack of toughness and determination with respect to Turkey, the relative absence of a long-term strategy, and the need to shore up national unity. The press constantly calls for a more energetic response to Turkey, more active efforts to influence the West in adopting a more pro-Greek stance, and the development of a more resolute and long-term strategy.

Similar events are observed in Cyprus. In November, 1992, around the time when the Cypriot Turkish and Greek leaders were involved in intense discussion at the United Nations on the future of the island as an independent entity, a huge uproar occurred in the Cypriot Greek press. The fuss was about the opening ceremony of the University of Cyprus in the Greek sector. A vitriolic attack against Nelly Tsouyiopoulos, the chairperson of the University Interim Governing Committee, was launched in the Greek press, especially the right-wing papers, because she had ignored the presence of the Greek Education undersecretary at the ceremony and had not provided proper seating for several important Greek academic representatives. Furthermore, the Greek Archbishop had not been asked to bless the university campus. Nelly Tsouyiopoulos was 'burned at the stake' for failing to protect Hellenism and Greco-Christian ideals.

In reality, this university had been envisaged as an academic institution. But someone discovered a book in the Turkish Studies Department which includes two maps depicting a 'divided' Cyprus. Apparently, the book was used in Germany to teach Turkish students about their roots, and the maps were intended to show the students that part of Cyprus is Turkish. However, to find this book in a Cypriot Greek academic institution was enough, along with the actions of Nelly Tsouyiopoulos at the opening ceremony, to preoccupy the Cypriot Greek press for many days.

Another feature of Greece's attitude towards Turkey is apparent in her constant monitoring of Western public opinion, making it seem as though Greece acts in ways calculated to gain Western approval. While it is common for countries to do this at moments of concentrated international media coverage, Turkey complains that Greece is extreme in the manner in which her public actions are committed to currying favour in the West. In addition, with respect to their bilateral relations with Turkey, the Greeks always seek to portray themselves as the injured party who is always in the right. This attitude was summed up in a Statement in *Ethnos* (31 May 1991): 'It is a wonderful feeling always to be right. But it is more important to make one's rightness acknowledged by others.'[281]

Obviously, the Greek public constitutes a great market for this sort of yellow, or more aptly, blue and white journalism. The Turkish public, on the other hand, is mostly indifferent to this situation as they are mostly uninformed about every trivial, insignificant development in Turkish-Greek relations. The Turkish press tends to concentrate on the news of current popular interest. Turkish-Greek relations, for the most part, are not high on the popularity chart. However, this does not hold true for the Cypriot Turkish press. In Cyprus there are daily reports on political processes dealing with the conflict. Turks publish the summaries of the Greek editorials and news, and the Greeks do the same with the Turkish press. Living on the same island, each side can watch both Turkish and Greek television. On Cyprus there is an active propaganda war.

Diplomatic Contacts
Two high-level Turkish diplomats who have been closely involved in dealing with present Turkish-Greek disputes and in their analysis, told us independently how the Greeks unanimously praise Turkish diplomacy and the long-term planning embodied in Turkish foreign policy. Greeks consider the conduct of Turkish foreign policy, based on a well-defined and immutable strategy, to be among the best in the world. One of these diplomats told us that whenever he travels to Greece to attend a multi-national meeting he 'always feels as though the Greeks treated (him) as if (he) was the most important person there. [He] was given precedence over the diplomats from other countries'.

A closer look at this phenomenon, however, suggests that there may be a correlation between the Greeks' praise of Turkish diplomacy and their obsession with 'the Greek Destiny', that is, the acceptance by Greeks of suffering as being an inheritance from all of their past 'chosen traumas' in history and, therefore, an inseparable part of life. In turn, this may have created 'the innate magnanimity and kindness in the Greek soul'.[282] In this case, if Turkish diplomacy is stable and good, the Turks will continue a policy of victimizing the Greeks. Just as Dr. Volkan's Greek psychoanalytic colleague expressed it, there does exist the feared expectation of a Turkish 'invasion'. The diplomats who spoke with us also describe how statements of Turkish politicians are carefully studied by the Greeks at all times, and all actions and reactions of Turkey are almost invariably denounced by Greece as provocations. One of the diplomats added: 'We cannot make any innocent remarks or even peaceful overtures without the Greeks finding some sort of overt aggression or provocation in them.' Under these conditions, the Turks believe that it is very difficult, in fact, impossible to have effective negotiations with the Greeks.

It seems to us that such highly emotionally-charged Greek public opinion on 'national themes' makes it extremely difficult for Greek politicians to move away from such emotional attitudes and the shared mood in the country. At the same time, the Greek politician is involved in politics that mobilizes people around him and around the same 'national themes'. This is not only true of their relations with Turkey but with other neighbours as well. Greece set as a precondition for recognition of Macedonia that the republic change its name. The entire Greek political class and people supported this unheard of demand to the consternation of Greece's friends and allies. In the light of such obtuse political behaviour, a former Greek deputy minister's suggestion in 1988 that an institute be established for the study of Turkey, since many Greeks feel it is impossible to understand the Turks, appears to miss the point. In fact, the number of existing institutes for Turkish studies in Greece is impressive, whereas, there is not a single institute in Turkey for Greek studies.

Contacts Among Citizens

While our focus has been on group phenomena and obsessions, we should note that when Turks and Greeks get together as individuals they find a great deal to share, such as food and music, so that the path to becoming good friends is facilitated. When a Turk and a Greek get to know each other on a personal level, usually in a 'neutral' country, they may notice that the 'other' is not a suitable target for their projections. Thus, they may focus on their similarities and become friends. Group psychology is different from individual psychology. When large groups interact, the 'reality testing' of the members about their projections and other shared mental mechanisms becomes blurred.

In discussing their lives in Greece, many Turks who have lived in Greece for long periods of time note that Greek citizens try to avoid discussing Greek-Turkish matters with Turks in both public and private. One may explain it away as prudence on the Greeks' part in order to avoid unnecessary quarrels. Those Turks whom we interviewed had the impression, however, that the Greeks did not want to find out directly what the Turks thought of Greek-Turkish problems. We believe that this is due to the group pressure on Greeks to keep the Turks as suitable reservoirs for projections. Friendships become more comfortable with the utilization of avoidance. As indicated earlier, the Greek press does not properly reflect Turkish views either. As a result of a lack of sufficient contact between both people and ideas, Greeks come to believe in what they themselves say. Their arguments gradually become severed from the Turkish reality while at the same time becoming intensified emotionally.

Often, casual meetings between Turks and Greeks have been affected by political obstacles. The Turkish government in 1984 took unilateral action against this by lifting visa restrictions on Greeks. Since then, however, some influential circles among Greek public opinion makers have been trying vigorously to restrict the number of Greek tourists travelling to Turkey. They accuse 'Turkey-goers' of spending scarce hard currency in an enemy country thereby contributing to its potential war effort. They are portrayed as harming their own country for the sake of some inexpensive leather goods or other similar items. When Turkey eased visa restrictions, the Greek government responded to these efforts by reducing the work hours of customs officials at some border points and tried to impose a tax on those Greeks who travelled to Turkey more than once or twice a year. Tourists from both sides of the border, however, continued to cross over. But then a tragic event occurred that once more inflamed emotions.

In 1991 a tourist bus was set on fire in Istanbul tragically killing twenty-five Greeks. This event was sufficient to 'concretize' in the Greek mind the savagery they expected from the Turks. The daily newspaper *Rizospastis* referred to the event as a 'genocide'. Upon investigation, it turned out that the criminal, who also died in the fire, was a mentally ill Turk who had been released from a mental hospital the day before. At a certain level, however, we think that this man might have 'acted out' the hostile tensions between the two ethnic groups.

'Other-directed' Cultures

In this chapter we have sought to illustrate the general mood of the public and officials in Greece reflective of the Turkish-Greek relationship. Turkish and Greek scholars, as well as investigators from other cultures, have consistently shown that the Turks and the Greeks belong to 'other-directed' cultures: each feels that something out there (for example, an 'out group') continues to frustrate them in spite of constant efforts to strengthen the 'in group' system.[283]

In the Turkish-Greek conflict, Greece is the smaller and weaker party; Greece has a population of ten million, while over fifty-eight million people live in Turkey. Although Greece expanded in the nineteenth and twentieth centuries at the expense of the Ottoman Empire, in 1922 she lost the war with the Turks in the western portion of Asia Minor. This is considered a tragedy in Greece, while for the Turks, the victory led to the foundation of modern Turkey. Moreover, in 1974 Greece remained a passive spectator as Turkish forces intervened militarily in northern Cyprus. It has been our observation that in conflicts between ethnic or national groups, the party which perceives itself as the loser or the victim becomes more obsessed with the opposing party than the opposing party does with the 'loser'.

The Greeks are involved in what Volkan calls 'pre-war rituals' in that seminal dehumanization of the opposite side can be prominently seen.[284] Thus, they call the 'other' snakes or other non-human, degrading terms. This act of dehumanization is usually projected backwards in historic time as well, as is evident in even such a scholarly work as Speros Vyronis' *The Decline of Medieval Hellenism in Asia Minor and the Process of Islamization from the Eleventh through Fifteenth Century*, in which the vocabulary used to describe activity by the Turks consists of terms usually associated with animals and insects.[285] This type of relationship is dominated by excessive polarized images, excessive projections and displacements, and a need to respond in a regressive fashion. These psychological mechanisms are, accordingly, geared more towards fantasy than reality while having more aggressively loaded aims than peaceful objectives.

This chapter offered signs and symptoms of intense, and sometimes malignant, obsessions. The psychology of an 'other-directed' culture coupled with the Greeks being the weaker party does not explain the obsessions adequately. The chosen traumas and chosen glories described in this book provide a foundation for the extremely strong psychological forces in the present Turkish-Greek relationships. The last chapter reviews the psycho-historical and psycho-political causes, and the meaning, of the signs and symptoms in neighbourhood interactions, and the intertwining of influences coming from internal and external worlds.

| 17 |

'Istanbul' not 'Constantinople'

Turkey and Greece have a crucial advantage in keeping peace between them when their situation is compared to the situations of many other states in regional conflicts. This advantage comes from their membership of the same alliance, NATO, but also from their traditional relationships. While this relationship is contaminated with intense psychological processes, its long history provides certain familiarity and caution. Since 1930, Turks and Greeks negotiated and concluded various documents, such as treaties, agreements, conventions, joint communiques, and so on. They have, at least, prevented wars, with the exception of the brief 1974 war on Cyprus which could be considered as a 'displaced war'. It was not a major war between Turkey and Greece; blood was shed on a location which, through the psychological mechanism of displacement, was the focus of a clash between the 'stand-in' parties, while the 'mother' countries remained outside a direct armed struggle.

The Turkish-Greek traditional relationship, however, does not allow a durable settlement between Turkey and Greece. Considering how, throughout world history, important conflicts of sovereignty generally result in war, the maintenance of peace between Turkey and Greece is no meagre success. Presently, drastic events in the surrounding areas—in the former Soviet Union, former Yugoslavia, the Middle East—and Turkey's attempt to emerge as a regional power are constantly influencing the Turkish-Greek relationship. The potential danger of a worsening Turkish-Greek relationship exists. It is, therefore, important that this conflict is studied in such a way that areas not illuminated by the traditional approaches of diplomacy, history, and political science can be examined.

Alongside the traditional and *Realpolitik* considerations in international relationships, there are always obligatory psychological—often unconscious—issues that are, in effect, tainted with irrationality. Economic, political, historical, and military events can, at times, become so psychologized and so 'stubbornly fixed' in the minds of the participants that without an understanding of the large group psychology that contaminates them, it might be impossible to establish newly channelled approaches towards finding solutions. All these factors have contributed to our underlying assumption that large group interactions involve processes, not just spontaneous 'magical' solutions. A more durable settlement between the Turks and the Greeks might not be achieved by 'logical' traditional approaches alone. Their relationship should be looked at through 'a psychological lens'[286] and findings from such a study should be 'aired out', i.e., discussed at conferences and included in art forms, such as novels and the cinema. In short, multiple meanings of events pertaining to both parties should be brought to Turkish and Greek mass consciousness. It is with such a belief that we undertook writing this book.

Throughout this book, while attempting to provide the historical flow of the Turkish-Greek relationship in a condensed form, our focus has been on the illumination of three factors: (1) chosen traumas and glories, (2) leader-follower interactions, and (3) identity problems. While we may be criticized for leaving out many historical events and references to important leaders, we would obviously need more than one volume to cover the details. We have chosen to discuss events and leaders who, in our estimation, have shaped the identities of both sides and their perceptions of the 'other'.

The Greek Identity

Western European nation-states have been products of long internal and international wars which raise national consciousness and bring about emotionally-invested frontiers. The Church and the Inquisition have helped create homogenized cultures by eradicating heresies. Economic development engineered by the bourgeoisie provided a strong network between classes, urban and rural populations, and regions. The Renaissance and the Enlightenment decisively contributed to the transition from feudal to nation-states in that this nationalist movement contained and reduced the power, status, and influence of the church and religion in society. Most western European countries created national churches especially as a result of the Reformation. It took revolutions to establish human rights and freedoms by restricting the absolute power of monarchies. Before the Western European nation-states came into being, the fatherland, the state structure, and the nation had already been created in a long evolutionary process. In contrast, in the Christian areas of the Ottoman Empire, the development of nationalism and the creation of nation-states took a different turn. At the moment of independence, the Balkan Christians belonged to the ecumenic Orthodox Church, which had political and judicial powers over the people transcending cultural and ethnic differences between the Greeks, Bulgarians, Albanians, Slavs, Romanians, and so on. These peoples lived intermingled in territories which were not ethically well-defined and which had no state structures. Those Christian nation-states which were born out of the Ottoman Empire had to fight (1) for independence against a declining imperial country, (2) for redeeming the members of its ethnic groups in the remaining territories of the Empire and in other countries (called irredentism) and (3) for creating a culturally homogeneous people. Certainly, modern Greece was involved in all three steps. Greece's movement in creating a national identity, however, more than the other nation-states which were established in the former Ottoman territories, had another element. The European countries, especially the British, the French, and the Russians, joined hands in 'demanding' and sponsoring the kind of identity modern Greece should have; it should be Hellenic. After their War of Independence, modern Greeks, in fact, embraced Hellenism. After forty years, when the *Megali Idea* became crystallized, they began to incorporate into their Hellenic identity their identity as the heirs of the Byzantine Empire. The modern Greek identity remains as the synthesis of these two elements and includes various chosen glories and chosen traumas.

Hellenism, as a national ideology, initially and essentially was externally-directed. At the time of the Greek War of Independence, this ideology was unrelated to the existing culture of Greece. As they quickly embraced Hellenism, they made it 'intimately personal'[287] and began to identify it in a mystical way that they felt could not be understood even by their Western sponsors. George Evlambios in

1843 stated that foreigners should not attempt the impossible by trying to understand the mysteries of Greekness. Evlambios observed:

> I do not know whether a foreigner can ever assimilate the spirit (*pnevma*) of another people (*laos*) to the point of daring to correct and alter the people's creations, especially when Greeks themselves - born and bred in their fatherland, and in contact from childhood on with their customs and language - do not give themselves such a right.[288]

It is ironic that the Hellenist thesis, although externally directed, should in practice cause the Greeks to be—psychologically speaking—'self-centred' and obsessively differentiated from 'others'. Because Hellenism was an imported ideology and as such facilitated an alien encroachment on highly personal matters of the self and identity, the Greeks, paradoxically, did their best to prevent foreign involvement and preserve their independence in a xenophobic manner.[289]

The embracing Hellenism could be crystallized by developing cultural links to the past. Greek scholars, as well as artists, provided the necessary links in finding a 'continuity' of people living in a span of twenty-five centuries. But the maintenance of Hellenism needed an unconscious group activity: wholesale projection of the old and unwanted Romeic identity which was perceived as oriental, therefore inferior, by the West. The Turks provided a suitable reservoir for the Greeks' massive projections. The Turks remained 'uncivilized', while the Greeks became 'civilized'. Due to the long history of their 'togetherness' and 'cross-identifications', the Greeks had to get rid of the Turk *within* themselves. No one explains this better than the great Greek writer, Nikos Kazantzakis, in his *Report to Greco*. In this book he describes his childhood memories in Crete and states:

> To gain freedom first of all from the Turk, that was the initial step, after that, later, this new struggle began: to gain freedom from the inner Turk—from ignorance, malice and envy, from fear and laziness, from dazzling false ideas, and finally from idols, all of them, even the most revered and beloved ... Overflowing the bounds of Crete and Greece, it (the struggle) raged in all eras and locales and invaded the history of mankind. Battling now were not Crete and Turkey but good and evil, light and darkness, God and the devil. It was always the same battle, the eternal one, and standing always behind the good, behind the light and God, was Crete; behind evil, behind darkness, and the devil, Turkey.[290]

This massive projection caused *Turkokratia*, the Greeks' common history with the Ottoman Turks, to be remembered in a stereotyped way. Our reading of the writings by Greek historians suggested to us that their work was intended to take revenge as much as document history. *Turkokratia* was transformed into a colossal chosen trauma. As the Turks were blamed for any negative perception of the Greeks by the West, it has become difficult for the Greeks to take responsibility for their shortcomings. The projection by a group of its unwanted parts on to some suitable target in order to bolster its own identity is only part of the psychological reaction; there is no guarantee in any case that such projection will continue and not boomerang. There is a need for shared mental activity to secure the stability of mass projections. Therefore, the Greeks continue to be obsessed with the Turks, and as they speak of having been victimized by them, they believe as a group that such victimization will be repeated. The expansionist, irredentist, and aggressive aim of the new Greek state is projected on to the Turks. Thus, the Greeks see Turkey as being governed by its army, and regard negotiation and dialogue with Turkish diplomats as futile—involvement with a powerless wing of the Turkish government.

Greek irredentism started with acceptance by modern Greeks of the Hellenistic thesis. While Hellenism provided a new sense of shared self-esteem and pride, it created a problem: the uncertainty regarding the frontiers of the new state. The ambiguity inherent in Hellenism as a national ideology based on the remotely past data of culture, language, and political configurations was not conducive to the determination of the borders. Moreover, since the Greek Kingdom continued expanding at the cost of the Ottoman Empire, it was politically impossible to set final territorial goals. The ambiguity about borders, we believe, created identity problems and became the fuel for irredentism. Modern Greeks tried to fill the vacuum created by denial of their Romeic identity and by incorporating 'Hellenic territories' and Greek-speaking individuals into the new Greek Kingdom.

As the Hellenic thesis was assimilated, the Greeks went through a process of purification. For example, they cleaned Turkish words and many words of Romeic origin from their language. They went back to the Hellenic source to form a language which was called *katherevousa*.[291] Hellenism is the regeneration of a two and a half millennia old ancient history. Hence, it is greatly dependent on historical memory created by deliberate efforts. This attitude toward history and nation building is not conducive to forgetting the chosen traumas and painful events in recent history. Therefore, the Greeks live in the past as much as in the present and consider the Turks as the ones who always frustrated their legitimate historical rights. The Turks were qualified as aggressive and expansionist even when they defended the regions they had inhabited for four to five centuries as the majority, for the Turks were not entitled to these lands from the Hellenic standpoint of history. In other words, aggressivity and expansionism were, and even now are, attributed to or projected onto the Turks on the grounds that according to Hellenism their holdings are illegitimate. Greek irredentism is rendered totally innocent in this context. Greeks seem to shy away from establishing a link between Greek irredentism and the concept of expansionism, and only feel the pain of deprivation of what is 'rightfully' their own.

After living with Hellenism for about forty years beginning with the Greek War of Independence, the cultural heritage of Byzantium, especially with the words of Spyridon Zambelios and Nikolas G. Politis, slowly entered into the Greek national identity intellectually.[292] It would become an appendix to the fundamentally Hellenic individual and group identity. With this development, further projection of the unwanted aspects of the Romeic identity on the Turks occurred. When the Byzantine culture condensed with the Hellenistic, starting around the 1860s, irredentism and the *Megali Idea* became inseparable. The Greeks, as a group, psychologically reached back to the fall of Constantinople as their prime chosen trauma. Every suffering since then was condensed with the event of 1453 and its mental representation. The inability to mourn the collapse of the Byzantine empire is expressed as a political ideology, found in the *Megali Idea*. It affects the Greeks' international relationships, especially their relationship with Turkey.

The seizure of Constantinople by the youthful and virile Turkish sultan after he opened a hole in the city wall was perceived as a rape, and Turks were considered lustful. The city, which was later named Istanbul, became over time the symbol of a fallen or grieving woman and was so celebrated in folk-songs and poems throughout many centuries. The seeds of the *Megali Idea* came soon after this Turkish conquest. Its ideology calls for the reverse of Eartha Kitt's song and has it 'Constantinople, not Istanbul'. Even today, whenever there are political problems between Turkey and Greece, the Greek press, as well as politicians and military men, often refer to the Turks as 'rapists'.

It proved impossible to fully realize the irredentist aspirations provoked by Hellenism and the *Megali Idea*; thus, Greek nationalism has remained unconsummated, unfinished, and unsuccessful despite its remarkable achievements. The Greeks always seem to gauge their success, not by what they gain, but by the perceived gap between their wished for objectives and reality. Since it is impossible in today's world to reach the 'ultimate borders' of Hellenism, the Greeks appear doomed to have a continuing sense of frustration regarding the present borders of Greece. The fact that the status of air space, territorial waters, and the continental shelf are disputed between Greece and Turkey exacerbate this feeling of frustration. The high number of events to mourn in Greece indicates a more likely preoccupation with chosen traumas than a preoccupation with chosen glories. Repeating mourning ceremonies suggest that attempts at mourning have been ritualized. The group's sense of being victimized prevails and this, paradoxically, supports the group's self-idealization and/or hopes for idealization. Being victimized also strengthens irredentist aspirations, keeps alive the *Megali Idea* and contributes to frustrations.

No clearly recognizable father figure appeared during the Greek War of Independence, although a charismatic leader (as defined by Max Weber) is essential in a time of crisis when a group is modifying or reforming its identity.[293] He confers legitimacy on a move from one shared belief system to another. Although there were Greek heroes during the War—even such foreign ones as Byron—no long-lasting charismatic leadership emerged, though President Ionnes Kapodistirias, who tried to consolidate reforms, was considered such a leader by some. Kapodistirias had been a close adviser to Tsar Alexander I, even acting as a joint Russian Foreign Minister along with Count Nesselrode. The Society of Friends (*Philike Hetaria*) sought to make him their head, but he refused. After falling out with Alexander he spent some time in Switzerland, and then in 1827 he was elected to a seven-year term as president of Greece. His attempts to turn Greece into a democratic, centralized state won the hostility of almost all groups in Greece; he became a hated man. The powers tried to oust him without success. Eventually he was assassinated by the Mavro Michili family, who were important landowners in the Morea.

The Greek War of Independence obviously cannot be reduced to the activities of the *Klephts*, but there is no denying the fact that the *Klephts* play an important part in this struggle. However, their role most likely had an adverse effect on the state structure. The *Klephts* had never really known a central government that was not foreign, physically and psychologically distant, and usually hostile. Koliopoulos states: 'The state of control and manipulated lawlessness demoralized and sapped the strength of the emerging new society. In the long run, that state of affairs did exercise a pernicious influence on both popular attitudes toward the emerging State and the actual functioning of that State.'[294] This is called *palikarism* in Greek politics. Indeed, in many respects *Klephtic*-style warfare survived up to the present; for example, during the Civil War of 1943-1949 they were self-proclaimed 'kings of the mountain' who were clearly more interested in plunder than in national or ideological struggles. Many of these men, such as Bellis, Tzavelas, and Karalivanos, later became resistance heroes. There was still another hero who was called Aris, whose real name was Thanasis Klaras. The role played by EOKA in the Greek Cypriotic struggle for *Enosis* can also be considered as the continuation of this style of warfare.

The story of *Klephts* and the possibility of their identification of the concept of the state with the sultan may explain partly the hostile and ambivalent attitude of Greeks toward the state, but this attitude may have a different cause: the absence of a charismatic leader during and after the War of Independence. At the time of the formation of the new Greek nation-state, the Turkish sultan was still the 'bad father', and since the Greeks had no acknowledged and long-lasting 'good father', they could not establish balance between 'good' and 'bad' and tame their perception of the sultan and his Turkish followers. Here we are not referring to the reality of the sultan and his government being the enemy and their actual wrongdoings. Rather, we are considering the Greeks' shared *psychic reality* about the Ottoman leader. In the long run, the psychic reality which is transmitted from generation to generation is more influential than the external realities in shaping a group's behaviour. We think that the unavailability of a charismatic hero at the time when the new Greek identity was established made it difficult for the Greeks to identify with each other and, in turn, with the leader and his or her aspirations for the group.[295] This situation most likely impeded the reconciliation of the Greek people with their own State which adversely affected their attitude towards political order, morals, and ethics in both domestic and international relations. Thus, it could be possible that the need for mass projections of unwanted parts onto other groups, especially on the Turks, remained most active in order to maintain cohesiveness of the Greek identity.

Hellenism and the *Megali Idea* underwent two catastrophes in this century. The first one occurred in Asia Minor in 1922, and the second one in Cyprus in 1974. In the first instance, the Greeks lost a war; in the second, they avoided a war (between Greece and Turkey proper). Markides suggests that the *Megali Idea* has an 'internal logic' and reinforces the moral foundations upon which traditional institutions, and we can add political institutions, are built.[296] Hellenism and the *Megali Idea* create such a shared emotional attitude and conviction that the Greeks feel entitled to the whole of Cyprus, the air space above the Aegean Sea, the continental shelf, and proprietary rights concerning the use of the word 'Macedonia'.[297] The *Megali Idea* and the idealization of Hellenism, on the one hand, and the psychology of the remaining victims, on the other, are the 'unseen' powers which are imbued in modern Greek group identity, and they complicate political negotiations, create psychological resistances to solutions, and make negotiations with the Turks difficult.

Greek accession to the European Community (EC) membership triggered another mass projection onto Turkey. This time Greece was becoming a truly European country; therefore, she needed to rid herself of all the non-European relics in her shared group identity. In the 1967-1974 Junta Era, Greece's international prestige was at its lowest ebb. The coup engineered by the Greek Junta in Cyprus prompted the Turkish military intervention which, in turn, led to the overthrow of the Junta and the return of democracy in Greece. Greeks then wished to forget the painful recent past. In 1981 when Greece was joining the EC, there was another Junta in power—this time in Turkey. Time was ripe to exploit the situation for foreign policy purposes, but there seemed to be also a psychological mechanism at work. Identifying their Junta with that of the Turks', the Greeks projected the ill feelings related to the repressive Greek military rule onto the Turks.

In 1975 the communists, who had been outlawed and outcast after the civil war, were incorporated into Greek political life. This helped to soften the domestic political polarization in Greece and resulted in withdrawing the old projections from the communists. The withdrawn projections laden with painful memories of the civil war, in turn, reinforced the new projections on to the Turks increasing their negative, brutal, oppressive, undemocratic image. The fact that Papandreou and his socialist party, PASOK, which have suffered most from the Junta, were in power enhanced the density and the scope of this projection.

Upon returning to democracy in 1984, Turkey tried to normalize its relations with the EC and eventually made its application for full membership in 1987. Greece perceived these attempts as against its foreign policy interests. In opposing the development of Turkey's relation with the EC, Greeks emphasized, perhaps more than other Europeans, the non-European character of Turks while highlighting their Muslim religion and 'fundamentalist' tendencies.

The Turkish Identity

Efforts at serious reform in political, cultural, and social areas within the Ottoman Empire go back to the last quarter of the eighteenth century. One crucial landmark of these efforts was the abolition of the Janissary corps in 1826 and attempts at the Turkification of the military at more or less the same time. During the 'longest century' of the Ottoman Empire, the nineteenth century, issues of cultural/social identity were approached in three different ways:

(1) To enlarge the Ottoman identity in all its citizens, regardless of their ethnic or religious adherence. This was unsuccessful since investment in ethnicity or nationalism increased in Europe, and within the Ottoman Empire, after the French Revolution.

(2) To put all Muslims in the empire under the umbrella of Pan-Islamism. Ethnic differences among Muslims precluded the success of Pan-Islam.

(3) To focus on expansion of the Turkish identity. Under this umbrella, Turks, and those who felt as Turks, would be combined. Since there were Turks and their adherents throughout Asia and Europe, the Turkish identity might be expected to have created a mighty political and cultural force.

All three options had one aim in common—to keep the sultan in place and in power. The drastic change involved in establishing a Turkish identity apart from the sultan and Ottoman traditions had to await the end of World War I and the Turkish War of Independence. During this time, Turks had to fight major Christian powers as well as Greeks and the Muslim Arabs in the Middle East. The environment was ready for a cohesive Turkish nation, and this came about under the leadership of Mustafa Kemal (Atatürk).

The modern Turkish identity has seen seventy years of history, revolution, and modification.[298] Atatürk's nationalist policies were predicated upon the concept of the National Pact, the *Misak-i milli*, first enunciated by the Sivas Congress of 1919 and then promulgated by the Ottoman Parliament under the domination of Mustafa Kemal's followers in January 1920. The National Pact in effect stipulated that all the territories of the Ottoman Empire inhabited by a majority of Muslim Turks formed an indivisible whole.

Upon the demise of the Ottoman Empire and the victory of Mustafa Kemal and his nationalists, Turkey was substituted for the Ottoman Empire, and the subsequent Treaty of Lausanne recognized the principles of the National Pact—the sovereignty and indivisibility of the Turkish nation, and the determination by plebiscites of the political future of certain areas of the former empire. In other words, the modern state of Turkey would harbour no irredentist aspirations with respect to former territories of the Ottoman Empire, nor towards territories outside the empire inhabited by Turks, such as Central Asia, with the exception of the Hatay (Alexandretta) which was incorporated into Turkey by means of a plebiscite in 1938. The National Pact basically corresponds to the *de facto* borders of the Ottoman Empire at the time of the Mudros Armistice, which ended the hostilities of World War I. Therefore, its realization did not necessitate the resumption of war against the victors of World War I. It marked the end of the multi-ethnic and multi-religious empire. The Turks who remained outside these borders did not constitute large groups; hence, the liberation of 'unredeemed brethren' was not a cause for concern.

The Ottoman Empire had broken up due to the question of nationalities. The unequivocal character of the new borders was essential to eliminate future wars and to concentrate on the socio-economic and political development of the new Turkey. As a result, the National Pact clearly defined the borders of new Turkey according to which the nationalist forces, under the leadership of Mustafa

Kemal, waged a war of independence. Irredentism and the National Pact were incompatible. Accordingly, the National Pact did not raise the problems that Hellenism had done in Greece. On the contrary, it contributed greatly to the new Turkish identity by distinctly shaping its outer borders.

Although more than ninety-five per cent of the citizens of the Turkish Republic are Muslims, their cohesion is based not on their religion but on their citizenship. This is one of the reasons why the ethnic Kurds, who played an important role in Atatürk's victories during the Turkish War of Independence, were put under the Turkish umbrella. Internal homogeneity was of utmost importance to the Turks. A large part of the population of the new state consisted of those who had been forced out of their centuries old Balkan lands through numerous ethnic purification or cleansing operations similar to those seen in Bosnia and Herzegovina today. The forced exchange of population between Turkey and Greece as envisaged by the Lausanne Treaty left a fairly homogeneous population in the country.

The new Turkish nation was not to be a continuation of Ottomanism; secularism sharply differentiated the Turkish Republic from the Ottoman Empire. During World War I and the Turkish War of Independence, the Turks fought mainly against Europeans. Paradoxically, however, under Atatürk's tutelage, Turkey became engaged in a vigorous process of westernization, and the West was, thus, both 'an enemy' and 'an ideal object'. Large groups in the process of developing a new mass consciousness usually adopt a 'purification policy'. This may include wholesale projection of the group's unwanted parts, and its attempt to cleanse itself from elements contaminated with them.

The Greeks won their independence one hundred years before the Turkish War of Independence and had massively projected, as we noted in the previous section of this chapter, their Romeic/Oriental identity onto the Turks as they evolved in their new Hellenic/Byzantine one. Modern Turkish nationalism evolved without massive projections onto the West. The new leaders of Turkey would not allow the enemy, the West, to become a suitable target for projection since the West was also idealized. Instead, in the initial phase of modern Turkey, Turks underwent a process of differentiating themselves further from the rest of the Islamic world, declaring themselves secular and closer to Western ideals and way of life. They used other

Muslims, notably the Ottomans and the Arabs, rather than Europeans as a reservoir for projections of their unwanted parts. This, of course, caused problems since it disturbed the continuity from past to present. The modern Turk relates to aspects of his past with a certain ambivalence. The westernized revolutionary elite of the new republic called themselves 'enlightened ones' and separated themselves from the traditional and conservative segments of the population. This led to a politically and culturally polarized society. The elite considered Islamic fanaticism as the main cause of the demise of the empire, whereas the conservatives accused the 'enlightened ones' of imitating the West at the expense of the real identity of the people. The ensuing 'identity crisis' took the form of a left-right dichotomy after 1960. This dichotomy, however, gradually lost its impact as a result of democracy. Nevertheless, the recent upsurge of Orthodox Islam among the newly urbanized population is the extension of this problem. The problem of Turkey's 'identity crisis', however, has nothing to do with Turkish-Greek relationships. The Turks' purification process, which was relatively harmless and included no malignant devaluation of others, mainly concerned the elimination of the Arabic and Persian influences in their language; they 'Turkified' many European words, and adopted the Latin alphabet. This, and other measures, such as accepting European criminal and civil laws and changing the dress code, further separated modern Turks from their Ottoman past and from other Islamic countries that continued using Arabic script and Islamic law.

The Turks' view of the Greeks describes their dilemma of having an enemy who is both devalued and idealized. Herkül Millas researched stories, novels, and plays written between 1909 and 1956 by the famous Turkish writer Yakup Kadri Karaosmanoğlu in order to understand the image of the Greek in Turkish literature.[299] The selection of Karaosmanoğlu is a good one. Not only was he an important literary figure but also a politician and a personal friend of both Atatürk and his successor, İnönü. Karaosmanoğlu's writings include references to the Greek invasion of Anatolia and he speaks of irresponsible and murderous Greek soldiers who terrorized the citizenry and dishonoured women. Karaosmanoğlu characterizes the Greek army as an unworthy opponent, the Greek men as greedy and ungrateful and the Greek women as flirtatious. Meanwhile, Karaosmanoğlu is very comfortable in comparing Atatürk to ancient

Greek gods and Atatürk's dining room to a gathering of Socrates.[300]
Unlike Europeans, the Turks, due to their long 'togetherness' with the
Greeks, never experienced the present day Greeks as a continuation of
the ancient ones.

Contrary to the Greek War of Independence, the Turks fought their
war under the indisputable leadership of Mustafa Kemal, an Ottoman
general. Apart from the benefits of a charismatic leadership in the
transition from Empire to nation-state, the War of Independence was
waged by a regular army under his command. The extremely limited
use of irregular forces in this war did not lead afterwards to the
lawlessness which had afflicted the new Greek state and political life.
The Ottoman state structure was transferred almost automatically to the
republic. Turkey has never faced the problem of state-building
experienced by the late-comer Balkan countries to the nation-state era.
Reconciliation of the state with the nation has never been a problem for
Turkey. All in all, the Turkish revolution largely resembled Western
European examples, mentioned earlier, in that the revolution aimed at
removing the monarchy and restricting the scope of religion.

There was a psychological price to be paid for all Atatürk's
innovations and his cultural revolution. Their idealization of Atatürk
and his perception of modern Turkey kept the Turks from grieving
over the loss of their Empire and brought about distancing from
selective aspects of their past. The inevitable psychological need to
integrate the past with the present would assert itself later, with all its
attendant psychological and real-world struggles. At the same time, the
victorious West, which found itself unable to impose its will on
Turkey at the conclusion of World War I, was still saddled with the
centuries-old stereotypes of the Turk.

Just before Atatürk's death, many Jewish scholars and artists
escaping from the Nazis went to Turkey. Most of them eventually
went to other richer countries, such as the United States, but they
contributed substantially to Turkey's westernization. For example,
many German Jewish physicians taught in Turkish medical schools;
German Jewish artists were central in the development of the Turkish
opera and ballet.

When Atatürk died in 1938, his friend, İsmet (İnönü) succeeded
him. We believe that İsmet İnönü was a more thoroughly Western man
in the European sense than Atatürk. Turkish educators began
translating the Western classics as well as ancient Greek writings in a

wholesale way, making them available in the schools at every level. Western culture and values came 'from the top'. Since Atatürk was 'the Eternal Leader' and, accordingly, 'alive', with his charisma still influential in educated circles as well as in public circles in general, İnönü's government found little opposition to the westernization, but unconscious resistance obviously remained among some.

Hottinger describes how Atatürk opened a wedge-shaped path through the thick forest of Turkish politics. During his time, and İnönü's, the end of the wedge 'was so wide that it seemed at first to be clearing the whole of the thicket. In the course of the decades that followed [Atatürk's] death, the broad path narrowed and trees and undergrowth grew tall on both sides'.[301] We agree with Hottinger, however, that the general direction of the path remains, and the Turks can yet advance along it.

Initially, Atatürk's own lonely but grand self was reflected in the new Turkishness. İnönü, having kept his country out of World War II, caused its further isolation and an illusion of greatness that fostered the denial of past losses and present realities. As the influence of the Atatürk-İnönü era weakened, Turks began to see their reality more clearly. However, it was still hard for them to mourn Atatürk, as it was difficult for them to mourn the Empire.

Meanwhile, the world did not stand still (Chapter 15), and external events began to challenge the new Turkishness and the grand loneliness at its core. After the Atatürk and İnönü eras, modern Turkey went through turbulent times due to internal opposing politics and ideologies, and searched for a newer identity. We suspect that attempts at mourning over the lost past identity and adjustment to the real world were among the causes of this turmoil. The exodus of millions of Turkish 'guest workers' to Europe challenged Turkey's self-contained existence. The Turkish reaction to Cyprus challenged emotionally, if not legally, the foundation of *Misak-i Milli* (The National Pact). Turks stressed their legal rights in 'the partition' of Cyprus that assigned Greeks to the south and Turks to the north. In spite of these events, the 'loneliness' lingered on. In 1975, Niyazi Berkes stated:

> Today's Turkey is neither a western nor a Moslem nation; it does not belong to a Christian, socialist, or capitalist community. It is neither Asian nor European.[302]

Berkes spoke about the 'loneliness' of Turkey in respect to its economy, politics, and culture. We believe that to some extent, two decades after Berkes described Turkey, some of the characteristics he attached to Turkey still remain. But Turkey has made great advances to turn this 'loneliness' into a 'uniqueness', as we shall see. Further events in the world forced the Turks to free themselves from some of the outdated original principles of Kemalism. Modification in economic principles and the encouragement of the private sector have tied Turkey more closely to the rest of the world. As mourning over the loss of Atatürk takes place, there has been more investment in the chosen glories and the chosen traumas of the Ottoman period. The external influence most telling in the modification of the present sense of Turkishness, however, is the collapse of the Soviet Union, the emergence of the Turkic Republics in Central Asia and Azerbaijan in the Caucusus, the events in Bosnia-Herzegovina, the burning of the Turks in Germany, and the activities of the PKK (Kurdistan İşçi Partisi—Kurdish Workers Party). The Kurdish issue called attention to such questions as: Who is a Turk? Who feels like a Turk? Presently, the Turkish news media is full of polls concerning these issues. Turkey, for some time now, has expressed an interest in becoming a full member of the European Community, and this brings the Greeks and other Europeans once more to the question: Istanbul or Constantinople? There seems to be no desire thus far on the part of Christian Europeans to have the Turks join their club. In fact, they are saying: 'As long as Constantinople is Istanbul, you don't belong to our kind!'

A Comparative Summary
Before we conclude, it is useful to include a summary comparing the psychological states of present day Turks and Greeks even though we repeat certain points. Turks and Greeks have certain common characteristics inherited from their 'togetherness'. Their similarities are related to food, music, folklore, traditional architecture, and some common words in their languages which are important but not essential to national identity. Culturally, they are dissimilar because of their different religions and languages. Although they have been 'together' for five hundred years, their histories before and after this togetherness are long and different.

Greeks waged an irregular warfare in order to gain their independence. Greek insurgence consisted of *klephts*, small local merchants and local priests, local and diaspora elite, as well as

European philhellenic liberals. They had many captains in the war but not one nationally recognized, charismatic leader. Except for their Asia Minor campaign (1919-1922), they largely employed irregulars in almost all expansionist undertakings against the Ottoman Empire. In contrast, the Turkish War of Independence was fought and won by an army of regulars under the leadership of an exceptionally charismatic person, an ex-Ottoman general. He was supported by the nationalist Ottoman elite, almost all of whom were military and civilian bureaucrats.

In the Ottoman Empire, the concept of the state was so overwhelming that the concept of homeland appeared only in the late nineteenth century with the advent of Young Ottomans and the concept of nation in the early part of the twentieth century with the appearance of Young Turks. At its establishment, modern Greece did not inherit a state structure of its own. Earlier, Greeks had identified the concept of state with the despotic Ottoman sultan. Therefore, when they formed a state, right from the beginning, they simply had misgivings about their own state concept. On the other hand, modern Turkey was the inheritor of the Ottoman state.

The above diametrically opposite attitudes of these two neighbours to the concept of the state, the place of the state in their wars of independence, and later in their respective societies, affected their relationships in some ways. The Turks, who associated the respect for state with ethics, morals, discipline, political order, and believed in the seriousness of state-to-state relations mistrusted the Greeks because they perceived the latter as lacking the same values. In turn, the Greeks, who had associated their irregular spirit with the independent-minded Homeric heroes and the democratic individualism of the West consider the Turks as servile and subservient to the state. They equated the Turkish army which, under the leadership of Mustafa Kemal, fought and won the war of independence, founded the republic, and played a role in the implementation of reforms, with the Turkish state. For them, the Turkish people, who they feel lack a democratic and individualistic spirit, could not control this expansionist aggressive force which, according to their perception, cruelly invaded Cyprus. Hence, there is a fear of Turkey among the Greeks. The absence of charismatic leadership most likely has prolonged the use of massive projection mechanisms against Turkey.

Hellenism was imposed by the West upon the people, who had

been cut off from its influence for two millennia. It was transformed into an ideology and became connected with the *Megali Idea*. It necessitated the denial of the Greeks' existing identity as 'oriental and uncivilized' and its whole projection onto the Turks. The *Megali Idea* aimed at the liberation of the 'unredeemed brethren' in the old Hellenic territories. This meant irredentism without clearly defined territorial objectives or, perhaps, simply infinite irredentism.

After their war of independence, the Turks also had their nationalistic 'mythology' which was based on the pseudoscientific 'Sun Theory' of language and history. This theory pointed at central Asia, the original home of the Turkic people, as the prehistorical birth place of languages and civilizations from where they spread all over the world. It had nothing to do with irredentism but was an obvious attempt at repairing the self-esteem of the Turks who felt humiliated by the defeats during the 'longest century' and the demise of their empire. This 'mythology' never became a national ideology and soon died a natural death.

The main thrust of Kemalist nationalism was to reach the level of contemporary western civilization. This objective had been repeated so often, not only by the leadership but by the rank and file of Atatürk's Republican Party, the press, and the 'enlightened ones' that it has become an integral part of Turkey's political culture. A foreigner who resides in Turkey for some time, gets the impression that the entire society is geared to an elusive objective of catching up with this 'contemporary civilization.'. We can say that Turkey is a country searching for 'utopia'. This search has put the priority of domestic socio-economic development well above foreign policy objectives. As a result, Turkish people have become inward looking, basically indifferent, even insensitive, to outside stimuli, unless they are really disturbed. The security provided by NATO strengthened this isolationistic attitude. The Turks wanted to be left alone with their search for utopia. This was one of the reasons for Turkish loneliness until the mid-1980s.

By contrast, Greeks do not seem to search for a utopia. For example, demands for Greece to become a post-industrial, high technology power never seemed to appear in the usually high sounding rhetoric of Greek political parties. Since Hellenism represents the peak of civilization, there has never been a problem of catching up with 'contemporary civilization'. It would be enough to go back to their old history to become superior to all civilizations.

The opposite traits of these neighbours has complicated their relationships and often confuses third parties. Usually the bigger and stronger party is more enterprising and the other more restrained and withdrawn in stirring up a conflict. In the Turkish-Greek conflict, it appears that Greece has often taken the initiative; whereas, Turkey has remained defensive. This unusual situation gives the impression that Turkey might be provoking Greece. In spite of its being the smaller of the two, Greece gives the appearance of being forced to shed its fear and choose a heroic path.

Apart from these differences, the two countries resemble each other in that neither of them has yet mourned their past losses and worked through their past hurts. For the Greeks, the loss of the Byzantine Empire and its capital, Constantinople, remain unforgotten. There is resistance to mourn over these losses since it would mean the acceptance of a different identity from that held by modern Greeks. Newer traumas (i.e., the tragedy in Asia Minor in 1922 and the tragedy in Cyprus in 1974) strengthen the Greek feelings of hurt. In this respect, the Greeks seem to have become perennial mourners. This increases the sense of victimization and entitlement, derivatives of which are observed not only with respect to Turkey but also Greece's other Balkan neighbours, in particular Macedonia and Albania. The Turks did not mourn their lost empire either. In this decade, working through the Turkish loss seemed more openly evident, but unless properly managed, it may not be free from complications. Unless Turks and Greeks remove the resistance to mourn their historical losses, they may not adapt themselves to new historical realities.

Assuming Responsibilities

We have noted that issues and elements in the evolution of modern Greek and Turkish identities are not similar. Turkey, with a population of sixty million persons, freed to a great extent from the emotional restrictions of the 'loneliness' she experienced at the beginning of the Turkish Republic and spurred by the geopolitical changes caused by the Soviet Union's collapse, is attempting to regain its past greatness. The greatness which is searched for is not military but economic and political. In 1992, Turkey possessed Europe's fastest-growing economy.[303] There are, of course, many obstacles against, as well as many good possibilities for, the Turks' aspirations.

For a long time, for practical purposes, Turkey had restricted her vision only to the west. She has now turned to the east (Turkic Republics), to the south (Persian Gulf), and to the north (Russian Federation) with a vigour that is rather new for the Turks.[304] Meanwhile, Turkey wants a better relationship with the West, which still remains Turkey's primary partner, and in this regard Greece is perceived as something of an impediment. Meanwhile, Greece is still obsessed with Turkey (and now with the Slavs) and has surpassed Portugal in becoming the poorest nation in the EC. Better neighbourly feelings between the Turks and the Greeks could benefit both countries. What is learned about the psychology of Turkish-Greek relationships described in this book might be included in the diplomatic, economic, and legal tools for modifying and enhancing positive outcomes when Turks and Greeks negotiate solutions for their differences.

In the Spring of 1992 and 1993, the authors attended meetings in Kaunas, Lithuania, and Riga, Latvia, where they and other Americans from the University of Virginia's Centre for the Study of Mind and Human Interaction met with interdisciplinary colleagues from Russia, Lithuania, Latvia, and Estonia. The aim of these meetings was to study the psychological meaning of the difficulties between the Baltic States and Russia.[305] When the Baltic peoples spoke of how they had suffered at the hands of the Russians, the Russians present wanted them to acknowledge that: (1) Russians and Soviets are not the same, and only the latter had been villains; (2) the crimes against the Baltic peoples had been committed not only by Russians but also by their own people; and (3) the Russians themselves had experienced horrors at the hands of the Soviet regime.

The Baltic people responded at first by reminding the Russians that, as far as they were concerned, the Russians were hunted down by their own people, and this, they insisted, was not the same as being hunted down by collaborators working with the intruders. As the meeting progressed, however, some Russian participants expressed profound understanding that one group cannot escape its own heritage, and that they would assume responsibility for what the previous generation in Russia had done to the Baltic nations. After that acknowledgement, the participants, regardless of national origin, could listen to one another with greater empathy.

Like the Russians under the Soviets who were linked to other ethnic groups, the Muslim Turkish communities under the Ottomans shared a similar fate with the Greek communities. This 'togetherness' has too often escaped the consciousness of Western observers of the Ottoman scene. Within the Ottoman Empire and modern Turkey, the Turks were, and are, in a dilemma similar to the one faced by the Russian participants in the aforementioned Kaunas and Riga meetings. The Turks constituted only one of the ethnic groups within the empire, but like the Russians, the heirs of the Soviets, the Turks are of the same 'stuff' as the Ottomans. This is so integral a part of their past identity that they cannot select what is 'good' from their heritage and deny and disregard what is 'bad'. Meanwhile, a responsibility falls on the Greeks' shoulders. Modern Greece has existed for over one hundred and seventy years, one hundred years longer than the existence of modern Turkey. *Turkokratia* can no longer, logically speaking, be blamed for Greece's difficulties, especially regarding the area of their economy. Farmers and shepherds constitute nearly a quarter of Greece's population, and Greece lags behind Europe on standards of modernization. As Turkey attracts more western investment, Greece experiences a sense of betrayal by the western countries. It seems to us that the continuation of the unconscious sense of victimization combined with the conscious idealization of Hellenism might be the underlying factors for the Greeks' obsession with the Turks (Chapter 15). Vast energy is spent to gratify the psychological needs of the group (i.e., extensive military expenditures), and this obsession has been costly for Greece. Turkey and Greece will be better neighbours if all join in singing Eartha Kitt's song, 'Istanbul, not Constantinople'. After all, this has been the reality since 1453.

Notes

1. *1991-1992 State of World Conflict Report* summarizes the present state of armed conflicts around the globe. This report comes from the International Negotiation Network (INN) of the Carter Center of Emory University.
2. Saunders, Harold H. (1990), p.30.
3. Volkan, Vamık D. and Itzkowitz, Norman (1984), and Volkan, Vamık D., Itzkowitz, Norman and Dod, Andrew (in press).
4. Rogers, Rita R. (1979) and Volkan, Vamık D. (1988, 1992).
5. Erikson, Erik H. (1966).
6. The 'other' appears in many ancient documents and languages. Even the ancient Chinese regarded themselves as *people* and viewed other races as *kuei* or 'hunting spirits'. In the United States, the apache Indians consider themselves to be *indeh*, the people, and all others as *indah*, the enemy (see L. Bryce Boyer, 1986). The Mundurucu in the Brazilian rain forest divided their world into Mundurucu, who were people, and non-Mundurucu, who were *pariwat* (enemies), except for certain neighbours who lived in close proximity with each other (see Murphy, R. F., 1957).
7. Stein, Howard F. (1990a), pp.72-3.
8. Pinderhughes, Charles A. (1979, 1982).
9. There are, of course, other and more sophisticated psychological processes that become condensed with *shared reservoirs* that foster the crystallization of the 'us' and 'them' dichotomy and the prejudice that is associated with it (Volkan, Vamık D., 1988, 1992; Thomson, J. Anderson; Harris, Max and Volkan, Vamık D., 1993).
10. Weber, Max (1968), p.389.
11. Horowitz, Donald L. (1985), p.53.
12. Stein, Howard F. (1990b), pp.1-2.
13. Shafer, Boyd C. (1976).
14. Freud, Sigmund (1923); Hartmann, Heinz (1939).
15. Greenspan, Stanley (1989); Emde, Robert (1991).
16. Stein, Howard F. (1986), p.248.
17. Ecevit, Bülent (1976), pp.76-9.
18. Volkan, Vamık D. (1991, 1992) and Volkan, Vamık D. and Harris, Max (1993a). Jews remember the Holocaust, the Navajo remember 'The Long Walk' of 1864, Mexicans and Guatemalans remember the conquest of their territory by the Spanish nearly 500 years ago, and Serbian slavs remember the 'betrayal' of Bosnian Slavs who converted to Islam under Ottoman rule. Memories may be preserved openly in public discourse or, in the case of still subordinate peoples, in concealed forms. Indigenous protests against the Spanish conquest, for example, are still enacted, throughout Mexico, Guatemala and Peru, in folk dances and dramas that officially celebrate the arrival of Catholicism but surreptitiously enact a defeat of the conquistadors (Harris, Max [1992]).
19. Freud, Sigmund (1917).

20. Volkan, Vamık D. (1992).
21. Maurer, David A. (1992).
22. Apprey, Maurice (1993); Apprey, Maurice and Stein, Howard (1993).
23. We should explain that shared past or present group hurts are not the only basis for the formation of various political ideologies. Sometimes they evolve out of a leader's conscious, but mostly unconscious, attempts to play out his intra-psychic dramas in historical inter-ethnic or international arenas.
24. Moses, Raphael (1990).
25. Soon after the independence of Estonia, physicians working in Estonia were required to speak a minimum of 1,500 Estonian words. This may be a form of purification. The non-Estonian (Russian) physicians were being forced to leave their professions or to be assimilated in the core group.Ethnic cleansing is an exaggerated and malignant form of common purification rituals. Evidence of ethnic cleansing appeared in Bosnia-Herzegovina, in regard to victimized Muslims; the experience there demonstrates how ethnic cleansing may become a form of genocide. As Montville, Joseph V. (1991) attempted to show, in certain circumstances, various factors converge to create an atmosphere where genocide may occur.
26. By way of illustration, reading the statements of contemporary Armenian leaders and witnessing their soul searching creates the impression that a shared unconscious masochistic ideology might have been developing in Armenia during the past seventy-five years, that permitted Armenians to 'idealize' victimhood (Libaridian, G. J. 1991).
27. Mack, John E. (1979), p.xvi.
28. For example, Britons remember D-Day; Jews remember the period of the Maccabees.
29. Volkan, Vamık D. (1991); Volkan, Vamık D. and Harris, Max (1993a).
30. Mack, John E., (1983), p.xvi; Volkan, Vamık D. (1988).
31. Quoted in Sherrard, Philip (1979), p.55.
32. Volkan, Vamık D. (1992); and Volkan, Vamık D. and Harris, Max (1993a).
33. Mack, John E. (1979).
34. Today Manzikert is known as Malazgirt and is located in eastern Turkey not far from Lake Van and Mount Ararat.
35. After examining the Greek historian Attaleiates' eyewitness account, Friendly, Alfred (1981) states that the confrontation occurred on either 24 or 25 August when the moon appeared as a small crescent just before dawn. Turkish scholars designate 26 August as the date of the battle while some European historians believed that it occurred on 19 August.
36. Cook, J.M. (1963).
37. Cook, J.M. (1963).
38. Cook, J.M. (1963).
39. Vasiliev, A.A. (1952).
40. Vasiliev, A.A. (1952).
41. Vasiliev, A.A. (1952).
42. Jenkins, Romilly (1966).
43. Jenkins, Romilly (1966), p.25.

44. Jenkins, Romilly (1966).
45. Hussey, J.M. (1937), p.37.
46. Vacalopoulas, Apostolos E. (1976).
47. North of the Great Wall of China, there were tribes known to the Chinese as *T'ou Kiu* (or *T'ü-chüeh*) or Turk. Cahen, Claude (1968) is practically certain, however, that the earliest Turks known to history (in the third century BC of the Chinese Annals) were the Huns. The specific term Turk can be found in the sixth century AD in both Chinese and Byzantine sources. They belonged to various tribes connected linguistically.

An old Chinese proverb says: 'A Turk is born in a hut, but dies on the prairie' (Lamb, Harold, 1940, p.24). The Turks were pagan horse nomads. The Turkic women dressed themselves in embroidered silks while remaining as active as their men and having equal status with men. The veil, harem, and polygamy for which Turks are typically known in the West (before the establishment of modern Turkey) were imported from the Arabs after the Turks became Muslim.

A Chinese source from AD 581 (Grousset, René 1970) describes the early Turk's arms as consisting of bows, arrows, whistling arrows, sabres, swords, and breastplates with their flagstaffs topped by the image of a she-wolf's head in gold. For them, the universe consisted of a series of levels, one stacked on top of another. 'The seventeen upper levels formed the heavens, a realm of light, and the seven or nine lower ones constituted the underworld, or place of Darkness. Between the two lay the surface of the Earth, where men dwelt. Heaven and Earth obeyed a supreme being who inhabited the highest level of the sky, and who was known by the name of Divine Heaven, or Tängri (*Tanrı*)' (Grousset, René, 1970, p.86).

48. The Turkish language, spoken in different dialects, dates back 5,500 to 8,500 years and is today the sixth most commonly spoken language in the world.

49. The Turkish tribes were known by different names, such as Karlıks (the snow dwellers), Kırgız (the fertile fields), Kıpcaks (desert men), etc. Here our focus is the Oğuz Turks. Historically, there has been controversy over the first identification of the Oğuz Turks (Grousset, René, 1970). It is difficult to know if the Uygur and Oğuz Turks were initially identical. Nevertheless, the name Oğuz appears in eighth century inscriptions.

The semi-mythological and semi-historical beginning of the Oğuz Turks can be found in *The Book of Dede Korkut* which 'must have been the creation of many hands over a long period of time, a matter of centuries. Numerous minstrels must have sung these legends ... either as individual stories or as units of a narrative style'. (Sümer, Faruk; Uysal, Ahmet E. and Walker, Warren S., 1972, p.XIX). This book, which contains poetry with prose, covers twelve legends bounded by their epic theme. The epic as a whole was first found in the Dresden Library in the nineteenth century, while a second copy was discovered in 1950 in the Vatican's library. It is interesting that the first English translation of the entire epic became available only two decades ago. (Sümer, Faruk; Uysal, Ahmet E. and Walker, Warren S., 1972).

According to our semi-historical knowledge, there were twenty-four Oğuz tribes each with a leader forming a confederation. Each leader, in turn, subjected themselves to the sublime leader, the Khan of Khans. Their original land is what is known today as Kazakhstan, Uzbekistan, and Turkmenistan. In the tenth century, the Oğuz came in contact with Islam, and by the end of the eleventh century, the great masses of Oğuz Turks were converted to this religion.

The stories of *The Book of Dede Korkut* suggest that the Oğuz's principal enemies were the Kıpcak Turks in the north, who still practised a shamanic type of religion. It is likely that the Oğuz either lost ground fighting the Kıpcaks and were forced to move westward, or they may have just been looking for more fertile ground. The irregulars of the Muslim Oğuz became known as *Turcomans*. A newer edition of *The Book of Dede Korkut*, on which all subsequent editions are based, suggests that the Oğuz' enemies eventually changed from the Kıpcaks to the Georgians and other Christians along the Black Sea as they began to settle in Azerbaijan and parts of Anatolia.

As far as can be determined, the Seljuks were an Oğuz clan which split off from the bulk of other Oğuz tribes before 985. Eventually, they captured Persia and moved into Asia Minor. It was the Seljuks who were victorious at the Battle of Manzikert.

According to Grousset, René (1970), the Seljuk sultans wished to protect their fine Iranian domain from the undisciplined Seljuk bands and encouraged them to march to Asia Minor. 'This fact explains why Persia proper escaped Turkification, while Anatolia became a second Turkestan' (p.154). The Seljuk kingdoms in Syria and Palestine, which were conquered soon after the battle of Manzikert, assumed an Arab character and the Turkish population that remained in Persia were absorbed by the 'host' Iranians. However, the above opinion should be modified due to the fact that a very large number of the population in Iran speak Turkish and that there are millions of Azeri Turks living there.

50. Cahen, Claude (1968) writes of the Turkification of Asia Minor as a source of astonishment. At that period in history, it is difficult to believe that the movements of peoples could involve more than a few tens of thousands of individuals. An optimistic estimate would not be more than two or three hundred thousand. Cahen states that what was important was not the number of immigrants, 'but the economic and social position that they held, and also the way in which relations between the two peoples became organized, particularly marriage and births' (p.144).

All indications are that the Seljuks who Turkified Asia Minor were not the nomads. Those involved in this process were sedentary. Cahen, Claude (1968) refers to thirteenth century travellers to Asia Minor who brought remembrances of wealth. If one takes into consideration the effects of the Crusades as well as the Mongol invasion, it would be impossible to consider the prosperity of the Turkified Asia Minor to be the work of nomads.

51. Schimmel, Annemarie (1992), p.44.

52. Schimmel, Annemarie (1992), p.31.
53. Duncalf, Frederic (1969). also see Setton, Kenneth M. (1955-1962).
54. Quoted in Garraty, John A. and Gay, Peter (1972), p.451.
55. Freud, Sigmund (1917). See also Pollock, George (1961); Volkan, Vamık D. (1981) and Volkan, Vamık D. and Zintl, Elizabeth (1993).
56. The term 'futureless memory' was coined by Tähkä, Veikko (1984).
57. Volkan, Vamık D. (1977, 1979, 1988, 1989).
58. Rogers, Rita R. (1979); Volkan, Vamık D. (1988); Harris, Max (1992); Apprey, Maurice (1993); and Apprey, Maurice and Stein, Howard F. (1993).
59. Schoebel, Robert (1967), p.14.
60. Schoebel, Robert (1967), p.9.
61. Young, Kenneth (1969), p.20.
62. Herzfeld, Michael (1986), p.119.
63. Markides, Kyriacos C. (1977), p.10.
64. Schoebel, Robert (1967) states that reference to Fabri, Felix, can be found in *Evagotorium III*, pp.236-9 and to Filelfo, Giovanni Maria, in *Monumenta Hungariae Historica*, XXIII, Part. 1, No. 9, pp.308, 309, 405 and 453.
65. In clinical studies, we see individual mourners who try to make 'contact' with a dead person by means of what Volkan, Vamık D. (1981) calls linking objects or linking phenomena. An object (i.e., a gift from the deceased or a photograph) is used in a *magical* way to control the relationship with the dead person. Linking phenomena are fantasies, sensations, songs or behaviour patterns that perpetuate the possibility of contact between the mourner and the one mourned without reference to any tangible object.
66. Berkes, Niyazi (1975).
67. Personal communication with Altan, Çetin (1992).
68. Clot, André (1990), p.20.
69. Blos, Peter (1979).
70. Adıvar, A. Adnan (1970).
71. von Hammer-Purgstall, Ritter Joseph (1835).
72. Babinger, Franz (1978), p.96.
73. Our book on Mustafa Kemal Atatürk, the founder of modern Turkey (Volkan, Vamık D. and Itzkowitz, Norman, 1984), devotes a chapter to the symbolism attached to Istanbul. We describe Atatürk's 'inhibition' when he could not visit the city for many years. At that time, Atatürk was fascinated by a poem called 'Fog', which was written by a well-known poet, Tevfik Fikret. In the poem, Fikret speaks of Istanbul as a woman who is either altogether pure or ready to prostitute herself. The establishment of such polarity (the Madonna/prostitute split) serves an oedipal theme—the mother/woman image is split on behalf of the oedipal son who can feel close to her in the absence of any possibility of sexual interaction, since he then need not anticipate being punished by the father. Interestingly, Halman, Talat (1992), a famous contemporary Turkish poet, also speaks of Istanbul as a prostitute in one of his poems, entitled 'Istanbul.'.
74. Rosenberg, Tina (1993).
75. Motolinía, T. de (1951).

76. Harris, Max (1992).
77. Arnakis, G. G. (1951).
78. Adıvar, A. Adnan (1970).
79. Altan, Çetin (1992).
80. Adıvar, A. Adnan (1970).
81. Kritovoulos, M. (1954), pp.181-2.
82. A story, reported by Adıvar, A. Adnan, (1970), possibly apocryphal, deals with Mehmet's being told that the corpses of some Christians did not decay but remained intact after burial. Greek priests opened some Christians' graves in Constantinople by the sultan's order and in his presence. Were this story true, it might indicate something more than the Conqueror's intellectual curiosity about Christianity; he might have unconsciously needed proof that the enemy—and, perhaps, the 'bad' oedipal father—had, indeed, rotted away.
83. Young, Kenneth (1969), p.114.
84. Volkan, Vamık D. (1977) has described mourning due to the loss of interaction with the enemy after the 1974 war on Cyprus.
85. Pollock, George (1977), p.29.
86. Kritovoulos, M. (1954), p.61.
87. Vogt-Göknil, Ulya (1953).
88. Şehzade Mosque was named for Sultan Süleyman's beloved son, whom he had executed as the result of an intrigue perpetrated by the sultan's wife, the famous Roxelana.
89. Sözen, Metin (1989), p.61.
90. Sözen, Metin (1989), p.82.
91. Stratton, Arthur (1972), p.127.
92. Pickthall, Mohammed Marmaduke, (publication date N/A), p.314.
93. Sözen, Metin (1989). p.90.
94. Köprülü, M. Fuat (1931).
95. Kelly, Laurence (1987).
96. For detailed information on Ottoman institutions, see Itzkowitz, Norman (1972).
97. Tusi, Nasï ad-Dïn (1964), p.230.
98. Lybyer, Albert H. (1913).
99. Clogg, Richard (1982), pp.185-207.
100. Suphi, Mehmet (1992).
101. Volkan, Vamık D. (1988).
102. Suphi, Mehmet (1992).
103. Nicolay, Nicholas (1577). Jews from Spain, Germany, Hungary, Portugal, and elsewhere sought refuge from 1478 through the reign of Süleyman the Magnificent, in the Ottoman Empire, settling in Thessalonika, Edirne (Adrianople), Skopje, Sofia, Monastir, Alexandria, and Istanbul. They were involved in economic and governmental affairs.
104. The writings of Abraham Woodhead (1608-1678), spokesman of Restoration Catholics, spell out the view of Islam (especially 'Turcism') as antichrist (reported by Gardiner, Anne Barbeau, 1991). When Martin Luther began to spread his ideas against Catholicism, it was said that he

was looking like a Turk.
105. Suphi, Mehmet (1992).
106. Bardakjian, Kevork B. (1982).
107. According to McCarthy, Justin (1983), 584,268 Armenians and 1,040,376 Muslims died in the six provinces where these events took place.
108. In this respect, it would be edifying to compare the demise of the Ottoman Empire with the recent end of the Soviet empire. As the end of the Soviet empire was being realized, it was discussed in many quarters as the Ottomanization of the Soviet Union. That comparison in those terms is untenable. The Ottoman Empire was brought down by a multiplicity of factors that included ethnic and national strife, foreign invasions, and participation on the losing side in the First World War that was followed by the invasion of the Turkish homeland by (greedy) European powers, including Greece, Britain, France, and Italy, seeking to realize territorial gains extended to them by secret treaties concluded pre-war and arrangements arrived at in the post-war peace process. The Soviet Union, on the other hand, was not invaded, was on the winning side in the Second World War, and (being interested, as empires are, in continuity and stability) had prevented the outbreak of ethnic and nationalistic struggles within its borders. The Soviet Union, in the final analysis, simply imploded, and the end results are still far from obvious.
109. Gladstone, William Ewart (1876).
110. Rose, Achilles (1898).
111. Eliot, Sir Charles (1908), p.273.
112. Vacalopoulas, Apostoles E. (1909), p.42.
113. *Third New International Dictionary* (1934), p.2465.
114. Mango, Andrew (1987).
115. For example, after the Greek War of Independence, hostilities continued such as those that broke out on Crete in 1896. These led Abdülhamit II to suspend the Organic Regulation that had governed Crete since 1878. In retaliation, the Greeks invaded Thessaly, only to be pushed back by Ottoman forces. Athens feared a general Ottoman invasion, and once again the European powers pressured the Ottomans in favour of Greece. A new autonomous regime was established in Crete which eventuated in Crete being absorbed into Greece in 1912.
116. Vacalopoulas, Apostoles E. (1909), pp.43-4.
117. Voyatzidis, Ionnis K. (1955), p.44. Also see Brice, W. C. (1955).
118. This information comes from Taki Berberakis, the Turkish daily *Milliyet*'s Athens correspondent. Berberakis' news release on Prof. Kichikis' appears in *Milliyet*, 14.12.1992.
119. Petropulos, John A. (1976).
120. Petropulos, John A. (1976), p.23.
121. Young, Kenneth (1969), p.123.
122. Sherrard, Phillip (1979); see also: Herzfeld, Michael (1986).
123. Woodhouse, C. M. (1968), p.101.
124. For example, in 1714 the Greeks welcomed the Ottomans back after the

Turks wrested the Peloponnesus from Venice. The Venetians had made inroads into Greek territory, imposed heavy taxes, championed Catholicism, and curtailed religious freedom.

125. Woodhouse, C.M. (1968), p.101.
126. Lewis, Raphaela (1971), p.189.
127. Vacalopoulas, Apostoles E. (1909).
128. İnalcık, Halil (1964).
129. Vacalopoulas, Apostoles E. (1909), p.29.
130. Vacalopoulas, Apostoles E. (1909), p.30.
131. The Ottoman Empire had a rigid dress code, one varied according to profession of the wearer; a judge would dress differently from a soldier or a clerk, for example.
132. Christians could not speak casually to a Turkish woman, and sexual relations were punishable by death. Such restriction was not designed to humiliate Greeks, however much as they might find it a snub. Islam governed all daily life in the Ottoman Empire and laid down many rules, regulations, and taboos for everyone in all ethnic groups. Some of these the Greeks thought of as hurtful and insulting, depending on where they lived and what they did.
133. Davison, Roderic (1990), p.119.
134. Petropulos, John A. (1976), p.18.
135. Hertzfeld, Michael (1986), p.3.
136. Hertzfeld, Michael (1986), p.5.
137. Hertzfeld, Michael (1986), p.5.
138. One Greek source insists that the *devşirme* system lingered on in some isolated areas until the early part of the eighteenth century. (Vasdravellis, 1954).
139. Vacalopoulas, Apostoles E. (1909), p.213.
140. Mango, Cyril (1973).
141. Mavrokordatos was appointed again in 1711.
142. Seton-Watson, R.W. (1934).
143. Mango, Cyril (1976), p.43.
144. Toynbee, Arnold (1922).
145. Clogg, Richard (1973), p.13.
146. Mango, Cyril (1973), p.14.
147. Clogg, Richard (1973), p.13.
148. Clogg, Richard (1973), p.16.
149. Clogg, Richard (1973), p.14.
150. Quoted by Clogg, Richard (1973), p.17.
151. Zatos, Stephanos (1969), p.242.
152. Kitromilides, Paschalis M. (1990), p.34.
153. We can say that what is happening now in the area known as Yugoslavia is a continuation of 'settlements' after the break-up of the Ottoman period. Under the Soviets, ethnic groups in this part of the world had to postpone ethnocentric activity. Greece is alarmed by the disturbances and sentiments in its neighborhood, especially about Macedonia.
154. Kitromilides, Paschalis M. (1990), p.35.

NOTES   205

155. Kitromilides, Paschalis M. (1990), p.45.
156. Kitromilides, Paschalis M. (1990), p.44.
157. Tatsios, Theodore George (1984), p.101.
158. Tatsios, Theodore George (1984), p.9.
159. Volkan, Vamık D. (1988).
160. Veremis, Thanos (1990), p.15.
161. Vacalopoulas, Apostoles E. (1979) and Xydis, Stephanos G. (1968).
162. Herzfeld, Michael (1986).
163. Zatos, Stephanos (1969).
164. Byron died at Missolonghi, a Greek harbour city, in 1824. 'When in Greece, the journey to Missolonghi is as imperative as the unavoidable visit to the Acropolis in Athens. If the Parthenon is a monument and a tribute to eternal beauty, Missolonghi remains a homage to a great human sacrifice.' (Zatos, Stephanos, 1969, p.200).
165. Herzfeld, Michael (1986), p.vii.
166. Herzfeld, Michael (1986), p.15.
167. Herzfeld, Michael (1986), p.60.
168. Herzfeld, Michael (1986) compares this with the emergence of the Finnish nation-state. The Finns also depended on folklore studies to create a national consciousness; their epic, *Kalevala*, (see Kirby, W. F., 1985) helped to bring cohesiveness among Finns. However, the Finnish national consciousness was established *before* their attaining statehood.

    At the time of consolidating a new identity, it is common for the large groups to be involved in a process called 'purification' (Volkan, Vamık D., 1992). In order to heighten the group's cohesion, the group 'cleans' itself of unwanted elements. One hundred years after the Greek War of Independence, with the establishment of the Turkish Republics, the Turks began to 'purify' their language. 'Ethnic cleansing' is a malignant form of purification.
169. Volkan, Vamık D. (1988).
170. Herzfeld, Michael (1981), p.65.
171. Koliopoulos, John S. (1990), p.93.
172. Koliopoulos, John S. (1990), p.92.
173. Koliopoulos, John S. (1990), p.97.
174. Baggally, John W. (1968), p.84.
175. Baggally, John W. (1968), pp.92-3.
176. The following is one of the dispatches of Sir Henry Layard, the British Ambassador in Istanbul, to Lord Derby describing the actual events which gave Gladstone the opportunity to make his famous 'bag and baggage' speech concerning the campaign which he proposed should be lodged against the Turks.

    The English people are not yet ready, perhaps, to endure hearing the truth about the events of last year, but it is my duty to state it in your Lordship.The marvellous cleverness displayed by Russia and her agents in misleading public opinion in England and elsewhere has been amply rewarded. It may still require some time to sift the true from the false, it will be too late when history shall have made that discrimination. The Porte [Ottoman government] has not had recourse to any efficacious means for presenting its case to Europe. It has not utilized for this purpose either the press or competent agents. A great proportion of the English public at this very moment is probably under the impression that the declarations upon which the first accusations were made against Turkey were true: 60,000 Christians violated or massacred, carts filled with human skulls, crowds of women burned in barns and other similar horrors. There are people, among whom I regret to say are Englishmen, who boast of having invented narratives with the design of discrediting, 'writing down' Turkey, to which they have been instigated by one who is well known. The public in England will find difficulty in believing that the most exact and competent inquiries into the events that occurred last year in Bulgaria have now reduced the number of the dead to about 3,500, including Turks who were in the first place assassinated by Christians. No impartial person is able today to deny that an uprising of Christians planned by its leaders to result in a general massacre of Moslems was projected, and that the insurrection was directed by Russians and Panslavist agents. ([İnönü], İsmet, 1923).

177. Gladstone, William Ewart (1876), pp.12-3.
178. The stereotyped idea of the 'rapist' Turk, the conqueror of Jerusalem and Constantinople, was condensed with the stereotyped idea of the 'oriental' (lazy, barbarous and dirty) Turk. The Turk appears harmless until he unleashes his aggression without any trace of humanity. Such remarks appear in books, such as the one titled *The Real Turk*, written in 1914 by an American (Cobb, Stanwood). He dedicates his work to his mother and states that he is a friend of Turkey. He blames the climate of Istanbul for the Turks' behaviour! He adds:

> In ordinary life, he [the Turk] is affable and dignifiedly curteous; kind to his children, to animals, and to strangers. He seldom loses his temper; but when he does, beware! He does not encourage street-fighting; yet, if he bears resentment, he may kill you. (p.31).

Since Cobb refers to the generation of Dr. Volkan's parents and grandparents, Volkan had a hard time recognizing his relatives in Cobb's descriptions. The stereotyping of the Turks by the Westerners had become so generalized that even the Father of Psychoanalysis (Freud, Sigmund, 1932), could not escape from this practice in spite of the long Turkish history of favourable treatment of the Jewish people.

179. Vaughan, Dorothy M. (1954).
180. Haslip, Joan (1958), p.221.
181. Volkan, Vamık D. and Itzkowitz, Norman (1984), p.60.
182. Adıvar, Halide Edib (1926).
183. Volkan, Vamık D. and Itzkovitz, N. (1984).

184. This information comes from *Encyclopaedia Britannica* (1910-1911).
185. Volkan, Vamık D. and Itzkowitz, Norman (1984), pp.123-4.
186. Erzurum and Sivas are two cities in eastern Anatolia. Before Mustafa Kemal arrived in Ankara, two important congresses took place at these cities. These congresses 'authorized' Mustafa Kemal's attempt to begin the new Turkish struggle against the enemy.
187. Aydemir, Şevket Süreyya (1969), vol.2, p.201.
188. The next chapter will explain the unconscious reason why the leader and his followers perceived Atatürk as the sun.
189. Atatürk, Mustafa Kemal (1952), p.174.
190. Kinross, Lord (1965), p.362.
191. Adıvar, Halide Edib (1928), p.367.
192. Kinross, Lord (1965).
193. Freud, Sigmund (1932).
194. Earlier (see Chapter 4), we wrote about Mehmet the Conqueror's life and indicated that certain psychological motivations within him played a role in the nature of initiation of the 'togetherness' between the Turks and the Greeks. We must admit that available historical data on Mehmet the Conqueror's life is not sufficient enough to present a detailed psycho-biographical portrait of him. Available data, however, strongly suggested the presence of the oedipal issues which we wrote about. In our understanding of Atatürk's personality and inner world we have more luck; there is sufficient material about him to enable us to present a sophisticated psychoanalytic portrait of him.

Much has been written about the difficulties entailed in writing sophisticated psycho-biographies of historical figures (Beres, David, 1959; Bergmann, Martin S., 1973; Erikson, Erik H., 1958, 1969; Greenacre, Phyllis, 1955; Mack, John E., 1971; Neiderland, William, 1965). There has been debate both about what data can substitute for the associations and transference reactions of actual analysands and the validity of those substitutes. Nevertheless, psychogenic factors which contributed to the personality make-up of a deceased person or a person who was never on a psychoanalyst's couch can be inferred with some confidence if autobiographical information combined with records contributed by other authors establish the existence of consistent and repeated behavioural patterns. In the case of Atatürk, such writings have been supplemented by information accrued from his own writings and speeches and from living people who knew him. The combination of data obtained from such sources has proved ample to provide a reliable picture of his actions and belief systems.
195. Abse, David Wilfred and Jessner, Lucy (1961).
196. Volkan, Vamık D. (1980).
197. Weber, Max (1925).
198. A leader may utilize the historical arena to find external solutions for his internal, mostly unconscious, wishes and conflicts. In that case, it is his wishes and conflicts that will modify the emotional and physical state of his followers. This is why we are baffled by maladaptive leaders, such as

Adolf Hitler, Joseph Stalin, Idi Amin, and Saddam Hussein. In trying to fathom the support they received, we forget that these leaders fulfilled certain needs of their followers.

Freud, Sigmund (1921), described the disappearance of individual personality and the acquisition of a common emotional focus when members of a regressively formed group identify with each other and idealize their leader. The group that is on the losing side of a heated conflict with another group regresses further and finds itself needing more protection and 'parenting'.

199. Volkan, Vamık D. and Itzkowitz, Norman (1984).
200. Aydemir, Şevket Sürreya (1969), vol.1.
201. Kinross, Lord (1965).
202. Aydemir, Şevket Sürreya (1969), vol.1.
203. Atatürk, Mustafa Kemal (1930), pp.77-8.
204. Atatürk, Mustafa Kemal (1929-1930).
205. Emin, Ahmet (Yalman) (1922).
206. Once Mustafa was caught fighting with another child and was badly beaten by his teacher, who was known to be religious. Atatürk recalled this incident: 'All my body was blood.' (Emin, Ahmet [Yalman], 1922) Mustafa's mother withdrew him from the school and enrolled him in another. He seemed 'different' in appearance and mood from his classmates. Parushev, P.(1973), his Bulgarian biographer, recounts one story about Mustafa's being asked to play leapfrog but refusing because he was 'too proud' to bend over and allow another boy to vault over his back.
207. Just before the Balkan War erupted, his mother went to Istanbul to live with her daughter, who by then had married. In making this move she left her husband, with whom she was never to be reunited; he eventually died in Salonika. Since Atatürk's mother was now separated from his stepfather (the union that had so enraged him was at an end), an extended family was re-established in a three-story house in Istanbul, with the mother living on one floor, and his sister and her husband on another. He was not a regular occupant but would live there in Istanbul whenever he could take time from the wars.
208. The Bulgarian king summoned the handsome young attaché to his box at the opera and then summoned him once again at a masked ball at which Mustafa Kemal wore a Janissary's costume obtained from an Istanbul museum (Parushev, P., 1973; Kinross, Lord, 1965). The king offered congratulations on his striking appearance and the excitement it caused. However brief were these confrontations with the king, they offered him, within the glitter of these great social events, a figure who seized his imagination. Later, as president of Turkey, Atatürk made a great effort to stage for the visiting Shah of Iran the first opera ever presented in modern Turkey, supervising the rehearsals himself (Tesal, Kıymet, 1975). By his order this opera was written and produced in twenty days. Later in life he had his last adopted daughter, a little child, dance for his entourage while dressed as Carmen (Aydemir, Şevket Süreyya, 1974).

In Bulgaria, Mustafa Kemal 'fell in love' with a Bulgarian girl, Miti, and wanted to marry her. Although her family permitted him to take her for walks in the park and take her dancing, when he asked for her hand her father spurned his suit on the grounds that he was Turkish (Parushev, P., 1973).

209. Many aspects of Atatürk's personality organization which are not relevant to the topic of this book are left out. Once again, the interested reader is referred to our previous work (Volkan, Vamık D. and Itzkowitz, Norman, 1984).

210. Evidence of his excessive self-esteem and self-determination (narcissism) can be found (besides seeing derivatives of them in his repeated behaviour patterns) in his own description of himself.

In 1927 Atatürk said:

Since my childhood, in my home, I have not liked being together with either my mother or sister, or a friend. I have always preferred to be alone and independent, and I have lived this way always. I have the peculiarity of being unable to tolerate being given advice by my mother, my sister, or any close friend according to their mentality and conceptions of the world. (Aydemir, Şevket Süreyya, 1969, Vol.1, p.484.)

The following self-description was written while he was in Karlsbad in 1918 for treatment of an ailment. World War I persisted and everything was grim for the Ottomans.

If I obtain great authority and power I think I will bring about with a coup—suddenly in one moment—the desired revolution in our social life. Because, unlike others, I don't believe that this deed can be achieved by raising the intelligence of others slowly to the level of my own. My soul rebels against such a course. Why, after my years of education, after studying civilization and the socializing processes, after spending my life and my time to gain pleasure from freedom, should I descend to the level of common people? I will make them rise to my level. Let me not resemble them; they should resemble me! (Aydemir, Şevket Süreyya, 1969, Vol.3, p.482.)

211. Lewis, Raphaela (1971).

212. To be born in a house of death is a burdensome situation. One might, on one level, feel in touch with the dead and, thus, immortal; but one might also wish to be free from such a burden. On 30 August 1925 Atatürk gave a speech to explain why he planned to close the *tekkes* (certain religious houses, chapels of the dervishes). (Atatürk, Mustafa, 1927.) He explained that he wanted the Turkish nation to become civilized, saying, 'It is necessary to tear down those perceptions that do not accept reality.' He continued to rail against religious beliefs and practices that 'numb the mind' instead of letting in the vigour of civilization and science, decrying especially, religious emphasis on attempting contact with the dead. *'To seek help from the dead is a blot on any civilized nation.'* [Italics added.] (Atatürk, Mustafa Kemal, 1952, Vol.2., p.217.)

Hamilton, James (1969, 1979); Pollock, George (1975); Volkan, Vamık D. (1981); and Volkan, Vamık D. and Zintl, Elizabeth (1993) studied the relation of a childhood coloured by death to positive outcomes in subsequent adult life. Pollock emphasized the relationship between this phenomenon and success in political leadership.He was impressed by the consequences of loss during childhood and the unconscious intimations of immortality that arise from grappling psychologically with such loss. His formulation applies to Atatürk, who faced object losses in childhood. An additional formulation is also applicable—the belief that where the early mother/child interaction is unsatisfactory to the infant because of the mother's grief, depression or other complications, he will subsequently be preoccupied with rescuing her— whether he sublimates this preoccupation (Olinick, 1969) or not (Searles, 1975). Those rescued are surrogates for the early mother. Under what seems altruistic lies a selfish hope of freeing the mother from grief and making her psychologically available and devoted to mothering her child.

213. Rustow, Dankwart A. (1970), p.229.

214. Rustow, Dankwart A. (1970), p.221.

215. Atatürk's rhetoric in Turkish strongly suggests a primary process feeling that he would live forever in a spiritual way. We are reminded of a description of immortality by Pollock, George (1975):

> A personal reunion with the broader idealized social system— Utopia, which lives on ideologically after the individual's physiological demise (p.348).

Perhaps Atatürk never consciously recognized his fantasies of resurrecting the dead and rescuing the grieving mother, but he might well have been aware of his creative urges. In a speech he made on 17 March 1937 (Melzig, H., 1944) he spoke of the pleasure of a gardener who cultivated flowers, and compared such a gardener with one (an obvious reference to himself) who liked to 'cultivate men.' Here he saw himself as 'the creator' of men, someone able to bring them to life and even to bloom. In this musing he might be saying that if he could 'raise' men in so omnipotent a way he could undo the death of his siblings and, thus, rescue his mother from her grief. He indicated that the man who cultivates men should act with the mentality of the flower gardener, who expects no tangible return for his efforts. When he saw himself anticipating no reward, his position had, of course, altruistic elements. Hidden underneath, however, was the wish to rescue himself from the effects of the traumas of his childhood.

216. This is Article 88 of the Turkish Constitution.

217. Volkan, Vamık D. and Itzkowitz, Norman (1984), p.320.

218. One exception was Atatürk's and his government's preoccupation with the Hatay province, which is located between Turkey and Syria. The Hatay had personal significance for Atatürk. It was there that he had stood with his men toward the end of World War I facing the enemy until the Turks

evacuated the area. The Hatay was not included within the borders of new Turkey and had remained as a disputed area. Eventually, on 30 June 1939, when Atatürk was already dead, it became a part of Turkey by decision of the French Mandatory Regime.

219. Berkes, Niyazi (1975), p.167.
220. The wish of some Arab leaders to be like Atatürk continues in present times. For example, Anwar al-Sadat (1979, p.12) stated that Atatürk's portrait hung in his parents' home in Egypt and that he grew up idealizing the Turkish leader.
221. Fromkin, David (1989).
222. A physical border, psychologically speaking, is like a skin around a large group, helping to preserve its identity. (Volkan, Vamık D., 1988, 1992).
223. The Turkish population census for 1927 shows Orthodox Greeks in Istanbul and nearby Gökçeada (Imbros Island) and Bozcaada (Tenedos Island) to be around sixty-seven thousand. Other sources put the number at one hundred thousand.
224. Stephens, R. (1966).
225. Quoted in Alexandris, Alexis (1986).
226. Freud, Sigmund (1921).
227. Volkan, Vamık D. and Itzkowitz, Norman (1984).
228. Alexandris, Alexis (1986).
229. Mango, Andrew (1987).
230. Turkey's position with respect to the EC was stated by President Turgut Özal (1991):

> Turkey wishes to integrate with Europe because she forms part of the European theater for defense and security. Since the European Community wishes to achieve not only an economic integration but, subsequently, a political and defensive union, Turkey's request is not only legitimate but logical and sensible. (p.343)

231. Turan means 'the land of all Turks'.
232. Bahcheli, Tozun (1990), p.1.
233. Adams, Thomas W. (1966). See also Volkan, Vamık D. (1979).
234. Rothman, J. (1991), in addition to the Cyprus conflict, includes in this class of conflicts the following: The Eritrean-Ethiopian, the Northern Irish, Israeli-Palestinian, the Lebanese, the Sri Lankan conflicts. All are protracted and apparently intractable. Rothman states that one of the serious obstacles to successful negotiation and conflict management in these conflicts is that compromise regularly appears unacceptable to the parties involved. He does not give a psychological cause for this correct observation. We believe that the idea of compromise unconsciously is a threat in that it erases the differences between the two opposing groups and, thus, makes their identities shaky.
235. İnalcık, Halil (1974), p.26.
236. For further background on the Cypriot Turks, see the excellent study of them and their culture, administrative systems, and politics by Gazioğlu,

Ahmet C. (1990).
237. The same also applies to much smaller Armenian, Jacobite, and Assyrian communities.
238. Luke, Sir Harry (1921).
239. Gazioğlu, Ahmet C. (1990).
240. Dixon, W. H. Hepworth (1879). Tradition and customs developed in ways that affected a bipolarity of the population with many similarities and with many dissimilarities, although Turks and Greeks were geographically scattered throughout Cyprus. A dual and balanced system of administration continued under British rule and was supported by the maintenance of the dual culture of Cyprus. Volkan, Vamık D. (1979) describes cultural customs and traditions. See also Gazioğlu, Ahmet C. (1990). For example, both groups consider inter-ethnic marriage as taboo as incest. When the Republic of Cyprus was created, it also was based on a dual system. Volkan, Vamık D. (1979), p.53, states:

> The term 'modern Cypriot culture' refers to the one in which, before the [1974] war, the two separate groups coexisted, divided by a psychological chasm and by certain customs, though not separated physically.

241. Gazioğlu, Ahmet C. (1990), p.248.
242. Ano Panayia is a Greek village, but not far away there were Turkish hamlets and one-third of the population of the nearest city, Paphos, was Turkish.
243. Mayes, Stanley (1981), p.11.
244. Blos, Peter (1979) who writes about the adolescent passage describes how the youngsters loosen up their emotional investments in their childhood idols as they search for new 'objects' to idealize while enlarging their world into their culture and society.
245. Mayes, Stanley (1981), p.13.
246. Mayes, Stanley (1981), p.18.
247. Mayes, Stanley (1981), p.24.
248. Mayes, Stanley (1981), p.24.
249. Markides, Kyriacos C. (1977), p.11.
250. Camp, Glen (1980), p.4.
251. Camp, Glen (1980), p.44.
252. Makarios III (1964). This statement appeared in *Apoyevmatini*, September 8.
253. Makarios III (1965). In a speech at Rizokarpaso, May 26.
254. From: Nedjatigil, Zaim (1982), p.196. The English translation of the *Akritas Plan* also can be found in Denktaş, Rauf R. (1988) The top secret *Akritas Plan* was drawn up by the Cypriot Greek leaders in collaboration with the Greek Army officers in 1963. It became known when it was first published in the Cypriot Greek newspaper, *Patris*, on 21 April 1966. The newspaper published this document in order to expose how Makarios III mishandled the Cypriot national cause.
   Polykarpos Yeorgadis, once Makarios' minister of interior, was the

EOKA area chief for Nicosia. Under the direction of Makarios, he became 'Chief Akritas' to implement the *Akritas Plan.*

255. Thirteen Proposals by President Makarios to Amend the Constitution, 1963:
   (1) The veto rights of the president and vice president to be abolished.
   (2) The vice president to be acting president during temporary absence of president or during incapacity.
   (3) The Greek Cypriot president of the House of Representatives and the Turkish Cypriot vice president to be elected by the House as a whole rather than by ethnic voting.
   (4) The vice president of the House of Representatives to be acting president of the House during temporary absence of incapacity of president.
   (5) Constitutional provisions regarding separate majorities for enactment of certain laws by the House of Representatives to be abolished.
   (6) Unified municipalities to be established.
   (7) The administration of justice to be unified.
   (8) The separation of the Security Forces into police and gendarmerie to be abolished.
   (9) The numerical strength of the Security Forces and of the Defence Forces to be determined by law.
   (10) The proportion of the participation of Greek Cypriots and Turkish Defence Forces to be determined by ratio of one to the other in the population.
   (11) The number of members of the Public Service Commission to be reduced from ten to five.
   (12) All decisions of the Public Service Commission to be taken by simple majority.
   (13) The Greek Communal Chamber to be abolished.

256. In a letter written in a crude tone to the Turkish Prime Minister İsmet İnönü, President Lyndon Johnson warned against any military operation on the island.

257. Sandler, Joseph and Freud, Anna (1983), p.67.

258. The shared narcissistic injury suffered by the Cypriot Turks was also dealt with through other shared mechanisms in the service of revising chronic hopelessness. For example, the Cypriot Turks 'believed', as was evident in children's play or adults' unguarded remarks, that there was some special weapon on the mountain-top site of an ancient castle, St. Hilarion, historically associated with heroism and strategically important for the Turks of that time. It was at the highest point under Turkish control. The likelihood of some sort of gun emplacement there provided a kernel of truth for this myth.

But, the helplessness of the Cypriot Turks would surface beneath their defensive bravado. For example, in his study of what mothers in the Nicosia ghetto were telling their children at bedtime, in 1968, Dr. Volkan found that the stories would begin in the usual way with the trials and tribulations of a hero; but, instead of the classic triumphant happy ending, there was usually an account of the hero's annihilation or dismemberment. (Volkan, Vamık D., 1979) Betwen 1968 and 1974, during the period of 'open' enclaves, old narcissistic defences had to take new forms; the great weapon became more like a nurturing breast then before, and a huge flag was flown near St. Hilarion on a wire stretched between two mountains. The Turks could see this red signal over great distances, and its sight 'refuelled' them. They obtained some relief from denying the Greeks' admission to the enclaves under absolute Turkish control. Whatever the military or political reasons for this, it was psychologically helpful to them in handling their shared low self-esteem.

259. Mayes, Stanley (1981), p.93.
260. Mayes, Stanley (1981), p.167.
261. Volkan, Vamık D. (1979).
262. Mack, John E. (1979), pp.xvi-xvii.
263. The Cypriot Turks' exodus to Northern Cyprus has been eloquently described by Pierre Oberling (1982). See also Volkan, Vamık D. (1979).
264. Utilization of the egoism of victimization mechanism did not keep the Cypriot Turks from mourning over the loss of their enemies (Volkan, Vamık D., 1979).
265. Paragraph 4 from the Report of the United Nations Secretary-General No. S/12323 of 30 April 1977.
266. Makarios' biographer, Mayes, Stanley (1981), writing about the Makarios-Denktaş guidelines, thinks that Makarios had accepted a Cypriot Turkish region on the island. However he was adamant that 'the central government must be strong enough to hold the two regions together, and he was not prepared to concede equality in this to the other community'. (p.268) Mayes is aware that Makarios' position was a threat for the Cypriot Turks since they feared being dominated by the Greeks again. Mayes further states that Makarios was essentially 'a simple man, for all the deviousness that his public role forced upon him' (p.277). But the British and the Turks considered him sinister because he condoned a barbarous kind of violence on the island.
267. Mayes, Stanley (1981), p.276.
268. For example, see Jacovides, Andreas (1966) and Tornaridis, Criton (1977) arguing the Greek side and Ertekün, Necati M. (1981), Nedjatigil, Zaim M. (1982, 1983) and Denktaş, Rauf R. supporting the Turkish side.
269. Track two diplomacy refers to an informal interaction between influential members of opposing groups. Its aim is to define and examine psycho-political impediments to the peace process, to develop strategies to influence public opinion and to organize resources in ways favorable to the resolution of conflict (see Burton, John W., 1987; Montville, Joseph V. 1987; Volkan, Vamık D., 1988; Volkan, Vamık D., Montville, Joseph V. and Julius, Demetrios, A., 1991; Volkan, Vamık D. and Harris, Max R., 1992, 1993b).
270. Dublin Summit Communique (June, 1990).
271. Volkan, Vamık D. (1988).

272. *The Wall Street Journal Europe* (March 27-28, 1992), p.1.
273. Filippopoulos, Alekos, on Antenna TV (April 4, 1991), p.9.
274. Zatos, Stephanos (1969).
275. Kolmer, K. in *Mesimrini* (April 4, 1991), p.9.
276. Kosonas, Akis, in *Kathimerini* (1991), p.10.
277. Athanasiadis, Titos in *Apoyevmatini* (April 29, 1991).
278. Panayiotos, Hristos in *ENA* (May 11, 1991), p.13.
279. This is not a phenomenon seen in recent years. For example, famous Greek writer Nikos Kazantzakis (1965) in describing his memories of his childhood writes that, in his imagination, Crete was 'The Virgin' while the Turk was a black devil.
280. *Athens News* (June 4-5, 1989), p.5.
281. *Ethnos* (May 31, 1991), p.6.
282. Zotos, Stephanos (1969), p.x.
283. The psychological reasons for the phenomenon of 'other-directedness' in both Turkey and Greece have been examined by Öztürk, Orhan, 1966; Öztürk, Orhan and Volkan, Vamık D., 1971; Skinner, J.D., 1966; Vassiliou, V.G. and Vassiliou, G., 1970; and Volkan, Vamık D., 1979.

Shared mental mechanisms of projection and displacement contribute to the establishment of shared social prejudices. A primitive type of projection, sometimes called externalization (Novick, J. and Kelly, K., 1970), is the unconscious transfer on a primitive level of an unwanted aspect of the self or group to another person or group. On a more sophisticated level, proper projection involves the unconscious assignment of unacceptable impulses, attitudes and thoughts to other persons or groups. Such transfers and assignments have a boomerang effect: unacceptable aspects or thoughts about one's self or one's group that are assigned to the opponent then are felt by the party of origin to be turned back against oneself, therefore, hostility that seems to have come from the outside is actually connected with the original feeling of antagonism held by the first party toward aspects of one's self and only secondarily towards the second party (the latter process is unconscious, the former conscious).

In displacement, feelings about one person or group are attributed to another. For example, someone might feel towards one's employer the hatred originally invoked towards one's father.

Although projection and displacement can, in some forms, be pathological, they are essential in child development. Children are not born with an integrated identity but slowly develop a sense of self by going through the necessary experiences of passing certain developmental phases, developing more sophisticated ego mechanisms and identifying with important others in the environment. One of the psychological manoeuvres a child uses as he begins to experience and maintain a cohesive sense of self is to project his personal unwanted and devalued aspects onto other people or things. Volkan describes elsewhere (1988) how and why children in the same ethnic group share 'suitable reservoirs' for their projections and displacement. For example, the symbols, landmarks, food, or songs of another group may be suitable targets for the reception of the shared projections of the first group's children. A child must first recognize the existence of the 'other' if he is to feel cohesive and secure inside. If he then shares his target with his peer in the same group, this sharing bonds them together in a gratifying way. The beginning of the development of 'us' and 'them' is due to these obligatory childhood experiences. (for further discussion of this topic, see Chapter 1.)

Volkan, Vamık D. (1979) considers child-rearing practices in both Turkish and Greek societies to be one of the reasons for their observable other-directedness. In societies where multiple mothering or the derivatives of multiple mothering exist, the upbringing of a child is not the exclusive prerogative of the mother. The other women (i.e., a grandmother, an aunt, an older sister, and even a wet nurse) in the household feel entitled to mother the child in their own way. In this way, the child has an opportunity to 'go' to a second or third 'mother' when he feels frustrated with the first one and 'expels' her from his emotional investment. He returns to her when another 'mother' turns 'bad'. In societies where the child has one-to-one experiences with a mother, he 'learns' that the same woman is sometimes 'good' and sometimes 'bad'. He tames both her loving and frustrating qualities. When a child has multiple mothers and can 'flee' from the 'bad' mother by quickly finding a 'good' one, his expectation of his caretakers remain exaggerated. The remnants of his childhood feeling that people out there can make or break him stay with him the rest of his life. Under such circumstances, the children in a specific society may have a tendency to be 'other-directed'. Such experiences occur in both Turkish and Greek societies (Volkan, Vamık D., 1979; Brown, L.C. and Itzkowitz, Norman, 1977, pp.126-141 for a similar scenario with respect to the child and mother in Arab-Muslim society).

In order to understand this concept better, consider the situation of a white child growing up in the 'Old South' of the United States under the devoted care of a black nanny. Here lies an important difference. The white southern child's natural mother is psychologically separated from the black nursemaid or nanny, whereas the Turkish (or Greek) women who share an interest in the child already 'share' their lives in general and can be extensions of each other (Volkan, Vamık D., 1979). The American child with both a white and a black 'mother' may experience more difficulties than the children in other-directed cultures (Smith, L., 1949; Volkan, Vamık D. and Ast, Gabriele, 1992).

Another aspect of child-rearing practices in traditional Turkish families is the abrupt removal of the male child, after the circumcision ritual during the latency phase (just before the attainment of puberty) of child development, from the world of women to the world of men. The integration of the two worlds becomes difficult and the child is subjected to lifelong negotiations with those two worlds. One world has to be perceived as being 'out there' in order for the child to feel comfortable within the second world.

Returning to both Turkish and Greek societies, the observable other-directedness is also explained by less psychologically clear reasons (Loizos, Peter, 1976; McNall, S.G., 1976). In the Turkish-Greek relationship the 'other' becomes the neighbouring country. Turks and Greeks, as groups, have jaundiced views of each other. When conditions are stressful, reality testing is flawed because each views the other as the frustrator. In this book we are especially interested in the psycho-historical influences of the expression of 'other-directedness.'

284. Volkan, Vamık D. (1988).
285. Vryonis, S. (1971).
286. Saunders, Harold (1990).
287. Herzfeld, Mikael (1986), p.32.
288. Evlambios, G. (1843), p.ii.
289. Herzfeld, Michael (1986).
290. Kazantzakis, Nikos (1965), p.68.
291. The evolution of *katherevousa* was unique among the uniform nation-states of the last century, such as Italy, Germany, and Finland. In these nation-states, court language was replaced with the vernacular language. The Turks also substituted vernacular for Arabic and Persian words. Hence, the 'language question' or *'ghlossikozitima'* in Greece created much sharper polarization in the society and influenced the identity problems.

   The 'purification' process of the Greek language is still going on. In recent decades, Greeks began claiming that things like yogurt, certain cheese, *Karagöz* (puppet shadow plays), and even coffee were of Greek origin. In this way, they deny the Turks any particularity. This may be due to a shared unconscious wish to erase any minor differences and render the Turks non-existent. In the United States, centuries old 'Turkish coffee' is disappearing and being replaced by 'Greek coffee'.

292. For samples of these two influential individuals, see: Politis, Nikolas G. (1872, 1876, 1882) and Zamblios, Spyridon (1856, 1859).
293. Weber, Max (1925).
294. Kolioupolos, John S. (1990), p.92.
295. Freud, Sigmund (1921) describes this group phenomenon.
296. Markides, Kyriacos C. (1977), p.10.
297. Kitromilides, Paschalis M. (1990) states that 'causal observers and propagandists' tend 'to associate the Great Idea with Greek "expansionism"' (p.59). While we agree with him that the *Megali Idea* was also motivated 'by concerns about social and ideological cohesion' (p.59), careful observation of the flow of Greece's history clearly indicates how the *Megali Idea* has been the emotional force uniting Greeks in the wish to (re)create a greater Greece. Thus, it has fuelled political aspirations.
298. Güleç, Cengiz (1992).
299. Millas, Herkül (1991).
300. For an extensive description of Atatürk's 'dining room', see Volkan, Vamık D. and Itzkowitz, Norman (1984). As president of Turkey, Atatürk

regularly invited his political colleagues, scholars, and friends to dine with him on a nightly basis. They would discuss revolutionary, cultural, and social issues as well as metaphysical topics.

301. Hottinger, A. (1977), p.81.
302. Berkes, Niyazi (1975), p.167
303. Coll, Steve (1993).
304. Fuller, Graham E. (1992).
305. Volkan, Vamık D. and Harris, Max (1992, 1993b).

Glossary

Armatoles	Greek bandits assigned by the Ottoman government to fight with other Greek bandits, the *klephts*.
Askeri	Military.
Ayan	Notables during the Ottoman period.
Beylerbeyi	(Bey of Beys) Regional commander.
Çete	Turkish word for a group of bandits.
Cizye	Special capitation tax.
Derebey	Lord of the valley, a notable.
Devlet	Turkish word for state.
Devşirme	The process through which a Christian youth, taken away from his family, becomes a Muslim and receives education to serve the sultan.
Dhimmis	People of the pact (*ahl al-dhimma*) who possess revealed and written religious scripture.
Divan-i Hümayun	The (Ottoman) Imperial Council.
Dragoman	A translator of the Porte.
EOKA (Ethniki Organosis Kyrion Agoniston)	National Organization of Cypriot Fighters - A Cypriot Greek terrorist organization.
Enosis	The Greek movement to unite Cyprus with Greece.
Gaza (Ghazza)	The raiding of non-Muslims by Muslims. The aim for the Muslims was to destabilize the enemy, gain booty, and, if they were killed in battle, to have a place in heaven.
Gazi (Ghazi))	The Muslim man who took part in the act of *ghazza*.
Ghulam	Slave educated for governmental services.
Haham başı	The chief rabbi.
Hatt-i hümayun	Imperial rescript.

Haydut	Turkish word for a bandit.
Hocabaşı	Turkish (and Greek) word for Greek notables in the Ottoman period.
High Islam	As a concept, High Islam refers to the urban Muslim civilization in *Sunni* Orthodoxy and grounded in the *Shariah* as expounded through the *Hanefi* School of Law. It also involves outward conformity with the institutions, way of life, and cultural expression of the ruling group.
İmaret	Soup kitchen.
İqta	Income derived from a share in agricultural taxation in return for military service.
Kadı	An Islamic juriconsult.
Kapıkulları	(Slaves of the *Porte*) Those individuals in the Jannissary Corps and Ottoman military/ administration collectively were called *kapıkulları*. They were originally recruited through *devşirme* and educated in the Ottoman palace school.
Karamanlı	A Greek who became Turcophone, speaking Turkish, but writing in Greek letters.
Katharevousa	Greek word for the neo-classical forms of the modern Greek language that required the rejection of words of Turkish and Romaic origins.
Klepht	Greek bandit.
Lala	Mentor.
Medrese	'College' for instruction in the Islamic science.
Megali Idea	(Great Idea) Greek words referring to the doctrine of Greek irredentism whereby all the lands of the classical-Hellenistic and Byzantine periods should be reclaimed for Greece.
Meta	A Byzantine agricultural tax consisting of a fifty-fifty split.
Millet	Originally it referred to an organized religious community within the Ottoman Empire. In the nineteenth century it meant a nation, i.e. the Armenian *millet*.
Millet-i Rum	The 'Greek' *millet*.
Misak-i milli	National Pact.
Molla	Religious (Muslim) person.
Nizam-i Cedid	A new military corps introduced by Sultan Selim III.
Oda	(Room) Training dormitories of the Ottoman Palace School where the Christian Orthodox youth taken in

	devşirme were educated.
Phanariot Greeks	Greeks from Istanbul's Fener district who held important positions during the Ottoman period.
Philike Hetaria	(Society of Friends) A Greek clandestine organization founded in Crimea in 1814.
Plevma	Greek word for the spirit; i.e., the spirit of Greeks.
Porte	The Ottoman government.
Reaya (Raia)	Ottoman subjects who paid taxes and supported the *askeri* group.Until the first half of the fifteenth century this term covered both Muslims and Christians alike. After this date the term designated only the non-Muslim subjects of the sultan. However, Muslims of the same class continued to pay the same taxes as before.
Rum	Turkish word for Roman. Greeks were called *Rums*. The Turkish word for *Hellene* is *Yunan* which comes from Ionian.
Rumeli (Rumelia)	The land of Romans, the Balkans.
Shariah	The religious (Islamic) law.
Strategos	Military governor in the Byzantine period.
Sürgün	(Forced exile) An Ottoman method of colonization.
TMT (Türk Mukavemet Teşkilâtı)	Turkish Resistance Organization, in Cyprus.
Taksim	Turkish for 'division'. It refers to Cypriot Turks' idea of dividing the island between Greek and Turkish sections.
Tanzimat	A new type of organization. *Perestroika* has the same meaning.
Tekke	Chapel of the dervishes.
Theme	Provincial structure in the Byzantine period.
Timar	(Fiefs) A grant constituting a stated share in the agricultural tax revenue of a stipulated area.
Turkokratia	Greek word for the period when the Ottomans ruled over the Greeks.
Ummah	The community of Allah or Muhammad; Muslims in the Ottoman Empire.
Vakıf	Ottoman Institution of pious endowments.
Voivodes	Russian word for governor or administrator. At one time Ottoman Greek governors were in charge of administering Moldovia and Wallachia.
Volkan	(Volcano) Cypriot Turkish resistance organization. See also: TMT.

References

Abse, David Wilfred, and Jessner, Lucie. (1961). The psychodynamic aspects of leadership.*Daedalus*, Vol.90, No.4, *Excellence and Leadership in a Democracy*, ed. S. R. Graubard and G. Holton. New York: Columbia University Press, pp.693-710.

Adams, Thomas W. (1966). The first Republic of Cyprus: A review of an unworkable constitution. *Western Political Quarterly*. 19:475-90.

Adıvar, A. Adnan (1970). *Osmanlı Türklerinde İlim [Science Among the Turks]*. Istanbul: Remzi Kitabevi.

Adıvar, Halide Edib (1926). *Memoirs of Halide Edib*. New York: Century Co.

___ (1928). *The Turkish Ordeal*. New York: Century Co.

Alexandris, Alexis (1986). Paper, Lehrmann Inst., 15 May.

Altan, Çetin (1993). Personal communication.

Apprey, Maurice (1992). The African-American experience: Forced immigration and transgenerational trauma. *Mind and Human Interaction*, 4:70-5.

___, and Stein, Howard F. (1953). *Intersubjectivity, Projective Identification and Otherness*. Pittsburgh, PA: Duquesne University Press.

Arnakis, G. G. (1951). Gregory Palamas among the Turks and documents of his captivity as historical sources. *Speculum*, 26:104-18.

Atatürk, M. Kemal (1927). *Nutuk* (The Speech). 3 volumes. Ankara: Türk Tarih Kurumu, 1967.

___ (1929-1930). Bağlılık (Solidarity), in *M. Kemal Atatürk'ten Yazdıklarım (My notations from M. Kemal Atatürk)* by A. Afetinan. pp.101-4. Istanbul: Milli Eğitim Basımevi, 1971.

___ (1930). Hürriyet (Freedom). In *M. Kemal Atatürk'ten Yazdıklarım (My notations from M. Kemal Atatürk)* by A. Afetinan. pp.77-97. Istanbul:

Milli Eğitim Basımevi, 1971.

___ (1952). *Atatürk'ün Söylev ve Demeçleri (Speeches and Statements by Atatürk)*. 3 vols. Ankara: Türk İnkilâp Tarihi Enstitüsü.

Aydemir, Şevket Süreyya (1963-65). *Tek Adam (The Singular Man)*. 3 vols. Istanbul: Remzi Kitabevi.

___ (1974). Interviews with V. D. Volkan, 20 November and 13 December, Ankara.

Babinger, Franz (1978). *Mehmed the Conqueror and His Time*. Tr. from German by R. Manheim, ed. W. E. Hickman. Princeton, N. J.: Princeton University Press.

Baggally, John W. (1968). *Greek Historical Folksongs*. Chicago: Argonaut.

Bahcheli, Tozun (1990). *Greek-Turkish Relations Since 1955*. Boulder, CO: Westview Press.

Bardakjian, Kevork B. (1982). The rise of the Armenian Patriarchate of Constantinople. In *Christians and Jews in the Ottoman Empire*, Vol.1, ed. B. Braude and B. Lewis. pp.89-100. New York: Holmes and Meier.

Beres, David (1959). The contributions of psycho-analysis to the biography of the artist: A commentary on methodology. *International Journal of Psycho-Analysis*, 40:26-37.

Bergmann, Martin S. (1973). Limitations of method in psychoanalytic biography: A historical inquiry. *Journal of the American Psychoanalytic Association*, 21:833-50.

Berkes, Niyazi (1975). Türk Düşününde Batı Sorunu *(The Western Question in Turkish Thought)*. Ankara: Bilgi Yayınevi.

Blos, Peter (1979). *The Adolescent Passage*. New York: International Universities Press.

Boyer, L. Bryce (1986). One man's need to have enemies: A psychoanalytic perspective. *Journal of Psychoanalytic Anthropology*, 9:101-20.

Brice, W. C. (1955). The Turkish colonization of Anatolia. *Bulletin of the J. Rylands Library*, Vol.38, No.1, September.

Brown, L. C. and Itzkowitz, Norman (1977). *Psychological Dimensions of Near Eastern Studies*. Princeton, NJ: Darwin Press.

Burton, John W. (1987). *Resolving Deep-Rooted Conflict: A Handbook*. Lanham, MD: University Press of America.

Cahen, Claude (1968). *Pre-Ottoman Turkey*. New York: Taplinger.

Camp, Glen D. (1980). Greek-Turkish Conflict over Cyprus. *Political Science Quarterly*, 95: 43-60.

Clogg, Richard (1973). *The Struggle for Greek Independence: Essays to Mark the 150th Anniversary of the Greek War of Independence*. London: Macmillan.

___ (1982). The Greek millet in the Ottoman Empire. In *Christians and Jews in the Ottoman Empire*, Vol.1, ed. B. Braude and B. Lewis. pp.185-207. New York: Holmes and Meier.

Clot, André (1990). *Mehmed II Le Conquérant de Byzance, 1432-1481.* Paris: Perrin.

Cobb, Stanwood (1914). *The Real Turk.* Boston: The Pilgrim Press.

Coll, Steve (1993). The Turkish question: How important is it? *Washington Post.* May 24, pp.A13-14.

Cook, J.M. (1963). *The Greeks in Ionia and the East.* New York: Frederick A. Praeger.

Davison, Roderic (1990). *Essays in Ottoman and Turkish History, 1774-1923: The Impact of the West.* Austin, TX: University of Texas Press.

Denktaş, Rauf R. (1988). *The Cyprus Triangle.* London: K. Rustem and Brother.

Dixon, W. Hepworth (1879). *British Cyprus,* London: Chapman-Hall.

Duncalf, Frederic (1969). *The Councils of Piacenza and Clermont - The First Hundred Years,* ed. M. W. Baldwin, pp.220-52. Madison: The University of Wisconsin Press.

Ecevit, Bülent (1976). *Ecevit'in Şiirleri [Ecevit's Poems],* ed. M. Kemal. Istanbul: May.

Eliot, Sir Charles (1908). *Turkey in Europe.* London: Edward Arnold.

Emde, Robert N. (1991). Positive emotions for psychoanalytic theory. Surprises from infancy research and new directions. *Journal of the American Psychoanalytic Association* (Supplement). 39:5-44.

Emin, Ahmet (Yalman) (1922). Büyük Millet Meclisin Reisi Başkumandan Mustafa Kemal Paşa ile bir mülâkat (An interview with Mustafa Kemal Paşa, President of the Grand National Assembly and Commander-in-Chief). *Vakit,* 10 January.

Erikson, Erik H. (1958) *Young Man Luther.* New York: W. W. Norton.

___ (1966). Ontogeny of ritualization. In: *Psychoanalysis - A General Psychology,* ed. R. M. Lowenstein, L. M. Newman, M. Schur, and A. J. Solnit, pp.601-21. New York: International Universities Press.

___ (1969). *Gandhi's Truth.* New York: Norton.

Ertekün, Necati M. (1981). *In Search of a Negotiated Cyprus Settlement.* Nicosia: Ulus.

Evlambios, George (1843). *The Amaranth: The Roses of Hellas Reborn: Folk Poems of the Modern Greeks.* In Greek and Russian. St. Petersburg: Academy of Sciences. (Greek Edition: Athens: Notis Karavias, 1973).

Freud, Sigmund (1917). Mourning and melancholia. *Standard Edition,* 14:237-58.

___ (1921). Group psychology and the analysis of the ego. *Standard Edition*, 18: 65-143.

___ (1923). The ego and the id. *Standard Edition*, 19: 3-66.

___ (1932). Why war? *Standard Edition*, 22:197-215.

Friendly, Alfred (1981). *The Dreadful Day: The Battle of Manzigert, 1071*. London: Hutchison.

Fromkin, David (1989). *A Peace to End All Peace: The Fall of the Ottoman Empire and the Creation of the Modern Middle East*. New York: Avon.

Fuller, Graham E. (1992). *Turkey Faces East: New Orientations Toward the Middle East and the Old Soviet Union*, Santa Monica, CA: Rand.

Gardiner, Anne Barbeau (1991). Islam as anti-Christ in the writings of Abraham Woodhead, spokesman for restoration Catholics. *Restoration*, 15: 89-98.

Garraty, John A., and Gay, Peter (1972). *The Columbia History of the World*. New York: Harper & Row.

Gazioğlu, Ahmet C. (1990). *The Turks in Cyprus: A Province of the Ottoman Empire (1571-1878)*. London: K. Rustem and Brother.

Gladstone, William Ewart (1876). *The Bulgarian Horrors*. London: John Murray.

Greenacre, Phyllis (1955). *Swift and Carroll: A Psychoanalytic Study of Two Lives*. New York International Universities Press.

Greenspan, Stanley I. (1989). *The Development of the Ego: Implications for Personality Theory, Psychopathology and the Psychotherapeutic Process*. Madison, CT: International Universities Press.

Grousset, René (1970). *The Empire of the Steppes: A History of Central Asia*. Tr. N. Walford. New Brunswick, NJ: Rutgers University Press.

Güleç, Cengiz (1992). *Türkiye' de Kültürel Kimlik Krizi (Cultural Identity Crisis in Turkey)*. Ankara: Verso Yayıncılık.

Halman, Talat H. (1992). Istanbul, In *A Last Lullaby*, pp.8-9. Merrick, N.Y.: Cross Cultural Communications.

Haslip, Joan (1958). *The Sultan: The Life of Abdul Hamid II*. London: Wiedenfeld and Nicolson.

Hamilton, James W. (1969). Object loss, dreaming, and creativity: The poetry of John Keats. *Psychoanalytic Study of the Child*, 24:488-531. New York: International Universities Press.

___ (1979). Joseph Conrad: his development as an artist 1889-1910. *Psychoanalytic Study of Society*, Vol.8, pp.277-329. New Haven: Yale University Press.

Harris, Max (1992). Hidden transcripts in public places. *Mind and Human Interaction*, 3:63-9.

Hartmann, Heinz (1939). *Ego Psychology and the Problem of Adaptation*.

New York: International Universities Press, 1958.

Herzfeld, Michael (1986). *Ours Once More: Folklore, Ideology, and the Making of Modern Greece*. New York: Pella.

Horowitz, Donald L. (1985). *Ethnic Groups in Conflict*. Berkeley, CA: University of California Press.

Hottinger, A. (1977). Turkey's search for identity: Kemal Atatürk's heritage. *Encounter*, 48:75-81.

Hussey, J. M. (1957). *Church and Learning in the Byzantine Empire, 867-1185*. London: Oxford University Press.

İnalcık, Halil (1964). Kıbrıs fethinin tarihi manası (The historical meaning of conquering Cyprus). In *Kıbrıs ve Türkler (Cyprus and Turks)*. pp.21-6. Ankara: Türk Kültürel Araştırma Enstitütüsü.

___ (1974). *The Ottoman Empire: The Classical Age, 1,300-1,600*. Tr. N. Itzkowitz and C. Imber. London: Weidenfeld and Nicholson.

İnönü, İsmet (1923). Statement at the Lausanne Conference. *Current History*, pp. 752-4, February.

Itzkowitz, Norman (1972). *Ottoman Empire and Islamic Tradition*. New York: Alfred A. Knopf.

Jacovides, Andreas J. (1966). *Treaties Conflicting with Peremptory Norms of International Law and the Zurich-London 'Agreements'*. Nicosia: n.p.

Jenkins, Romilly (1966). *Byzantium: The Imperial Centuries, 610-1071*. New York: Random House.

Kazantzakis, Nikos (1965). *Report to Greco*. Tr. P.A. Bien. New York: Simon & Schuster.

Kelly, Laurence (1987). *Istanbul*. New York: Atheneum.

Kinross, Lord (1965). *Atatürk: A Biography of Mustafa Kemal, Father of Modern Turkey*. New York: William Morrow.

Kitromilides, Paschalis M. (1990). 'Imagined communities' and the origins of the national question in the Balkans. In *Modern Greek Nationalism and Nationality*, ed. Martin Blinkhorn and Thanos Veremis, pp.23-65. Athens: Sage-Eliamep.

Koliopoulos, John S. (1990). Brigandage and irredentism in nineteenth-century Greece. In *Modern Greece: Nationalism and Nationality*, ed. M. Blinkhorn and T. Veremis, pp.67-102. Athens: Sage-Eliamep.

Köprülü, M. Fuat (1931). *Alcuni osservazioni intorno all'influenza delle instituzioni byzantine sulle instituzione ottomane, Roma: Instituto per l'Oriente*, 1935 (Turkish edition: *Bizans Müesseselerinin Osmanlı Müesseselerine Tesiri (The influence of Byzantium Institutions on Ottoman Institutions)*. Istanbul: Ötüken Yayınları, 1931)

Kritovoulos, M. (1954). *The History of Mehmet the Conqueror*. Tr. C. T. Riggs. Princeton: Princeton University Press.

Lamb, Harold (1940). *The March of Barbarians*. New York: The Literary Guild of America.

Lewis, Raphaela (1971). *Everyday Life in Ottoman Turkey*. London: B. T. Batsford.

Libaridian, G. J. (ed.) (1991). *Armenia at the Crossroads: Democracy and Nationhood in the Post Soviet Era*. Watertown, MA: Blue Crane Books.

Loizos, Peter (1976). Notes on future anthropological research on Cyprus. In Regional *Variation in Modern Greece and Cyprus: Toward a Perspective on the Ethnography of Greece*, ed. M. Dimer and E. Friedl, *Annals of the New York Academy of Science*, 268:355-62.

Luke, Sir Harry (1921). *Cyprus Under the Turks*. London: K. Rustem and Brother (reprinted 1969).

Lybyer (1913). *The Government of the Ottoman Empire in the Time of Suleiman the Magnificent*. Cambridge, MA: Harvard University Press.

Mack, John E. (1971). Psychoanalysis and historical biography. *Journal of the American Psychoanalytic Association*, 19:143-79.

___ (1979). Foreword. In *Cyprus - War and Adaptation* by V. D. Volkan, pp.ix-xxi. Charlottesville, VA: The University Press of Virginia.

___ (1983). Nationalism and the self. *Psychohistory Review*, 2:47-69.

Mango, Andrew (1987). Greece and Turkey: Unfriendly allies. *The World Today*, 43:144-7.

Mango, Cyril (1973). The Phanariots and the Byzantine tradition. In: *The Struggle for Greek Independence*, ed. R. Clogg, pp.41-6. London: Macmillan.

Markides, Kyriacos C. (1977). *The Rise and Fall of the Cyprus Republic*. New Haven: Yale University Press.

Maurer, David A. (1992). A long road to rebuilding hope - missionary collects supplies for Navajo. *The Daily Progress*, Charlottesville, VA, June 18.

Mayes, Stanley (1981). *Makarios, a Biography*. New York: St. Martin Press. London: Macmillan, 1981.

McCarthy, Justin (1983). *Muslims and Minorities*. New York: University Press.

McNall, S. G. (1974). Value systems that inhibit modernization: the case of Greece. *Studies in Comparative International Development*, 9:46-63.

Melzig, H. (1944). *İnönü Diyorki* (İnönü Speaking). Istanbul: Ülkü Basımevi.

Millas, Herkül (1991). Türk edebiyatında Yunan imajı: Yakup Kadri Karaosmanoğlu (The Hellenic image in the Turkish literature: Yakup Kadri Karaosmanoğlu.) *Toplum ve Bilim*, 51 & 52:129-52.

Montville, Joseph V. (1987). The arrow and the olive branch: A case for track two diplomacy. In *Conflict Resolution: Track Two Diplomacy*, ed. J. McDonald and D. Bendahmane, pp.5-20. Washington, D.C.: U.S. Government Printing Office.

___ (1991). The pathology and prevention of genocide. In *The Psychodynamics of International Relationships*, Vol.2, ed. V. D. Volkan, J. V. Montville and D. A. Julius, pp.121-43. Lexington, MA: Lexington Press.

Moses, Raphael (1990). Shame and entitlement: Their relation to political process. In *The Psychodynamics of International Relationships*, Vol.1, ed. V. D. Volkan, D. A. Julius and J. V. Montville, pp.131-41. Lexington, MA: Lexington Press.

Motolinía, T. de (1951). *History of the Indians of New Spain*, tr. F. B. Steck. Washington, D. C.: Academy of American Franciscan History.

Murphy, R. F. (1957). Intergroup hostility and social cohesion. *American Anthropologist*, 59:1018-35.

Nedjatigil, Zaim M. (1982). *The Cyprus Conflict: A Lawyer's View*. Nicosia: Tezel.

___ (1983). *Turkish Republic in Northern Cyprus in Perspective*. Nicosia: Tezel.

Nicolay, Nicolas (1577). *Les navigations, peregrinations et voyages, faicts en la Turquie*. Paris: Anvers.

Niederland, William G. (1965). An analytic inquiry into the life of Henrich Schliemann. *Drives, Affects, Behavior*, Vol.2, ed., M. Schur. New York: International Universities Press.

Novick, J., and Kelly, K. (1970). Projection and externalization. *Psychoanalytic Study of the Child*, 25:69-95.

Oberling, Pierre (1982). *The Road to Bellapais: The Turkish Cypriot Exodus to Northern Cyprus*. New York: Columbia University Press.

Olinick, Stanley L. (1969). On empathy and regression in the service of the other. *British Journal of Medical Psychology*, 42:41-9.

Özal, Turgut (1991). *Turkey in Europe and Europe in Turkey*. London: K. Rustem and Brother.

Öztürk, Orhan M. (1966). Folk interpretation of illness in Turkey and its psychological significance. *Turkish Journal of Pediatrics*, 7:165-79.

___ , and Volkan, Vamık D. (1971). The theory and practice of psychiatry in Turkey. *American Journal of Psychotherapy*, 25:240-71.

Parushev, P.(1973). *Atatürk, Demokrat Diktatör (Atatürk, Democratic Dictator)*. Tr. into Turkish from Bulgarian by N. Yılmazer. Istanbul: E. Yayınları.

Petropulos, John A. (1976). Introduction. In *Hellenism and the First Greek War of Liberation (1821-1830): Continuity and Change*, ed. N.

P.Diamandouros, J. P.Anton, J. A. Petropulos and P.Topping, pp.19-41. Thessaloniki: Institute of Balkan Studies.

Pickthall, Mohammed Marmaduke. *The Meaning of the Glorious Koran.* New York: New American Library.

Pinderhughes, Charles A. (1979). Differential bonding: toward a psycho-physiological theory of stereotyping. *American Journal of Psychiatry*, 136:33-7.

___ (1982). Paired differential bonding in biological, psychological, and social systems. *American Journal of Social Psychiatry*, 2:5-14.

Politis, Nikolaos G. (1872). Khelidhonisma (Swallow Song). *Neoellinika Analektà* 1:354-68.

___ (1876). (In Greek) The First of March. *Estia* 1:142-3.

___ (1882) (In Greek) *Introductory Lecture for the Class in Hellenic Mythology.* Athens: Aion.

Pollock, George H. (1961). Mourning and adaptation. *International Journal of Psycho-Analysis*, 42:341-61.

___ (1975). On mourning, immortality, and Utopia. *Journal of the American Psychoanalytic Association*, 23:334-62.

___ (1977). The mourning process and creative organization. *Journal of the American Psychoanalytic Association*, 25:3-34.

Rogers, Rita R. (1979). Intergenerational exchange: Transference of attitudes down the generations. In *Modern Perspectives in the Psychiatry of Infancy*, ed. J. Howells, pp.339-49. New York: Brunner/Mazel.

Rose, Achilles (1898). *Christian Greece and Living Greek.* New York: Peri Hellados Publication Office.

Rosenberg, Tina (1993). *The Washington Post*, March 28, p.13.

Rothman, Jay (1991). Conflict research and resolution. Cyprus, *Annals of AAPSS*, 518:95-108.

Rustow, Dankwart A. (1970). Atatürk as founder of a state. *Philosophers and Kings: Studies in Leadership*, ed., D. A. Rustow. New York: George Braziller.

Sadat, Anwar al- (1979). *In Search of an Identity: An Autobiography.* New York: Harper Colophon Books.

Sandler, Joseph, and Freud, Anna (1983). Discussions on the Hamsptead Index of the ego and the mechanisms of defence. *Journal of the American Psychoanalytic Association (Supplement)*, 31:19-146.

Saunders, Harold H. (1990). An historic challenge to rethink how nations relate. In *The Psychodynamics of International Relationships*. Vol.1, Eds. V. D. Volkan, D. A. Julius and J. V. Montville, pp.1-30. Lexington, MA: Lexington Books.

Schimmel, Annemarie (1992). *I am Wind, You are Fire*. Boston: Shambhala.

Schwoebel, Robert (1967). *The Shadow of the Crescent: The Renaissance Image of the Turk (1453-1517)*. New York: St. Martin Press.

Searles, Harold G. (1975). The patient as therapist to his analyst. *Tactics and Techniques in Psychoanalytic Therapy, Vol.2 - Countertransference*. Ed. P.L. Giovacchini. pp.95-151. New York: Jason Aronson.

Seton-Watson, R. W. (1934). *A History of the Roumanians*. Cambridge, England: Cambridge University Press.

Setton, Kenneth M. (1955-1962). *A History of the Crusades*, 2 volumes. Philadelphia: University of Pennsylvania Press.

Shafer, Boyd C. (1976). *Nationalism: Its Nature and Interpretation*. Richmond, VA: William Byrd Press.

Sherrard, Philip (1979). *The Wound of Greece, Studies in Neo-Hellenism*. New York: St. Martin Press.

Skinner, J. D. (1966). Symptoms and defence in contemporary Greece: a cross-cultural inquiry. *Journal of Mental and Nervous Disorders*, 141:478-89.

Smith, L. (1949). *Killers of the Dream*. New York: W. W. Norton.

Sözen, Metin (1989). *Mimar Sinan ve Tezkiret-ul-Bunyan (Architect Sinan and a Book about Buildings)*. Istanbul: MTV.

Stein, Howard F. (1986). On professional allegiance in the study of political psychology. *Political Psychology*, 7:245-53.

Stein, Howard F. (1990a). The indispensable enemy and American-Soviet relations. In *The Psychodynamics of International Relationships, Vol.1*. Ed. V. D. Volkan, D. A. Julius and J. V. Montville, pp.71-89. Lexington, MA: Lexington Books.

Stein, Howard F. (1990b). The international and group milieux of ethnicity: identifying generic group dynamic issues. *Canadian Review of Studies in Nationalism*, 17:107-30.

Stephens, R. (1966). *Cyprus, A Place of Arms*. London: Pall Mall Press.

Stratton, Arthur (1971). *Sinan*. New York: Charles Scribner's Sons.

Sümer, Faruk; Uysal, Ahmet E.; and Walker, Warren S. (Tr. and ed.) (1972). *The book of Dede Korkut*. Austin, TX: University of Texas Press.

Suphi, Mehmet (1992). The expulsion of Safarad Jews: Regression in the development of modern society. *Mind and Human Interaction*, 4:40-51.

Tähkä, Veikko (1984). Dealing with object loss. *Scandinavian Psychoanalytic Review*, 7:13-33.

Tatsios, Theodore George (1984). *The Megali Idea and the Greek-Turkish*

War of 1987: The Impact of the Cretan War on Greek Irredentism, 1866-1897. New York: Columbia University Press.

Tesal, Kıymet (1975). Interview with V. D. Volkan, 13 May, Ankara.

Thomson, J. Anderson, Jr.; Harris, Max; and Volkan, Vamık D. (1993). *The Psychology of Western European Neo-Racism. Monograph No.2.* Charlottesville, VA: Centre for the Study of Mind and Human Interaction.

Tornaridis, Criton G. (1977). *Cyprus and Its Constitutional and Other Legal Problems.* Nicosia: Proodos.

Toynbee, Arnold (1922). *The Western Question in Greece and Turkey.* London: Constable and Co. Ltd. London.

Tūsi, Nasīr ad-Dīn (1964). *The Nasirean Ethics,* tr. G. M. Wickens. London: George Allen and Unwin.

Vacalopoulas, Apostoles E. (1909). *The Greek Nation, 1453-1669: The Cultural and Economic Background of Modern Greek Society,* tr. Ian Moles and Phania Moles. New Brunswick, N.J.: Rutgers University Press, 1976.

Vasdravellis, I. (1954). *Istorika Makedonias II: Arkheidon Veroias-Naousis (1598-1886).* Thessaloniki.

Vasiliev, A.A. (1952). *History of the Byzantine Empire 324-1453.* Madison: University of Wisconsin Press.

Vassiliou, V. G., and Vassiliou, G. (1974). Variations of the group process across cultures. Journal of Group Psychotherapy, 24:55-6.

Vaughan, Dorothy M. (1954) *Europe and the Turk: A Pattern of Alliances, 1350-1700.* Liverpool: University Press.

Veremis, Thanos (1990). From national state to the stateless nation. In: *Modern Greece: Nationalism and Nationality,* ed. M. Blinkhorn and T. Veremis, pp.9-21. Athens: Sage-Eliamep.

Vogt-Göknil, Ulya (1953). *Les Mosquées Turques.* Zurich: Origo.

Volkan, Vamık D. (1977). Mourning and adaptation after a war. *American Journal of Psychotherapy,* 31:561-9.

___ (1979). *Cyprus—War and Adaptation: A Psychoanalytic History of the Ethnic Groups in Conflict.* Charlottesville, VA: University Press of Virginia.

___ (1980). Narcissistic personality organization and reparative leadership.*International Journal of Group Psychotherapy,* 30:131-52.

___ (1981). *Linking Objects and Linking Phenomena: A Study of the Forms, Symptoms, Metapsychology, and Therapy of Complicated Mourning.* New York: International Universities Press.

___ (1988). *The Need to Have Enemies and Allies: From Clinical Practice to International Relationships.* Northvale, N.J.: Jason Aronson.

___ (1989). Cyprus: Ethnic conflicts and tensions. *International Journal of Group Tensions*, 4:297-316.

___ (1991). On chosen trauma. *Mind and Human Interaction*, 3:13.

___ (1992). Ethnonationalistic rituals: an introduction. *Mind and Human Interaction*, 4:3-19.

___ , and Ast, Gabriele (1992). *Eine Borderline Therapie*. Göttingen: Vandenhoeck and Ruprecht.

___ , and Harris, Max (1992). Negotiating a peaceful separation: A psychopolitical analysis of current relationships between Russia and the Baltic republics. *Mind and Human Interaction*, 4:20-29.

___ , and Harris, Max (1993a). *Shaking the Tent: The Psychodynamics of Ethnic Terrorism. Monograph No.1*. Charlottesville, VA: Center for the Study of Mind and Human Interaction.

___ , and Harris, Max (1995b). Vaccinating the political process: A second psychopolitical analysis of relationships between Russia and the Baltic States. *Mind and Human Interaction*, 4:169-90.

___ , and Itzkowitz, Norman (1984). *The Immortal Atatürk: A Psychobiography*. Chicago: University of Chicago Press.

___ , Itzkowitz, Norman and Dod, Andrew (in press). *The Psychic Rage of Richard Nixon*.

___ , Montville, Joseph V. and Julius, Demetrios (1991). *The Psychodynamics of International Relationships, Vol.2, Unofficial Diplomacy at Work*. Lexington, MA: Lexington Books.

___ , and Zintl, Elizabeth (1993). *Life After Loss: The Lessons of Grief*. New York: Charles Scribner's Sons.

von Hammer-Purgstall, Ritter Joseph (1835-1843). *Histoire de L'Empire Ottoman*, 18 volumes, tr. J. J. Hellert. Paris: Ballitard Barthes.

Voyatzidis, Ionnis K. (1955). The Rupture of Greek-Turkish Relations, (Reported in *The Greek Nation, 1453-1669: The Cultural and Economic Background of Modern Greek Society*, tr. Ian Moles and Phania Moles, pp.44 and 306. New Brunswick, N.J.: Rutgers University Press, 1976).

Vryonis, Speros, Jr. (1971). *The Decline of Medieval Hellenism in Asia Minor and the Process of Islamization from the Eleventh Through the Fifteenth Century*. Berkeley, CA: University of California Press.

Weber, Max (1925). *Wirtschaft und Gesellschaft* (2 vols). Tübingen, Germany: J. C. B. Mohr.

___ (1968). Ethnic groups, in *Max Weber, Economy and Society: An Outline of Interpretive Sociology*, ed. G. Roth and C. Wittich, p.389. New York: Bedminster Press.

Woodhouse, C. M. (1968). *The Story of Modern Greece*. London: Faber.

Xydis, Stephen G. (1973). *Cyprus: Reluctant Republic.* The Hague: Mouton.

Young, Kenneth (1969). *The Greek Passion: A Study in People and Politics.* London: J. M. Dent and Sons.

Zamblios, Spyridon (1856). (In Greek) Some philological researches on the modern Greek language. *Pandora:* 7:369-380, 484-94.

___ (1859). (In Greek) *Whence the Vulgar Word Traghoudho? Thoughts Concerning Hellenic Poetry.* Athens: P.Soutsas and A. Ktenas.

Zatos, Stephanos (1969). *The Greeks: Dilemma Between Past and Present.* New York: Funk and Wagnalls.